LIGHT FROM MANY CANDLES

By
Rev. Don Jennings

Cover photography: Perry Struse

*To Marty & Hank
With Love*

*Don Jennings
Rom. 8:28
also my love
Thelma*

WH books

WALLACE-HOMESTEAD BOOK CO
1912 GRAND
DES MOINES, IOWA 50305

ISBN # 0-87069-213-5
Library of Congress Catalog
Card No. 77-71018

Cover photography: Perry Struse

Published By
Wallace-Homestead Book Co.
1912 Grand
Des Moines, Iowa 50305

Face Forward

THE MONTH of January, the beginning of the New Year, was so named by the Romans. They named it in honor of one of their gods whose name was Janus. It is said that Janus had two faces. With one he looked forward and with the other backward; thus, he was able to see both the past and the future.

It seems that it is human nature for man to keep looking backward. There are certain joys and experiences of the past that we enjoy living over again and again in memory. Some good comes from looking back if we profit by our mistakes of the past. However, those who live on past worries wake up to find that they have dissipated the present and endangered the future.

Few, if any of us, can foretell what lieth ahead of us. Only through the telescopic lens of faith can we see the future, for what lieth in the New Year ahead only God knows.

Long ago I made a list of New Years resolutions. Each year I get them out and study them. I like to see how well I have rated during the past year. Below are some of them that I endeavor, by God's help to practice.

In the New Year ahead I purpose to be more sincere. Someone has said that what you do speaks so loud I can't hear what you say. It is true that our deeds are remembered longer than our words.

In his State of the Union message the late President Kennedy said, "We are judged more by what we do at home than by what we say abroad." Insincerity is easily detected. For many years the following words have been my prayer: "I would be true, for there are those who trust me; I would be pure, for there are those who care."

I also purpose to be more optimistic in this New Year ahead. A pessimist lacks faith, an optimist exemplifies it. He has faith in himself, in others, in the future and above all in God with whom all things are possible.

It was Paul, the apostle, who said, "I can do all things through Christ who strengtheneth me" (Philippians 4:13). Paul had an optimistic faith. He had tried it and found it had not failed him.

Long ago, Charles Sheldon, minister and author, wrote the book, *In His Steps*. After much prayer and thought he purposed to live his life in the light of the question, "What would Jesus do?"

The above book has influenced many lives. It helped me to endeavor to live my life in the light of God's plan for me. It can be done if our lives are saturated with prayer for ourselves and others. Only by this formula will we be able to keep resolutions. If we measure our resolutions by the words, "What would Jesus do?" ours can be a Happy New Year.

Lord, you know what the future hath in store for me. I pray, help me to trust you for each day, knowing that you will be our Guide. AMEN.

1

Right Or Privilege?

"WELL, DAD, according to the law I'm old enough to have the right to a driver's license." These were the words of a wide-awake farm boy. I came upon the father and son in the dairy barn as they were talking. I heard only a part of the father's answer as he responded, "Sure, Bill, according to the law you are old enough, but you will have to prove your right drive. Let us say it is a privilege that everyone your age has."

I would like to have heard more of the discussion from this wise young father and his eager son. What the son had said was true. His age gave him the right, but his father wanted him to see that it was a privilege which must be proven.

Someone has said that with each opportunity comes responsibility. Most of us have, long ago, decided that our country does not owe us a living, but an opportunity to make a living.

Recently, we stood at Plymouth Rock. We could vision those courageous men and women as they came ashore, knowing not what they faced. They were sure of one thing. They would now have the privilege of worshiping God as they felt led to do. They would now have the privilege of reading their Bible for instruction and faith.

Every child has a right to an education, either in our public or parochial schools. It isn't as though we were going to be given an education, but rather a privilege to make the most of it.

Abraham Lincoln included in his Gettysburg Address the words, ". . . our fathers brought forth upon this continent a new nation, conceived in liberty and dedicated to the proposition that all men are created equal." To me, this means that all of us have certain rights that are ours only so long as they do not infringe upon the rights of someone else. In no country in all the world are the privileges as great as in America. God has blessed us with many opportunities.

A new year is upon us. It was John, an early follower of Jesus, who, in exile on the Island of Patmos had some great visions of what lay ahead. At one time he heard a Voice saying, ". . . behold I have set before thee an open door, and no man can shut it . . . (Revelations 3:8)

As it was in those early days, so it is in our day. There are doors opening before us. We may not have deserved to live on, but God in His mercy is giving us this privilege.

It is our prayer and hope that the New Year ahead may bring peace and a new life for many in our troubled world. That the New Year may see hate, violence and destruction change to mutual understanding. May the year before us be a time in which we shall learn to share more of our opportunities together. May it be that we shall make more of the need for a foundation of truth and honor. This was the Master's way of life. He gave His all for the cause of truth. We can, by our dedication to Him, give new hope to His cause.

We believe, O God, that you have brought us to this new day. Help us in the year ahead that we may know and follow your will. AMEN.

The Future Is Now

"TOMORROW'S WORLD is already upon us," so observed Roy L. Smith, pastor and author. The future is now. We are a part of it. What may come tomorrow is already beginning. That bomb that could destroy us may already be prepared, but the formula that can save us is in our hands.

Another New Year is upon us. What it may bring to us, we may have already determined during the past year. We can look into the New Year with doubt or with hope and faith. Someone has observed that yesterday is a cancelled check; tomorrow is a promissory note; today is the only cash we have, spend it wisely. The future is now.

The writer of Proverbs has left us with many words of wisdom. This writer speaks wisdom when he says, "Boast not thyself of tomorrow; for thou knowest not what a day may bring forth." (Proverbs 27:1) On the other hand, Katharina Von Schlegel, poet, has written, "Be still, my soul; thy God doth undertake, To guide the future as He has the past."

The future, without faith, may look dismal. True, what may come tomorrow is already beginning, but it need not all be discouraging. As the angel said to John, on the Island of Patmos, he says to us, ". . . behold, I have set before thee an open door, and no man can shut it . . ." (Revelation 3:8) Each New Year is an open door of opportunity. New discoveries are being made in medical science. Proven formulas for better relationship with our fellowmen are waiting to be put into practice.

It is somewhat like the boy who was trying to interest a farmer in a book on better ways of farming. "Sir, if you will buy this book," urged the young salesman, "you can learn how to be a better farmer." The man looked at the boy, smiled and said, "Son, I already know a lot more than I have ever put into practice." Most of us know much more about the good way of life than we have ever put into practice.

Most of us know the formula for health of body, strength of character and peace of mind. These are not beyond our grasp but will take determination and discipline. "Blessed are the pure in heart: for they shall see God," taught Jesus (Matthew 5:8). A pure heart comes only from seeking, finding and serving God.

Life in the New Year ahead, to be rewarding, must not only be lived perpendicular, reaching up to God, but also horizontally, reaching out to man.

Perhaps someone nearby is fearful of the days ahead of them. There is that one who has been disillusioned in some condition that has faced them. God still holds the key. His plan can never be defeated. The future is now. Enter it with faith.

O God of every age, we thank Thee for the hope we have, through Thee, of the future which is upon us. Help us to go forth with courage.

AMEN.

Looking Ahead

THE FROST came before we were prepared for it. My neighbor hurried outside to gather some seed from some of his favorite flowers to plant again the following May.

I watched my good friend from my side of the fence as he prepared for the future. I smiled to myself and called out, "Uncle Orlo, you are always looking ahead." What better words could be said of anyone. Here was a neighbor who had enjoyed the past, but lived in the present, while he prepared for the future.

3

We have seen many harvests come and go. Whether we shall see another new one, only God knows. But, we shall save some seeds from the past to be ready for the future.

This is true not only of material and physical things, but of the spiritual as well. As Uncle Orlo once observed, "we should work as though we will live forever, but live as though we might die tonight."

As I look ahead into a new year, I do so with anticipation. I have reached some goals during this past year. Other hopes and plans have not materilized. God willing, I shall keep striving. I still have other goals ahead. I once heard Gabriel Heatter, radio commentator, say, "Life begins when a man fixes a goal for himself. It ends when there is no goal ahead."

The Author of the Epistle to the Hebrews was one who, with faith and hope, was always looking ahead. He entreated his listeners to remember the faith of those of the past. He also reminds us that we are to ". . . run with patience the race that is set before us, looking unto Jesus, the Author and Finisher of our faith . . . (Hebrews 12:1-2)

In the last Bible my mother used, before her eternal departure, I found a piece of paper on which she had written, "I know not what the future holds, but I know who holds the future." It was this confidence she had in her Lord that kept her faith alive each day while she looked forward to better days ahead.

As we complete the living of another year, we look ahead to a new one. We pause to thank God for His bounteous blessings of the past. We look ahead and pray that the New Year may be a year of not only material and physical prosperity, but a year when peace shall reign again in our troubled world. The kind of peace and prosperity that comes when we submit our will to God's will.

O God of today and tomorrow as well as the past, help us to keep our eyes on Thee. We know that you will lead in right paths of duty and blessings. AMEN.

Suffering

"SON, PREACH on the trouble — you will always find people who know what you are talking about." The above advice was given me, by a grand old pastor, when I first entered the ministry.

I have found through these many years that my good pastor friend was right. There is much trouble and suffering in the world. One is often tempted to say with Job, the great sufferer of long ago, "Man is born unto trouble." We suffer from illness, sorrow, tragedy, the wrong doing of others, and our own sin and evil.

As we enter into this season of the year we cannot forget that there was also suffering at Calvary. Here a man suffered not for the evil He did, for it is said that He went about doing good, but He suffered for each of us.

Most of us have stood by someone we loved dearly and saw them suffering. We knew that, short of a miracle, they could not continue to live. This is what took place at the cross. Here a mother shared the suffering of her Son, yet could do nothing except, with Him, pray for His enemies.

Without a doubt, the saddest words the world has ever heard came from the suffering Christ when He cried out, "My God, My God, why hast Thou forsaken Me?" (Matthew 27:46)

No greater suffering can come to anyone than to feel that he has been forsaken. This is often the feeling of a little child. It is also in the thoughts of many of the elderly. It is certainly the cry of a wounded soldier far from home. Someone penned the words, "There was the veil through which I might not see."

But there can be no rose without the thorn. There could be no Easter without Calvary. Someone has said that the nails of Calvary form the keys by which heaven may be opened.

As sure as there is a reason for our suffering, so sure is there a Companion Who stands with us when we feel forsaken. "For He hath said I will never leave thee nor forsake thee" (Hebrews 13:5). All great causes are won through the suffering of their crusaders.

Two Manchurian Christians were arrested and led out to be tortured. As they faced death one of them cried out, "It is finished, it is the end." The other knew what was said to be the Manchurian translation of the fourth Gospel. He cried, "No, that is not what the Master said when He was dying. He said it is accomplished."

When we suffer we can give up in despair or we can, by God's help, feel that something is being accomplished by our suffering. Suffering can mean tragedy. It can also, in the end, mean victory. By Calvary's road it was the latter. Through faith in Him who conquered it, may be so for each of us.

O Thou who faced suffering with courage, help us to realize that you will stand by us in our most difficult hour. AMEN.

Life's Purpose

RECENTLY, ON a stormy night, I was cautiously making my way to my destination. On passing a brilliantly lighted church bulletin board I read, "A man without a purpose is like a ship without a rudder." As I drove on through the night I pondered on those words. I concluded that the important thing about life is not how fast we are moving, but rather the direction.

I never come to this season of the year but what I try to think of what it must have been like, to Jesus, facing those last forty days. Here was a Man with a purpose. He knew the direction that He must go. He moved without hesitancy toward His goal; toward the trial and the cross. The cross was not His purpose, but He had to go by the way of the cross to reach His goal.

There can be no crown without a cross, and no victory without conflict. Any worthwhile purpose in life calls for courage of our convictions. William Shakespeare, English dramatist and poet, in one of his plays has a father, Polonius, giving some parting advice to his son. The father completes the advice by saying, "This above all: to thine own self be true, and it must follow, as the night the day, thou canst not then be false to any man."

The enemies of Jesus tried to get Him to compromise, but He could not do so and still be true to His own purpose, as well as those He came to save. As Jesus stood before Pilate, and His unjust trial, He said, ". . . To this end was I born, and for this cause came I into the world, that I should bear witness unto the truth . . ." (John 18:37)

5

As He could not compromise, no more can we lower the flag, and still be faithful to things that we know are true.

Faith does not depend upon ideal circumstances or surroundings. Faith conquers when men of faith act. Being a true Christian in these days may not be dangerous but it still takes courage. This age in which we live calls for great faith in the present, the future; in ourselves, and above all, in God. With God, all things are possible.

Esther, a courageous queen of Old Testament days, felt inadequate to champion her own people's cause. She was inspired to go before her husband, the king, by the words given her by Mordecai, her cousin. He challenged her by saying, ". . . who knoweth whether thou art come to the kingdom for such a time as this?" (Esther 4:14)

Each of us are challenged, at times, to do something or to face some decision that we have felt that we were not capable of doing. We cannot turn away and still be true to ourselves and to others whose future destiny may be dependent upon our decisions.

Help me, Father, to know Thy will. Give me then the determination to do it without compromising. We ask this in the Name of Him who was not afraid to do Thy will. AMEN.

Emblem Of Freedom

ONE DAY, several years ago, we found ourselves on Arch street, in Philadelphia. Before us stood a little frame house. It was dwarfed by the buildings on either side. This modest building had been the home of Betsy Ross. It was in this house in 1777, at the request of the Continental Congress, that Betsy Ross made the first flag of the United States of America. That flag has been known by many as the Emblem of Freedom.

From that day to this our Emblem of Freedom has been through many trying times. Most of us know that there are many sacrifices connected with freedom. To be worthy of all its benefits demands discipline, sacrifice, and dedication.

I never witness the Passion Play but what I recall what one man, who portrays the part of Christ, had to say about the cross. Someone asked him if the cross which he carried in the Passion Play was real heavy. He answered that it most certainly was. "If it were not heavy," he replied, "I could not feel the part."

The storms of adversity, like the storms on the ocean, test the fortitude of the voyager. We are, likewise, made stronger by them. A philosopher of long ago observed that men are often slaves because freedom is too difficult.

Moses, leader of the liberation of the Israelites, did his best to lead his people out of Egypt and into the Promised Land. Whenever they were confronted with hardships, they grumbled. Many of them complained that it would have been better to be slaves in Egypt than corpses in the wilderness.

The last day of Jesus' life on earth drew near. Ever before Him loomed the cross. He could not turn aside from it for it was to be the emblem of freedom for the whole world. But freedom demanded sacrifice. It was as He once said, ". . . For this cause came I into the world . . ." (John 18:37)

Through this sacrifice on the cross, man was set free. But he was set free to serve a higher Authority. Freedom's cost is never lost, providing it brings a challenge to a more worthy cause. In all our lives, a cross is the emblem of our freedom. With its weight our lives are tempered. For it is not alone something to which we cling, but which we must carry.

A young couple had set out to build their home. The plans and most of the construction work was accomplished with their own hands. The work was finally completed. They were to move in the following day. That night lightening struck the house. It burned to the ground along with their life's dreams. In the ealy morning light they noticed the red rambler rose, nearby, was blooming. They discovered that the heat which was generated through the destruction of the house had caused the rose to bloom over night.

This is a parable of many of our lives. The cross can be a challenge or a stumbling block. Jesus made it a challenge and won. He proved to us that it need not be the weapon of defeat, but rather the emblem of freedom.

Surely I must fight, if I would reign: Increase my courage, Lord; I'll bear the toil, endure the pain, supported by Thy word. AMEN.

Eternity's Garden

IT SEEMS only yesterday that I laid our flower garden to rest. The beautiful clematis, the fragrant peonies, both now seem as if they were dead, along with other favorite parennials that added so much in their season. But, there is a hint of Spring in the air. I know that down there in the earth there is already a stirring of God's natural laws. Our garden will soon be alive with beauty again.

If the great Creator is so mindful of the beauty of the earth, that He directs the seasons to bring renewed life to nature, certainly the immortality of His highest creation is no problem to Him.

Easter is not a problem to be proven, it is rather a fact to believe. We do not base our faith upon an empty cross, alone, but also on an open and empty tomb. The miracle of Easter is a glorious victory for all who have placed their faith in Christ, the Lord of both the Cross and the Grave.

Often, in our Palm Sunday Hosannas, and our Easter Victories, we tend to forget the days in between. There never could have been an empty tomb had it not been for the Man on the cross. There never would have been a Resurrection had there not have been a death.

God's love for His disobedient creation and the willingness of Jesus to do the will of His heavenly Father, is one of the amazing truths about that last week. Many of us, with humility and wonder, still sing with the author, John Newton, his words, "Amazing Grace! How sweet the sound, that saved a wretch like me." This, however, is what it is all about. It is a story that will only be finished in eternity.

It seems only yesterday that we laid to rest our beloved mother and father. However, in the light of what God has done for us through Christ, I know that in His own good time we shall see them again.

The Gospel according to John, records that the final words of Jesus from the cross were, ". . . It is finished . . ." (John 19:30) Many of the followers of Jesus, hearing these words, must have thought that this was the end of their hopes. Nevertheless, some of them would not give up the hope they had received through Him.

Amongst those who went to the tomb, early on that first day of the week, was Mary Magdelene. Her life had been changed. Jesus had truly been her Saviour. She wanted to be near Him in death as she had in life. Jesus spoke to her. She made haste to tell the disciples. Life, now, could never be the same. It would never end.

As you and I walk in the garden of the dead, our hearts are often heavy with loneliness. We are thinking of those whom we have loved and lost awhile. In the midst of all of this our faith speaks to us just as Jesus spoke to Martha in the death of her brother, Lazarus, "Whosoever liveth and believeth in me shall never die" (John 11:26)

Easter, then, is not a day of sadness. It is a day of rejoicing, for it is a day of victory for eternal life.

We thank Thee, Lord, for the blessed promise of eternal life through Jesus Christ our Redeemer. AMEN.

God's Tomorrow Begins Today

ON A well lighted bulletin board, standing on the lawn of a beautiful country church, I read the following words, "God's tomorrow begins today." It was Easter Sunday. The first flowers of the Springtime were in blossom. The church was freshly painted. Everything, including the well kept cemetery adjacent to the church, seemed to speak of hope.

I entered that church that beautiful morning. The entire service, up to the time of my message, spoke of faith and hope. As I began my message the words on the bulletin board were fresh in my mind. "God's tomorrow begins today," I said. I then continued, "Is not this the message of Easter?"

As I read again the reports of that first Easter, I asked, "What meaning would all the rest of the Gospel story have, if it were not for the resurrection news?" God's tomorrow really begins today. The Christian religion begins with the birth of the Saviour and continues with His life and teaching. But the Christian's real faith comes to its climax in the resurrection. This is the victory.

It is this realization that helped a dear friend of mine, who was suffering with a terminal disease to say, "I just live a day at a time and trust God for tomorrow." God's tomorrow does not end today. Life with God never ends.

The message of Easter is a message of haste: "Go quickly and tell His disciples that He is risen from the dead . . ." (Matthew 28:7) It is a message of joy: "And they departed from the sepulchre with fear and great joy, and did run to bring His disciples the word" (Matthew 28:8)

The Easter message is the unfailing promise of the ever present Lord. My mother, like many others, loved to sing at her work. In doing so she made her own burden lighter and helped to encourage those around her. One of her favorite songs was, "Peace, Peace, Wonderful Peace," written by Will Cornell. I can hear her now singing, "What a treasure I have in this wonderful peace, Buried deep in the heart of my soul; So secure that no power can mine it away; While the years of eternity roll."

To my mother, God's tomorrow begins today. This was what Easter meant to her. I believe that she is singing it today, along with the great hosts who, likewise, believed that eternity begins today.

Take heart, dear friend, when day's dark shadows seem to blot out hope's determined light. The victory of Jesus over death and the grave gives new hope to all who believe that, "God's tomorrow begins today."

We thank Thee, Lord, for the promise of tomorrow and we are grateful for the hope that is ours today. AMEN.

Life After Death

"SEE YOU, darling, see you in the morning." Those were the last words spoken by Catherine Marshall to her beloved husband, Peter Marshall, the famous minister. Dr. Marshall had suffered a heart attack in the night and was being carried on a stretcher from their home to be taken to the hospital.

Little did Catherine Marshall think that those were the last words she would have the opportunity of saying to her husband in this life, "See you, darling, see you in the morning."

Many of us have spoken those words to some dear one not realizing that, "in the morning" could very well mean, after the night of death we shall see those whom we loved and lost awhile.

One of the deepest needs of every bereaved person is to believe in life after death. In the darkest hour there is comfort in the thought that this life does not end with that which we call death.

Jesus, endeavoring to reassure Martha in the death of her brother, Lazarus, said with compassion, "Whosoever liveth and believeth in Me shall never die" (John 11:26). Even if those, who have been near and dear to us, have not been restored to life in this world, like Lazarus was given life again, we have the promise of Jesus, "I am the resurrection and the life; he that believeth in Me, though he were dead, yet shall he live" (John 11:25).

The resurrection of Jesus was the most reassuring proof of life after death. He came forth from the tomb, on that glorious morning; to walk amongst those who had known and loved Him. Finally, in the presence of His disciples, He ascended back to His Heavenly Father from whence He had come.

Before the trial, crucifixion and resurrection, Jesus comforted His followers with the promise, ". . . because I live, ye shall live also" (John 14:19) He lives! Therein is the eternal promise and hope for each of us.

Those dear ones, whom I have loved and lost awhile, are no less dearer to me now than they were when I was able to take them in my arms in this world. Because Christ lives, I believe that I will see them in the morning.

Elizabeth Barrett Browning, English poet, died in June 1861. It was in the autumn of that same year that Robert Browning, out of his depths of grief and loneliness, wrote "Prospice," one of his most famous and inspirational poems. The last lines of the poem read, "O thou soul of my soul, I shall clasp thee again, and with God be the rest."

The ties that bind us, to those who have been dear to us in this life, are not broken when they leave us in death. We too, can say with faith, "See you, darling, see you in the morning."

O God, we thank Thee that through our faith in the Resurrection that we too may say to those we have loved and lost awhile, "See you, darling, see you in the morning." AMEN.

The Nation's Hope

ROGER BABSON, American statistician and business forecaster, was once asked why North America prospered and grew so much faster than did South America. Mr. Babson's reply was that he had observed that those who went to South America, did so to find gold, but that our forefathers came to North America to find God. It has been proven, many times, that a nation's growth and endurance depends upon its goal and faith.

The time of a birth, whether it be when the breath of life is given a human form, or a new idea is born; each is an occasion filled with excitement, wonderment and hope. It is no less true of the birth and growth of a nation.

One has only to study the history of the birth and development of our own nation to discover how it fought its way through tribulation and depression. Even in its human imperfections it never lost sight of from whence it came and its hope for the future. Its basic foundation of freedom of worship under God could never be forgotten.

The Nation's hope has often been expressed by many of our own presidents. President Woodrow Wilson, addressing a gathering of recently naturalized citizens in 1915, said, "You have just taken oath of allegiance to the United States. It was an historical accident, no doubt, that this great country was called the United States; yet I am thankful that it has that word "United" in its title." President Wilson went on to explain that in unity there is strength, without which no nation can long endure.

Almost forty years later, General Dwight D. Eisenhower, having been elected to the highest office in the Land, sought out God in prayer for wisdom and strength for his overwhelming responsibilities as the nation's thirty-fourth President.

The hope of the future of any nation is its determination for unity with one another and its faith and dependence upon God. The Psalm writer reminds us of this when he says, "Blessed is the nation whose God is the Lord; and the people whom he hath chosen for his own inheritance" (Psalm 33:12)

We approach the day when we again remember that crucial occasion of the signing of the Declaration of Independence. As we do so we note that there are those on every side who spend their time in criticism of the Country that has nurtured them. It is true that we are passing through a time when our Nation's future seems to be in peril.

Our beloved Country never has, nor will it ever be perfect. It is only when we recognize our imperfections, work with unity and pray for God's grace, that we shall be given wisdom and courage to solve the problems and be adequate for our day.

Isaac Watts, hymn writer, saw his nation passing through a fearful experience when he wrote, "O God our help in ages past, our hope for years to come." This should be the prayer of every faithful American.

O God, our help in ages past, Our hope for years to come, Be Thou our guide while life shall last, And our eternal home. AMEN.

Liberty

IN OUR tour of Independence Hall, Philadelphia, several years ago, our greatest thrill came when we beheld the Liberty Bell. I ran my finger down the crack in the old bell. I then read the words inscribed thereon, "Proclaim liberty throughout the Land and unto the inhabitants thereof."

Liberty, freedom, independence, what mighty words are these. I often wonder if they mean as much today as they did to those courageous men and women of 1776. The possession of liberty means more than being free to do as we please.

Many American citizens think of Independence Day as nothing more than the Fourth of July, just another holiday. I remember, as a boy growing up on the farm, that the Fourth of July was one of the holidays to which we looked forward. I always tried to be the first one up in our neighborhood to shoot the first firecracker. On growing to manhood I realized that the Fourth of July meant more than shooting fire crackers and sky rockets. To gain liberty much was sacrificed in blood, sweat, and tears. To keep that freedom, we need courage, discipline and a devotion to the cause of right against wrong.

The best example of the One who has brought more freedom, to more people of the world than any other, is Jesus of Nazareth. The kind of freedom He represented is the kind the world of today needs. He would have us not only pray for peace, but be peacemakers. He would have us remember that we cannot really have freedom for ourselves unless we would be willing to give it also to others. His golden rule of doing unto others as we would that they should do unto us, has never been improved upon.

The founding fathers were serious when they said that they were establishing this nation on a belief in a Supreme Being. In the very beginning they appealed for the defense of these rights and for the truth that, "all men are created equal." If we would continue to enjoy this freedom we would do well never to forget this truth.

America has experienced many obstacles in its climb to freedom. Throughout our history there have been some things that have been indestructable. We have weathered all of the storms and tragedies because of them. One is the faith in a worthwhile cause, "with justice for all," and the courage to see it through. Another is a faith in God who is the champion of justice and mercy for all, and the courage to let this be known. When we lose sight of these we will have lost our way. If we keep these truths ever before us we cannot fail.

"Proclaiming liberty throughout the land," is not done by words alone. This is done by deeds also. We would do well as a nation of people, so fortunate in material blessings, to turn back to God who has never failed us. His way is the way of true and lasting liberty.

Father in Heaven, keep us ever mindful of Thy wise providence that brought our fathers to this land and will keep us and make us what Thou wouldst have us to be as a nation. AMEN.

The Nation's Strength

THE nation's strength lies not in her material riches alone, but in her moral and spiritual integrity. The proof of our strength is not how much we possess, but how we use our possessions.

The greatness of any nation depends upon the foundation laid within the home. As someone has said, as goes the home, so goes the nation. No country is stronger than its individual citizens. If there is a breakdown of the family the strength of the nation is jeopardized.

Elton Trueblood, Quaker philosophy professor, once said, "There is a withering away of the family life, as we once knew it." In this fast moving, complicated age, we have about every modern convenience to make a house a home. Everything except all of the family at home at the same time.

If the family life is no longer centered around the home, as it was intended to be, then the family is in decay. Is it true that we have become so tied up in the affairs of life that we seldom have time together as a family?

A mother and father, who reared eight children, were asked to give their formula for a successful achievement.

The mother said, "There are two words which Dad and I learned early in our married life. We have tried, by God's help, to be an example of them to our children. We have expected our children to observe them, likewise. The two words are discipline and love." The practice of those two words, discipline and love, have nurtured many a happy family. The lack of their use has caused the shattering of the hopes of many others.

It is not always easy to say, "No, you must not," when our children want us to say "Yes." However, discipline given with love for those children will, in years to come, cause them to reverance such parents.

Jesus, early in His childhood, exemplified these two words. When He was twelve years old He was left behind in Jerusalem. When they returned looking for Him, they found Him in the Temple, about His Father's business. The outcome was that, "He went down with them, and came to Nazareth, and was subject unto them" (Luke 2:51) His entire life was one of discipline and love. He taught that these should be learned early in life, in the home where they were exemplified by father and mother.

Paul, the apostle, was once writing to Timothy. In this letter he reminded Timothy that he was the kind of young man that he was, because of the faith of a grandmother and mother. We owe more than we can ever express, for what we are or what we may become, to the faith of those who have gone before us and have nurtured us in that faith.

It is true, and it will ever be so, that the ingredients for a strong Christian character, home and nation, will be found in the sincere practice of discipline and love.

O God, you have set aside the families in groups and blessed them. Help us to be worthy of the honor of being a part of your great family. AMEN.

Ties That Bind

THERE IS a vivid battle scene of the Civil War described by Burke Davis, author and lecturer, in which soldiers from Georgia and Texas were rushing up to the fighting line in support of their gray-clad comrades. Interestingly enough, a curious diversion took place. Standing just aside from the stream of men, a soldier waved a bundle of mail, letters from home. For a moment men forgot the battle and rushed over toward the soldier and crowded around him.

No matter where we go, who we are, or what we are doing, there is a strange tie that binds us with the family. This is as it should be. An old Latin proverb says, "He that flies from his own family has far to travel." The influence of a good home, parents who loved us, and watched over us, is something that we can never forget.

The writer of Proverbs says, "Train up a child in the way he should go; and when he is old he will not depart from it" (Proverbs 22:6) This writer is speaking of an indelible influence that impresses itself upon us to remind us, in years to come, of ties that can never be fully forgotten.

The hope of our nation is not found, alone, in her material riches, or scientific achievements. The true hope is found in the sacred sanctuary of the home. It is in the home that the foundations are laid that shall build the men and women who will continue to help preserve our nation's heritage. As long as we have mothers and fathers who feel that they have a duty to mold the moral characters of their children, we need not lose hope.

With prayer and Bible reading being banned from our public schools, it is up to the homes of our beloved country to come to the rescue of our children. For many of us, our first recollection of the Lord's Prayer and the Twenty Third Psalm, dates back to our childhood in the home. These are the ties that bind. This is as it should be.

It is in the home where we first learn to share. It is here that we first learn the real meaning of love. If we learn our lessons well the future homes will profit by our experiences.

"Home and religion are kindred words," said Horace Bushnell, author and statesman, "a house without a roof would scarcely be a more indifferent home than a family without religion."

Paul, the apostle, writing to Timothy, his associate in spreading the Christian gospel, bears witness to the influence of a Godly home. Paul says, "when I call to remembrance the unfeigned faith that is in thee, which dwelt first in thy grandmother Lois, and in thy mother Eunice; I am persuaded that it is in thee also" (II Timothy 1:5) This is one of the many examples of how Christian parents make investments that continue to produce Christian character. These are the ties that bind us into an eternal fellowship.

O God, we thank you for the influence of our homes where Thy Name is kept in reverence. AMEN.

Family Influence

"THE SPIRIT of a person's life is ever shedding some power, just as a flower is steadily bestowing fragrance upon the air," so wrote Starr King, author and lecturer. How true, the blossom cannot tell what becomes of its odor, and no man can tell the outcome of his influence and example.

Influence is a word that cannot be measured. Whether good or evil, its power is without limit. Time and eternity cannot erase its effect.

My father and mother have been gone these many years. Never a day goes by, however, but what some thought comes to me, of their influence on my life. For this I shall ever be grateful. The words that parents speak to their children, in the privacy of the home are not heard by the world. But, in the end, the influence of those words are felt, for they are echoed again and again in the lives of those who heard them.

How often the elements that move and mold society are the results of a wise mother's prayer and a diligent father's counsel. The size of the house and its rich appointments does not make a house a home. Only love, understanding and wise counsel insure the making of a home.

True wisdom is found in one of Solomon's Proverbs which begins with, "Hear, ye children, the instruction of a father, and attend to know understanding" (Proverbs 4:1).

One of the most familiar of the Ten Commandments says, "Honor thy father and thy mother: that thy days may be long upon the land which the Lord God giveth thee" (Exodus 20:12). Paul, the apostle, referring to the above words, goes on to write, "And, ye fathers, provoke not your children to wrath: but bring them up in the nurture and admonition of the Lord" (Ephesians 6:4).

A worthy, lasting influence makes strict demands on the lives of parents as well as the children. My good neighbor, Uncle Orlo, referring to his mother's influence on his life, recalls that it was not so much what she said but how she said it and the way she lived, that made a lasting impression on his life.

A good example is the best teacher. Exemplifying our instruction, as parents, gives added weight to our influence. Jesus practiced this, and the influence of His life can never be measured.

How often we have heard the words, "The family that plans, plays and prays together, stays together." This means, to me, that the family that counsels together about all of the concerns of life, both material and spiritual, stays together. God has a way of strengthening the bonds of a family like this. Their influence upon each other creates eternal ties that cannot be broken.

Our Heavenly Father, we are grateful unto Thee for the heavenly influence that rested upon our parents. In turn their lives have influenced ours. May it ever be so with each of us. AMEN.

The Value Of Home

IT IS GOOD to be happy with one's place of abode. Someone has said that home is where you hang your memories. What about that house in which you live? Not, how much is its tax valuation. Rather, what is the value of its memories? Is it a house with so many rooms and a place where three square meals are prepared each day? What kind of a contribution is it making to those who call it home?

One of my favorite poems, about home, was written by Eddie Guest. Its theme follows the thought that it takes a heap of living in a house to make it home. Sometimes you have to roam before you really appreciate the things you left behind. By the time you have read the poem you come to the conclusion that it takes more than a house to make a home.

Home is never an accident, but rather an achievement. Young families, striving for the home of their dreams, realize this. Parents and grandparents, looking back over some achievements and other disappointments have discovered this.

It was Plato, the Greek philosopher, who wrote, "Let parents bequeath to their children not riches, but the spirit of reverence." Home is the Master's workshop. The hope and safety of the world's future will depend upon the environment of our homes. Foundations of our governments will continue to be laid in our homes of the world.

John Stuart Mill, English philosopher, tells in his autobiography of his unusual education. His father educated the boy at home. But his father, James Mill, had no religious faith. He would not allow any religion to be taught the boy.

Many years later, when John Stuart Mill became famous, he looked back over his education with a great sense of loss. He said that his mind was stuffed with information, but his soul was starved. "I was left at the commencement of my voyage with a well equipped ship but no sail." John Stuart Mill, like many others, knew that if his ship was to move it must have a sail to help connect it to the power.

Joshua, who led the tribes of Israel across the Jordan River into the Promised Land, gave credit as it should have been, to God's providence. This faithful follower of Moses had been like a father to many of these descendents of Abraham.

He now was admonishing them in this new land. Joshua urged them to "serve God in sincerity and in truth." "And, if it seem evil unto you to serve the Lord, choose you this day whom ye will serve . . . but as for me and my house, we will serve the Lord" (Joshua 24:15).

If you read the account of the faithful father's proclamation, you will note that the people answered that they would not forsake the Lord who had brought them thus far.

If we are to have a nation that will not forsake the Lord who has not forsaken us, a great deal will depend on the stand of our leaders. Much will depend upon the God fearing family and its importance in the life of our nation.

Grant us faith and wisdom to so live that our homes may be a small haven of heaven here on earth. AMEN.

Expressing Our Gratitude

IT WAS the year 1918. So many were losing loved ones, not only from World War I, but the flu. Everyone in our family who were living at home had "come down" with the dread epidemic, except my father and me. Mother had nursed them all back to health again.

Thanksgiving came. We had little of this world's goods, but much for which to be thankful. Our immediate family was spared and restored to health again. We had food to eat and shelter from the storm. Parents who loved us, showed their concern for our welfare. God had been good to us.

It was not always to be this way. Heartaches, material loss, death and other sad experiences came to us, just as they do to all families. But, thanks for the memories, they have helped to hold us steady. They have kept us believing that God does not forsake us.

Martin Rinkhart, theologian and musician of the sixteenth century, spent the greater part of his life at Eilenburg, Saxony, amidst the horrors of the Thirty Years

War. Here, in the presence of suffering, he ministered to the sick and dying. Through it all he was inspired to write: "Now thank we all our God, With heart and hands and voices."

In the presence of that dread pestilence he led his people in grateful praise to God. Thanksgiving may not minimize our troubles, but it tends to magnify our blessings.

The wise man of Proverbs once wrote, "Trust in the Lord with all they heart; and lean not upon thine own understanding. In all thy ways acknowledge Him and He shall direct thy path" (Proverbs 3:5-6). With famine facing a large percent of the world's population; with crime on the increase, and promiscuous living so prevalent in today's society, we would do well to take serious thought on the words of wisdom above.

From the birth of our nation, down through its development, our national leaders, as well as our spiritual advisers, have called us to times of thanksgiving and praise. Acts of thanksgiving, however, contain not only praise for blessings received, but prayers for guidance in the years ahead.

We pause in the presence of another beautiful bountiful harvest. As we do so, we will do well not only to thank God for the rich harvest of field and flock, but give grateful praise for the love of families; freedom of worship; and a nation once again at peace with the world, if not completely with ourselves. The Psalm writer expresses the sincere feelings of all of us when he says, "Bless the Lord, O my soul: and forget not all his benefits" (Psalm 103:2).

We thank Thee, O God, for the many blessings that you have bestowed upon us. Help us to be worthy of these gifts. AMEN.

My Cup Runneth Over

RECENTLY I paused beside the wheelchair of a man who has been paralyzed from his waist down for five years. He spends his days and nights either in his chair or his bed. As I laid my hand on his shoulder I asked, "Paul, how are you today?" His eager response was, "Just fine, Reverend, I'm thankful for my many blessings, my cup runneth over."

Most of us have known or know others like this courageous man who count their blessings and feel that their cup is running over. There are those, however, who have given up in despair.

I have found that it is not just those who possess the most who are the most grateful. Gratitude is not born in abundance, but rather through evaluation. The real joy of gratitude and happiness comes when we let our cup overflow unto those around us. God's blessings we cannot hoard.

Someone has said that comparing our problems and sad experiences with those whose lot has been far worse than ours helps us to be grateful for our own. Counting our blessings instead of our disappointments helps us to smile through our tears. In so doing we notice that our cup runneth over.

The composer of that most familiar and beloved Twenty Third Psalm says, "Thou anointest my head with oil; my cup runneth over." That is, the Lord refreshes my spirit and cheers my countenance and fills my cup to overflowing. I cannot help from being thankful.

A husband of twenty years was short on expressing his love and gratitude to his faithful wife. One day he blurted out, "Peg, I just can't keep it to myself any longer.

I've just got to tell you how much I appreciate you and love you for all you have done for me." This may seem amusing but there are times in all of our lives when we recognize that our cup is running over. It is then that we realize that we have forgotten to show our gratitude.

We Americans have so much for which to be thankful. God has richly blessed our Land. He has filled our cup to overflowing. The sad part of it is that we have been so busy complaining about the size of our cup that we have not noticed the overflow.

The most grateful are not those who have the largest number of blessings, but who place the highest value on the benefits they receive.

The Psalm writer says, "Bless the Lord, O my soul and forget not all His benefits" (Psalm 103:2).

Blessing the Lord and showing gratitude we cannot save for one day of the year. Every day is Thanksgiving Day. When we make it so, it is then that we notice that our "cup runneth over."

Forgive us, our Father, if we have failed to thank you for our cup's overflow. We do give thee sincere thanks for all thy blessings. AMEN.

Thankfulness

ALICE JENNY celebrated her one hundredth birthday this past summer. As has been my custom, I was in her hospital room to talk with her and have a prayer and, of course, to congratulate her.

She is now blind and her hearing is weakened, but her spirit is as fresh as ever. After reading some of her favorite Bible verses, I concluded with the Twenty Third Psalm.

As I finished Alice smiled and said, "He leadeth me, He leadeth me, that's the best part." Then she continued with, "I have so much for which to be thankful. Although I cannot see, I have friends who see for me. Even though I cannot walk alone, I have One who leads me."

As I came away from her room, I thought of a verse that I had just read for her. "Why art thou cast down, O my soul? and why art thou disquieted within me? Hope thou in God; for I shall yet praise Him for the help of His countenance" (Psalm 42:5).

There is much for which we can complain, with conditions, physically, materially and nationally. But there is also much for which we can be most grateful.

Each morning, at our home, I raise the stars and stripes to the top of our flagpole. As I do so, it is with a sense of gratitude for a country in which I can perform this act unafraid. I sit behind the wheel of my car and thank God for the privilege, not the right, to drive where I choose. I open my Bible and read it in peace, knowing that in our Country we still have freedom of worship.

I know that these privileges I have mentioned, and many others, are not to be taken lightly. These opportunities could be taken from us as they have in other countries. Therefore, I know that with freedom comes discipline and dedication.

As another national Thanksgiving Day draws near, I will express my gratitude to God and my fellow citizens. I will, also, pray that God will give us the courage to stand up and be counted against that which would destroy us and for that which will continue to make us strong.

I will pray that, as we gather together with our families around our bountifully laden tables and our generous harvest, that we shall never forget that all that we hold dear comes from God who is the giver of all that is worthy of praise.

The Guiding Light

THE CELEBRATION of Christmas is exemplified in many ways. It would not be Christmas without music and song, which tells us of the Christ Child in Bethlehem's manger. Christmas is observed as a joyful occasion. That first Christmas was heralded by the angel chorus with their message of joy to the world the Lord has come. Each of these give meaning to the Christmas story.

But the story of Christmas could not be told without light. There are no more picturesque figures, in the imagination of that first Christmas, than those of the three wise men from the far east, following the star. They did not see nor hear the angel chorus as did the shepards. They did not know where the Christ Child was to be born but they did see His Star. These men of wisdom followed its light until it stood over the place where the Child lay.

Many songs have been written concerning the Wise Men who followed that divine light. William C. Dix, English poet, wrote, "As with gladness of old — Did the guiding star behold — As with joy they hailed the light — Leading onward, beaming bright — So, most gracious Lord, may we — Evermore be led to thee." Years later, a young minister who was to become the famous Phillips Brooks, sat on the hillside overlooking Bethlehem. The stars shown high above him and Bethlehem lay in the shadows of the valley below. As he sat there he was inspired to write, "O little town of Bethlehem — How still we see thee lie — Above the deep and dreamless sleep — The silent stars go by — Yet in thy dark streets shineth — The everlasting light — The hopes and fears of all the years are met in thee tonight."

How true and assuring are the above words. The star that was hung in the heavens, that glorious night long ago, still shines. No age needs its light more than ours. Even though we live in a day when man's knowledge is greater than ever before, we desperately need the wisdom the Light of the world can give.

The prophet Isaiah, foreseeing the birth of the Messiah, wrote, "The people that walked in darkness have seen a great light; they that dwell in the land of the shadow of death, upon them hath the light shined" (Isaiah 9:2).

The Child in Bethlehem's manger grew up. Seeing those who were walking in darkness, Jesus counseled, "I am the light of the world. He that followeth me shall not walk in darkness, but shall have the light of life" (John 8:12).

We live in a day when hate, violence, and frustration seems to overshadow love, compassion, and devotion. What has the event of Christmas to offer? The same as on that night long ago. The angels gave it to us and the conclusion of their message is as true today as then: "Glory to God in the highest, and on earth peace, good will toward men" (Luke 2:14). The Light still shines as a Guide in a darkened world. That Light, Jesus, still has the formula for "Peace on Earth, good will toward men."

Grant, O God, that the Light that came to Bethlehem long ago may shine anew in our hearts. AMEN.

18

Begin With The Sky

"I ALWAYS begin with the sky," explained Miss Ruby Brown, as with her brush in her hand she pointed to her easel. She was the only art instructor of my youthful days that made me feel that I wanted to become an artist. Whatever the landscape picture was to be, Miss Brown taught us to always begin with the sky.

The inspired artists who have painted the picture of the first Christmas story began with the sky. The heavenly light, the angels from above, and a Star over Bethlehem.

There were shepherds keeping watch over their flock by night. "And, lo the angel of the Lord came upon them: and they were sore afraid" (Luke 2:9). "And suddenly there was with the angel a multitude of heavenly hosts praising God and saying, Glory to God in the highest, and on earth, peace, good will toward men" (Luke 2:13-14). When Jesus was born in Bethlehem wise men came from the east, saying, "Where is He that is born King of the Jews? For we have seen His Star in the east and are come to worship him" (Matthew 2:2)

Not only the Christmas story begins with the sky, but the Creation itself. "In the beginning God created the heaven and the earth" (Genesis 1:1). God first created the heavens with the sun, moon and stars. Without heaven our earth would be void and useless.

After Miss Brown taught us to paint the blue sky, with the sun and the clouds, she exclaimed, "Now, we will paint the landscape." I have never become an artist, with brush and paint, but I learned that the landscape will never be right until we have finished with the sky.

What has this to do with Christmas? I believe that one of the reasons that Christmas never seems quite complete for many, is the fact that they have not looked up. They have not let the Light from above guide them to the Bethlehem Child from heaven. It is He who makes Christmas complete.

The true spirit of Christmas comes in both looking up to God and reaching out to those about us.

"We had the best Christmas party last year that we have ever had," explained a factory worker to me recently. He went on to say, "Instead of a party for ourselves alone, we took our party to a Children's Home. It was an experience I shall never forget." In bringing joy to others, a lasting peace came to their own hearts.

Can we forget what we think the world owes us and remember little children and those growing old? Can we remember that the Baby who was born in Bethlehem is still the Guiding Star that hovers over our darkened world? If we can, our picture of Christmas will be complete and satisfying, and the true joy of Christmas will linger in our hearts.

O God, as we look up to Thee, help us to look round about us that we may help to bring joy to others as Thou has done for us. AMEN.

"Christmas – Give It Away"

IT WAS Christmas Eve and Nurse Alma Jenkins was on duty at the hospital. Nurse Jenkins had served at City Hospital for many years. She was one of those whom you can't do without, but one whom many take advantage of.

An emergency had arisen. The nurse that was to come on duty was ill and Nurse Jenkins was asked to stay on a "few hours" longer. It really didn't matter that she had plans for her children that Christmas Eve. They and their father would wait for her. With a smile in her voice she said, "I have decided long ago that if you would keep Christmas you must give it away."

This faithful nurse had said more than she realized. She was right, we can't really keep Christmas unless we give it away. We can observe, spend it, and make it a time of exchange. However, that which brings the greatest joy is when we realize that it is more blessed to give than to receive.

On that first Christmas Eve, long ago, there were Shepherds on the hillside near Bethlehem. After these lowly shepherds saw and heard the exciting news from the heavenly angels, they hastened to Bethlehem. Here they found Mary and Joseph and the Babe lying in a manger.

When they had seen this glorious sight they could not keep it to themselves, they too, had to "give it away." The Bible tell us that "they made known abroad the saying which was told them concerning the child" (Luke 2:17)

The familiar Christmas story also contains the account of the coming of the Wise Men from the east. After they had presented their gifts to the Christ Child, "Being warned of God in a dream that they should not return to Herod, they departed into their country another way" (Matthew 2:12).

When we experience the true spirit of Christmas, we are never the same again. We too, will return to our every day living a different way. Life will never be the same again.

Someone has said that you can always tell how much one values their Christmas by the way they show it and share it with others. The truth about Christmas is that it is to be shared with others.

One of the experiences to which I look forward each year is Christmas caroling. Through the years our youth groups, like many others, have gone about singing the carols for the shut-ins.

One evening, near Christmas, we sang in the corridor of one of our nursing homes. One women who heard us thought we were doing it especially for her. Later she said to me, "It gave me new hope. No one will ever know how much I needed it that evening."

When Christmas comes to you with all of its joy, its message of peace on earth, and the truth that the Christ of Bethlehem cares, give it away to others and it will come back to you.

Help us, Lord, to have the true spirit of wanting to do unto others as we would that they should do unto us. AMEN.

Automation

IT IS a cold winter evening. The snow is drifting against the window. Outside, the thermometer registers five above zero. When I was a boy it would have been necessary to see that there was plenty of fuel in the wood box or nearby, against a cold stormy night like this.

But not so tonight. The thermostats are set in each room. There is no wood to carry in or ashes to carry out. Electricity heats our house, cooks our meals, washes and drys our clothes. What a change from fifty years ago.

There is a new word born into our language in recent years. The word is automation. The word refers to automatic handling by machinery and electronic control of what used to be done by human hands and brain.

What has this to do with thoughts for better living? First of all, this is not an exhortation for the return to the backbreaking tasks of yesterday for man and woman.

What about this age of automation and leisure time? Spare time already fills a sizeable part of man's waking hours. This spare time can be destructive or creative. Someone has said that man should have as much to show for his leisure time as he does for his labor.

In Milan, Italy, tourists are taken to the Church of Santa Maria where Leonardo da Vinci painted the Last Supper. This great artist spent many hours in the Church, painting, but also many hours in the Chapel meditating. Some of the monks resented his seeming idleness. They wanted him to get on with his work. Da Vinci's answer was, "When I pause the longest I can then make my most telling strokes with my brush."

Jesus believed so much in the need of turning aside from the heavy pressures of life, for a time, that He said to His disciples, "Come ye yourselves apart in a desert place, and rest awhile . . ." (Mark 6:31)

Automation, however, should not mean that we lose contact with our fellowmen. Life and living is not best done as a solo. It is easy for us to send a generous check to the United Fund or our church and feel that we have paid our debt to society. Having had the responsibility of helping to "raise the budget" in public life for many years, I know how those generous checks gave a lift to both the budget and the committee.

"Bear ye one another's burdens and so fulfill the law of Christ," urged the Apostle Paul (Galatians 6:2). I can see this exhortation in action in this day of automation. We must never forget, however, that nothing will take the place of personal concern. In these days of the automatic computer, man is in danger of becoming only a number instead of a person.

Those around me are persons, whether they be next door or ten thousands miles away. If I cannot go, I can send, but I can remember that they are God's creation just as I am.

The more we reach out in the Master's name to bring relief to the suffering, comfort to the sorrowing, and love to the unloved, the larger and richer will our world become. It cannot be done alone by the pressing of a button, but by the warming of the heart.

Dear Lord, forgive us if we have not had the compassion for others as You have taught us to have. AMEN.

Antidote For Deception

RECENTLY, WHILE we were visiting in Florida, my brother-in-law called my attention to a tree on the lawn. He pointed to a mass of leaves high in the treetop. He then informed me that those green leaves were not a part of the tree, but mistletoe. "If that mistletoe is left to grow up there," Warren explained, "it will spread and eventually kill the tree."

Webster's dictionary says that mistletoe is an evergreen parasitic shrub that lives off of oak and other trees to its liking. The mistletoe, growing in that oak tree, was an interesting phenomenon. It taught a lesson on how something, though pleasing to the eye, is often most deceptive.

From the time of the Creation, evil has always been deceptive. First in the Garden of Eden. Eve was tempted to partake of the forbidden tree in that, ". . . it was pleasing to the eyes, and a tree to be desired to make one wise . . ." (Genesis 3:6) Even the subtle serpent deceived Eve by convincing her that she would not die, but would rather become wise.

Evil has always made its most devastating gains by deceiving the weak. Like the mistletoe, which always suggests romance but is also a parasite, evil lives by temptation.

The old-fashioned morning glory that grew in our garden was beautiful to the eye. If left to its own design, however, it would soon choke out the fruit and vegetables that grew there. Sin, like the morning glory and the mistletoe, may at times be pleasing to the eye, but it does not always show the finished product.

One of the subtle evils of our day is the drug traffic. It attacks and tempts youth at an early age. It promises to pick one up, but in the end it leaves one hopelessly defeated. It seems, at times, like a way out of trouble but in the end trouble destroys its victim. It is like the man of wisdom who wrote long ago, "Wine is a mocker, strong drink is raging and whosoever is deceived thereby is not wise" (Proverbs 20:1).

Paul, the apostle, gives us the conclusion to this whole matter. He points out the way and our only hope. In writing to the Christians at Rome concerning sin and the escape from it. He says, "For the wages of sin is death; but the gift of God is eternal life through Jesus Christ our Lord" (Romans 6:23).

Someone has observed that man in his own hands is a mess, but in the hands of God he can be a message. Most of us have had the experience of being deceived by evil desires. Many of us have had the experience of being deceived by evil desires. Many of us have discovered that the only way out is God's way. Sin deceives and destroys but God receives and saves. His remedy is the antidote for deception.

Father in Heaven, give us the wisdom to know right from wrong, and the courage to take the right stand. In the name of Jesus. AMEN.

"Attention Please!"

I MUST confess that my hearing is not quite as sharp as it used to be, but it is much better than it might be. The long-suffering lady in my house, who has put up with my peculiarities for over fifty years, expresses her views of the matter. She says that I may not hear quite as well, but it is more because I do not pay attention as I should.

The above words were not spoken in unkindness. The fact is there is more truth than fiction in them. From many observations, that I have made recently, I am not alone. In these days we have so many aids to hearing that we are losing our attention to hearing.

There was a time when a listener responded to the sermon with an "Amen." Now, being so used to the blare of the loud speakers, they have grown less used to giving attention.

I recall reading about the preaching of Phillips Brooks in Trinity Church, Boston. This was long before the days of amplifiers. Those who heard him said that his words rushed by like an express train. In those days the hearers had to be really listeners and pay attention to what was being said.

It is not that we cannot hear. But we have grown so used to listening to those things that seem to please us that we fail to pay attention to the more important.

Jesus often called His listeners to attention by saying, "He that hath ears to hear, let him hear." Even this Master of men's interest said that He had to speak to them in parables for in "hearing they hear not . . . for their ears are dull in hearing."

In my early youth we had a pastor who was called a repeater, by some. To make his point he would often say, "Now let me repeat." At least, he made his point clear. Another preacher came our way whose sermons were short and to the point. He got our attention and held it.

In Gerald Green's novel, *The Last Angry Man,* one character makes this complaint, "We're drowning in bad talk. The most overwhelming fact of the twentieth century is the assult on the public ear and eye with the relentless avalanche of useless information." He has a point. There are times when we need to close our ears.

But with all of the trash that permeates the air, it is no time to close our ears. We would do well to continue to train our ears to heed the still small voice that begs our attention. All of those voices that would destroy all that is good cannot drown out the Voice that has outlived them all. He and those who follow in His train still have the remedy for our day. "He that hath ears to hear, let him hear."

Father, forgive us for not listening when that still small voice speaks to us. Help us to have ears to hear as well as tongues to speak. AMEN.

Anchors That Hold

CHARLES STEINMETZ, electrical engineer, was born, reared and educated in the face of tremendous difficulties. It was said of him that during his early life of preparation the winds blew from the wrong direction against him. Someone remarked, "This was what made him strong."

We have discovered this in the lives of many people. It is not the strong winds that would destroy them, but the anchors that hold in the face of the storms.

Most of us remember the story out of the life of Paul, the apostle. They were taking Paul and other prisoners, under guard, to Rome. Their ship ran into a storm. They were in danger of being shipwrecked. Under direction from Paul, the Scripture says, "And fearing that we might run on the rocks we let out four anchors from the stern and prayed for the day to come" (Acts 27:29).

As we study the life of Paul it seems that all of the elements of life were against him. He had to learn to live with bad health, and continually face cruel enemies. The winds seemed to ever blow against him from the wrong direction. However, he learned that there were anchors that held him steady.

As a lad on the farm I watched my father fasten cleats on the underside of a flat ladder. He laid it on the roof where we were working and said, "Donal*, it is safe, the more you bear your weight on it, the safer it is." So it is with certain anchors in life; the more we put our faith in them, the safer they are.

The ship of State has been in danger of shipwreck. This has been true, also, with the fate of the Church. It is likewise true of the home as we have known it. The destruction of anyone of these would leave us destitute on the stormy sea of life.

---

*My father always called me "Donal" . . . not "Don" or "Donald", just "Donal" without the "d".

It is a great day for pessimists. I can sympathize with the boy whose teacher asked, "Jim, what is the shape of the world?" The lad answered without hesitation. "My dad says it is in the worst shape it has ever been in."

Remember, however, it is not the winds that blow against us that would destroy us, rather it is the anchors that are available, that can save us.

What are those four anchors? Faith in an eternal God who created us. Faith in an eternal Book whose words have been, and will ever be a guide on the treacherous sea or on the quiet waters. Faith in an ever living Christ, who proved that nothing, not even death, could destroy Him and His teachings. Faith in an eternal plan, of which we are a part.

Horace Bushnell, preacher and writer, once said, "Every man's life is a plan of God." We are here, each of us, for a purpose. There may be many crises that we must face in life, but if we cast out the four anchors and pray for the day, we will come through the storm victoriously.

O Divine Creator, keep us ever mindful that you have a plan of life for each of us. Help us to be willing to be led in that plan, that our lives may be complete in Thee. AMEN.

Accomplishment

DR. ROBERT F. GREEN, one of the most successful physicians in his field, was confined to the hospital. In visiting with him he told me of a telelphone conversation he had with his young son that very day. Dr. Green had called his home and this young son had answered with, "Dr. Green's residence. May I take a message?" When the doctor informed him that the caller was his father, the son eagerly responded, "Dad, guess what, I learned to swim today, and without my life jacket too."

As Doctor Green and I discussed this incident and others, our conversation seemed to center around the one hope of all our lives; a sense of accomplishment.

Those first steps of our children, or the first words spoken by them, were as thrilling to us as the day they graduated from high school or college. The sense of accomplishment is inspiring music to our ears and a tonic to our souls. However, accomplishment comes not as a bequest, but rather a conquest. It is gained by overcoming many hazards, by substituting faith for fear.

Matthew, the author of the first Gospel, tells of the occasion when Jesus was walking on the water towards the disciples on the sea of Galilee. When the Master sensed the fear of His disciples in the boat He said to them, "Be of good cheer; it is I, be not afraid." Peter answered Him by saying, "Lord, if it be Thou, bid me to come unto Thee on the water" (Matthew 14:27-28).

At the invitation of Jesus, Peter started to walk toward his Master on the water, but when he saw the turbulent waves about him he was afraid and began to sink. Jesus put out His hand and saved him. Peter failed because he feared.

Peter's life, for sometime, was a battle between faith and fear. He finally, through God's grace and his own determination, reached the high plateau of accomplishment. He became the rock that Jesus knew he would be, and that Peter had hoped that he could be.

There is a little of Peter in every one of us. We have all been defeated many times by fear and the lack of confidence. Most of us, however, have felt that sense of accomplishment that has come when we have given life our very best.

24

"Hitch your wagon to a star, keep your seat and there you are," was a motto used by many graduating classes of long ago. However, becoming an accomplished farmer, doctor, lawyer, or a success in any field, is not quite that easy. Keeping one's seat is not as easy as it sounds.

One learns the satisfaction of prayer by continuing the practice of prayer. One realizes the benefits of applying the Golden Rule, of doing unto others as we would that they do unto us, only by continuing to apply this rule to everyday living.

A great baseball pitcher once said that a pitcher does not last long on past victories, but by continuing to deliver.

It is good to talk of that long line of splendor of Christian victories, but is is far more important that we continue what they have begun. Each new generation profits by the faith and courage of the past and present one.

Dear Lord, you know how often we have tried and failed. We ask that You might take control of our whole being that what we do may be as You would have it to be. We shall praise Thee. AMEN.

A Cup Of Cold Water

"FREE ICE Water at the Wall Drug Store, 168 miles." I had heard of this drug store long before I read this sign out in South Dakota. This unique store is located in a little town of Wall, at the gateway to the Bad Lands.

Business had been poor for this drug store. People were passing by the store, but not many of them stopped. The wife of the proprietor had an idea one day. She had a large sign made and placed several miles down the road. The sign read, "Free ice water at the Wall Drug Store." It worked like magic. The store became world famous; all because of a free glass of ice water.

Most of us have found that the profitable returns of life are greater when we have discovered the joy of what it means to share. The courteous word, the friendly smile, are like the frosting on the cake. They are like the free glass of ice water.

Sam Walter Foss, the poet, became famous with his poem, "Let Me Live by the Side of the Road and Be a Friend to Man." What more worthwhile motive for living could there be than to "be a friend to man." To feel that a part of your life had been given to others without thinking of the returns.

Dr. Tom Duly practically gave his life to the unfortunates of Laos. Just before he died, he wrote to a young medic, in whom he was interested, the following words: "Dedicate some of your life to others, your dedication will not be sacrifice. It will be an exhilarating experience, because it will be a sincere effort applied toward a meaninful end." This is good counsel for each of us, "dedicate some of your life to others," your dedication will not be in vain.

Jesus, in speaking of rewards said, "Whosoever shall give to drink unto one of these little ones, a cup of cold water only in the name of a disciple, verily I say unto you, he shall in no wise lose his reward" (Matthew 10:42).

The "reward" often is not seen, but felt. It is the feeling that comes to one when he has gone the second mile and more. It is a reward that cannot be measured.

Away back in Old Testament days there is an incident in the life of Elijah, the prophet. The poor widow who had, "but a handful of meal in the barrel, and a little oil in a cruse," was asked by Elijah to bake him a little cake first. Believing the promise of Elijah, she did so. Her reward, for her faith and action, was that, "the barrel of meal wasted not, neither did the cruse of oil fail" (I Kings 17:16) until the end of the drought.

It may be the first little cake, or a glass of water. Whatever the good deed may be, if done in the spirit of the Master, the reward, though unasked for, will be given.

Help us, Lord, to see the joy that comes in giving a cup of cold water in Thy Name, as we go about doing good for others. AMEN.

Assurance

THE OCCASIONS that caused me the greatest fear, as a child growing up on the farm, were the thunder storms in the night. Mother knew how we feared them. As the thunder grew louder and the lightning more blinding we trembled in our beds upstairs. We waited and longed for one thing. As the first drops of rain began their rhythmic beat on the tin roof we knew what to expect.

We listened for the lifting of the latch on the stair door and the words, "Children, do you want to come down?" Did we? Down the stairs and into Mother's room we bounded. We knew that we would be safe now. Mother's presence gave us complete assurance that all was well.

There is one word that gives added power to our faith in the present and our hope for the future. Without that word our whole future would limp. That word is assurance. From early childhood, through the hopeful years of youth, and into the fading years of age we seek for assurance.

The common confession that many make is that so often their cherished dreams have crashed at their feet. Disappointment has confronted them and there is nothing to which they can cling. Life is not all smoothness for any of us. We find ourselves groping for a sense of security. We all need something to give life stability.

On a ship coming across the ocean to America was a family of four. There was a father, a mother, a daughter age three, and a son of six. During a storm one day, the six-year-old boy clung to his father. He looked up with tears in his eyes and inquired, "Daddy, when will we have a house that won't shake?" The father answered, "Not until we get to America."

We know, as long as we travel the high seas of life, our houses of faith may shake at times. But they need not come crashing down about us. It is not necessary that we be controlled by fear, but rather by faith. A faith that does not control life cannot save it.

Someone has said that it is not by struggle but by yielding that we find security. In the Song of Moses he says, "The eternal God is thy refuge and underneath are the everlasting arms" (Deuteronomy 33:27). Trusting in this truth gives stability to our faith.

Jesus was with the disciples on the sea when a storm came upon them. The water almost filled their boat. Jesus was sleeping in one end of the boat. In fear His disciples awakened Him. He arose and took command of the waves. When they saw how He was able to calm the seas, they said, "What manner of man is this that even the winds and the sea obey Him?" (Matthew 8:27)

The secret of their safety was that Jesus was in their boat. All was well, it gave them complete assurance. It is no secret that we, likewise, can have complete assurance if we recognize that "God is our refuge." Jesus can quiet the stormy seas around us and bring calmness of faith and a courageous spirit, just as He did for the disciples. We too can have this assurance if we will but let go and let God.

We thank Thee, Lord, for your power to bring peace out of turbulence. AMEN.

Accentuate The Positive

"ACCENTUATE THE POSITIVE" was a song quite popular many years ago. Like most songs of this type it soon lost its popularity, but its message is still relevant for this day.

"Accentuate the positive, eliminate the negative," so went the song. In all experiences of life, this is a good practice. It is easy enough to be negative; to look on the dark side; to look for mistakes, and to be a prophet of failure. To be positive one must possess wisdom, courage, and above all, faith.

Norman Vincent Peale, nationally known pastor and author, wrote a book several years ago on, *The Power of Positive Thinking.* His philosophy in this book was that you need be defeated only if you want to be. This is true in all the avenues of life.

On the wall above the office desk of the body shop where my car was repaired were these words, "Making the best of a bad mess is our business." He who accentuates the positive has this kind of attitude concerning life.

Most of us know that there are many things wrong with our country, our church, and our community. But, negative talk alone will not right the wrong. Being negative only emphasizes the wrong but does not solve the problem.

A couple, on the verge of breaking up their marriage, came to me recently. They began to enumerate all the things that were wrong with each other. I listened patiently. I then suggested that they take a few minutes to see if they could list some good points about each other. In spite of the imperfections in life about us, it is surprising how much good there is if we look for it.

Jesus and His ministry was positive. When we read the Beatitudes and the Sermon on the Mount, we recognize this truth. Hate is negative, Jesus taught love which is positive. An eye for an eye, or getting even with one's enemies is negative. Jesus taught that we should do unto others as we would that they should do unto us. This is positive.

True, the Master's eye was not closed to the sins of His day. His life, however, was an example of victory over defeat and love over hate. Those who have sought His help and followed His formula have experienced victory.

Paul, the apostle of faith, gave us ageless advice when he said that whatsoever things are honest, just, pure, lovely, and of good report, "if there be any virtue, and if there be any praise, think on these things" (Philippians 4:8). He too believed in accentuating the positive. This prescription for life has never been improved upon.

Help us, Lord, never to give up to despair. Grant that each day may be a day of victory for our good and Thy glory. AMEN.

Achievement

RONNIE was a nine year old boy who sang in our cherub choir. One Sunday he had a solo part in the children's anthem. He forgot his words and failed, so he thought. Ronnie cried, just as many of us do when we feel that we have failed.

The next week Ronnie's director urged him to try again. That Sunday the cherub choir had another anthem ready. Ronnie sang his part without mistake. As this fine, determined little lad, took his seat, he had a broad smile on his face. It was quite an achievement to turn failure into victory.

Achievement often comes by the way of failure and tears fraught with determination. Someone once observed that difficulties are the things that show what men are.

Peter, the disciple, was one of the most human of the Twelve and one of the most valuable to Jesus. The history of his life seemed to be a struggle between failure and victory. His name signified the rock while his actions were often like the waves of the sea.

Peter wanted to walk on the water but his fears overcame his faith. The time came, however, when his faith finally conquered his fears. In triumph he became Peter, the rock. His was an achievement realized only when he gave himself up to that greater power. Peter was always getting in the way until the Spirit took control.

As a child, in the first grade in school, I had one great ambition. I wanted, more than anything else, to be able to write my own name. In my childlike mind I visioned myself going home from school and showing my mother that I could write my own name.

I struggled each day with my pencil as I watched Miss Zona, my teacher, write my name. I wanted to do it myself. When finally I let Miss Zona guide my hand, it was then that I achieved my ambition.

Life, for most of us has been a series of battles going on within. Wanting to achieve certain ambitions and make a name for ourselves, has often taken precedent over the real values of life. It is only when we have given up and over to God that we are able to accomplish the things that really endure.

Peter, with Christ's guiding hand, became the rock he was intended to be. He finally came to the place where he was in control of every situation, but only as he was controlled by that greater Power, the Spirit of God. This, each of us may achieve and in the same number.

Lord, help us this day, to give up and over to Thee, that we may accomplish those things that will make our lives more fruitful for your sake and our good. AMEN.

A Good Teacher

ONE SINGLE action is worth a thousand words. It goes without saying that most of us have been influenced more by examples than pronouncements. Often, the examples that have influenced us most have come to us in our early youth.

I shall always treasure the memory of my first public school teacher. Not just because she was the first to teach me to write my name and to read my first words. It was Miss Zona Graves whose example for the first three years of my school career that made an indelible impression on my life.

Miss Zona's philosophy, which she taught by precept and example was, "Stand tall, walk straight, keep clean, and be honest." She taught this, but best of all she illustrated it. It was not unusual to see her walking with her arms folded behind her back. By so doing she stood tall and walked straight. She believed and practiced that, "cleanliness was next to Godliness," and that honesty was the best practice.

This world is far from perfect. We are appalled at the utter disregard of common decency and the lack of integrity on all sides. But when I stop to enumerate those whom I know are still standing tall, walking straight, keeping clean, and being honest, it gives me encouragement for the present and hope for the future.

The Apostle Paul's relationship with Timothy was almost like father and son. Paul's life made an eternal impression upon young Timothy. Paul, likewise, was often encouraged through the relationship with Timothy and his family.

In writing to Timothy, Paul spoke of ". . . the unfeigned faith that is in thee, which dwelt first in thy grandmother Lois, and in thy mother Eunice . . . " (II Timothy 1:5) Paul was sure that with examples, such as Timothy's grandmother and mother had set, he could not help from having their kind of faith also.

We do not become active believers in God through inheritance. Parents cannot bestow upon their children character; however, we parents, by the lives we live and the example we set, can make an indelible imprint upon their lives.

The disciples were never the same, though they were not perfect, after they had walked in the presence of Jesus those three years. The lessons their Master taught and the example He set made a lasting impression upon their lives. The influence of His life shall never cease.

His teaching, example and presence in the lives of millions will continue to help men and women walk straight, stand tall, be honest and keep clean.

O Great Teacher of all who will come to Thee, we thank you for those whose teaching and lives have influenced ours. May we be always mindful of your blessed Presence with us. AMEN.

A Good Image

RECENTLY at one of the commencements, where I had the privilege of speaking, I met a man who caused me to think. This man, a faithful reader of my column, shook my hand and said, "I see your face and read your column every two weeks." Then, with a smile he added, "I'd know that face any place, you leave a good image."

We cannot help what our facial features are like. Much of this we have inherited and can well be proud of it. However, the kind of image we leave is, to a great extent, up to us. The man's statement set me to thinking. What kind of an image do I portray?

An eight-year-old boy, with all the self confidence of an artist, was drawing a picture one day. His mother asked him what he was doing. The boy answered, "I'm drawing a picture of God." The mother, with doubt in her voice said, "Why, Billy, no one has ever seen God."

The self-styled artist without looking up replied, "They will when I have finished."

The artist must have an image in his mind if he is to produce a picture. The poet, likewise, if he would write a poem. So it is with everyone who would perfect a life. Most of us, unconsciously, are the images of what we believe, do and say.

The disciples of Jesus came to Him one day and implored the Master to show them the Father. Jesus responded by saying, "He that hath seen me hath seen the Father."

The Master's great purpose in coming to this world was to show, in deed and word, what God was like. He came to be the image of our Heavenly Father. Jesus portrayed the Father's image in His acts of forgiveness, His dealings in justice and His examples of mercy.

What do we mean by a good image? A likeness, a model to go by or a picture of our ideal. I well remember one of my teachers in public school when I was a youngster. She was not only my image of a good teacher, but my ideal of what I thought an angel must be like.

It is true, whether we intend to do so or not, we leave a good or a bad image in the minds of those with whom we come in contact day by day.

Peter, the big fisherman and a disciple of Jesus, often left the wrong impression on those who observed his actions. Impetuous though he was, it is said by some that he was the most human of the Twelve. When he was finally transformed from a wave to a rock he became a living image of his Master.

None of us will ever be able to leave a perfect image for we have too many imperfections. But, as Peter became an example of his Master's life, so may we through prayer and discipline do likewise.

Give us the wisdom, O God, and the humility of spirit that others may see Jesus, Thy Sons, in us each day. AMEN.

Being Relevant

THERE ARE many words being used today that seem to be taking on a new meaning. One of those words is "relevant." On all sides there are those who are saying that writers, speakers, and teachers "are not speaking to our day. Their books and philosophy are not relevant." However, keeping up with the times means more than going modern. Seeing the need of the present is more than talking the language of the day.

We hear so often that we need a new set of rules. Some of us have a feeling that we have not outdated the Ten Commandments. A closer look and a sincere study of them would help us all to discover that they are far more relevant to our day than we realize.

Dr. Paul R. Woudenberg, effective pastor in California, reminded his congregation that there were precedents for the "growing ethical anarchy" in this country today. He said that ancient Israel went through the same debacle. The prophets, Isaiah, Amos, Hosea, and Micah showed the only way out of it. Their words have meaning for Americans today.

Whether the time is ripe for such wise counsel, as these early prophets gave to their day, we too would do well to see that it is the only way back. There is danger in making our belief and religious practice so broad that it becomes so thin that it has very little meaning.

My father practiced soil conservation fifty years ago. He may have used different methods than are used today; nevertheless, his concern was the same. He practiced the principle that "if one expects fertility of the soil tomorrow, one must conserve what is ours today." There is a trend today toward destroying and not conserving, not only the soil, but the soul.

Jesus, called a revolutionist by some, came saying, "Think not that I am come to destroy the law, or the prophets: I am not come to destroy, but to fulfill" (Matthew 5:17). We who would compare our modern activities to Jesus, must remember the change, which He brought about, came through compassion, not hate. He may have hated the sin, but He loved the sinner.

A peaceful and responsible society cannot come through anarchy or lawlessness. It will come only through those whose lives are disciplined for the concern of others' welfare and not their own alone. This was the plan of Jesus. His formula is still relevant for our day.

Help us, Lord, that we may once again listen to those, who out of the past have words of wisdom for our day. In Jesus' Name we pray. AMEN.

"Brevity"

I HAD conducted a funeral service in a little country church one afternoon. On my return to the village in which I lived, I met a man who had attended the funeral. Ben Moses was not a member of my congregation, but a good friend of mine.

Ben shook my hand and said very seriously, "Reverend, I liked that sermon this afternoon." I was curious and inquired, "Ben, would you mind telling me what you liked about it?"

Ben Moses, who with his brother, were well respected businessmen in the community replied, "When you got through you quit." I shall never forget that compliment and have tried to this day to live up to those words.

A dear old friend of mine, who had many years of experience, gave me good advice in the early years of my ministry. He laid his hand on my shoulder one Sunday morning and with kindness in his voice he said, "Brother Don, if you can't preach a sermon in twenty minutes it is sure you never will in forty."

It is not the length of our prayer, but rather the depth of our faith and the sincerity of our petition that really counts. The greatest prayer ever prayed, the Lord's Prayer, contains only about sixty-five words. It was Martin Luther, the great reformer and preacher, who said, "The fewer the words, the better the prayer."

A little girl taught her father a lesson, one night, that he has never forgotten. As she said her bedside prayer she prayed, "God is great, God is good, and that's enough, Amen." This was enough. Not because she had forgotten the rest of the prayer, but because she believed that God was great and God was good. This was all that was necessary for a child's faith.

Long arguments for the Church, the Bible, or for God shows man's ability. It convinces many that he knows what he is talking about. However, the truth is not in how much we say, but rather how we do that counts.

In the Sermon on the Mount, Jesus advised His hearers that, "When ye pray, use not vain repetitions, as the heathen do; for they think they shall be heard for their much speaking."

Jesus gave many words of wisdom during His brief ministry; words to which we cling for inspiration and guidance. The Beatitudes, found in the fifth chapter of Matthew are words spoken to the point, with brevity, by Jesus. Those words, however, bear more weight because of the fact that it was said of Him, "He went about doing good."

It was said of a pastor of my childhood days, "You knew he had something to say. When he stood up he said it; when he had finished he sat down. As you went on your way, what he said stayed with you." God bless those who know when they have said enough; the light of their witness shall live on.

O God, teach us to weigh our words and apply our hearts unto wisdom. In Jesus' Name. AMEN.

Beyond The Horizon

THE DAY was drawing to a close. The sun, like a great ball of fire, seemed to be slipping beyond the western horizon. The disappearing sun was sending its final rays across the evening sky. The reflection through the scattered clouds was breathtaking.

All of those present, at the lakeside, were talking of the beauty of the evening. One of the guests was sitting quietly by. He was blind. Finally he spoke, "It is a beautiful sunset. Even though I am blind I have been seeing it through your eyes. I can see beyond the sunset. I am sure it will even be a more beautiful day tomorrow."

This man's words not only inspired the writing of a song, but gave faith to those present for a better day ahead.

So it is with the closing of a year. As the old year drifts away into memory we, in faith, look beyond the horizon to a better year tomorrow.

What is ahead? This we do not know. But we, like Abraham of old who, "went out, not knowing whither he went," (Hebrews 11:8) can do likewise with faith in God who does know what the future has in store for each of us.

Henry David Thoreau, American philosopher and writer, once said, "I live in the present. I only remember the past and anticipate the future." This is good philosophy for each of us.

It is good to look backward and be grateful for the blessings of the past. It is well that we ponder over failures of the past that we might profit by them in the future. As we look back in memory we should never forget that the present is ever with us. We can live only a day or a year at a time, but by God's help, we can make the most of the opportunities or disappointments that come our way.

A follower of my column wrote me recently, "During the past year I have had a heartbreaking tragedy and several disappointments, but I did not give up. God has seen us through. I have found that keeping busy at something worthwhile compensates for the heartaches of the past, and gives hopes for the future."

This letter came as I was preparing to write this column. How true were the above words. As we look into a new year we must walk with courage and faith in the future.

From the wisdom of Solomon comes the following words, "Whatsoever thy hand findeth to do, do it with thy might . . . " (Ecclesiastes 9:10) This wise man was warning of the brevity of life and the temptation to waste those years instead of investing them.

The year 1976 will mark the two hundredth year of our nation's birth. It could well mark the beginning of the end of our democracy or it could well be a year in which our beloved nation experiences a rebirth of realization of why we are here. If we look beyond the horizon with faith in God and concern for our fellowmen, the years ahead could well be the best years of our lives.

O God of eternity, we know what lieth beyond our horizons, but we know that Thou art there. We will trust Thee for whatever Thou seest best for us and ours. Through Christ we pray. AMEN.

Bearing The Unbearable

TO ELIZABETH GILBERT, October 26 started out to be just another Saturday for a busy farm wife and mother of several children. Little did she think that by evening one of her children would be in the hospital, having been struck by a car.

It was a tragic day and night. This distraught mother and father had to bear the unbearable ordeal of standing by helplessly, to await the verdict of the next few hours. Trusting the outcome, of one of those they loved more than their own lives, into the hand of competent, concerned hospital staff and above all into the hands of God.

It was not easy for this mother to "cease pleading and demanding," as she said, that Tammy's life be spared.

"I prayed the hardest prayer of my life," said this mother. "Lord, she is your child. You love her too. You know what is best for her. Please, help me to bear whatever happens."

Tammy's life was spared. Elizabeth Gilbert will always remember that night, and especially her prayer of relinquishment to God's will and wise providence.

Experiences, though not like unto the above, could be related by many of us. Many of our prayers were not answered in the way we had hoped, but they were answered. The grace and courage that comes to us to bear the unbearable is that which comes from trusting God's wisdom and power.

Mark, the gospel writer, tells of the father that brought his sick son to Jesus. He pleaded with the Master that if Jesus could do anything to " . . . have compassion on us, and help us."

I can see Jesus looking with compassion upon this concerned father whose son had fallen on the ground before them. "Jesus said unto him, If thou canst believe, all things are possible to him that believeth" (Mark 9:23).

With tears in his eyes and a burden on his heart that had been unbearable since his son was a child, the father cried out, " . . . Lord, I believe; help thou mine unbelief" (Mark 9:24). The boy was healed by Jesus. The father's faith was strengthened. In the confessing of his weak faith, he was made strong.

Tragic experiences come to each of us; we believe in God; we pray for His help in our helplessness. We try our best to believe that all things work together for good to those who love God. We plead with Him for what we think is best for those we love.

Finally, not knowing what else to do we cry out, "Lord, I believe, help my lack of faith." With that confession of our weakness and trusting His wise providence, we are given strength to bear the unbearable. The will of God becomes our will. Life's darkest day becomes life's brightest hope.

Thy will be done, O Lord, we pray. For we know if Thy will is done in our lives, all things will work together for our good. AMEN.

Birthplaces

IT IS just a little log cabin. It is not attractive in itself, but thousands come each year to gaze upon it.

We, like many others, had made our way to Hodgensville, Kentucky. We climbed the steps that led to that beautiful shrine, built there on "Sinking Spring Farm." Within the walls of that memorial we beheld a small log cabin. Why did I remove my hat, as I stood there, on that rainy morning? Because Abraham Lincoln, sixteenth President of these United States, was born there.

Many birthplaces of great men and women have been honored in one way or another. It is well that they should be. However, those places of their birth have not become famous within themselves. These places are held in reverence because new ideals, goals, and determinations were born within the lives of these men and women that molded their entire future.

I have often thought that every inspiration that comes to me is the birthplace of a future goal. Abraham Lincoln, as well as many others, had those birthplaces. As Lincoln saw his brothers and sisters of another race being sold into slavery, there was born within him the determination to strike this wrong with all of his might.

What has made some occasions and places mean so much to us? Isn't it because on those occasions some things were born within us that gave new hope and courage to us for tomorrow?

Most of us will never have a shrine built over our birthplace. We may, however, because of a courageous decision of faith, cause those who know us to say, "He was born there."

Down a dusty road moves a cavalcade of men. It is the road that leads to Damascus. The leader of these men had been commissioned to go down this road and destroy those whom he found who dared worship a man who called himself the Son of God. Something happened to this man on that road.

Years afterward, legend tells us, two men were seen walking along this same road. One of them stops and kneels in the dust. If you would have been close enough you might have recognized this man as the apostle Paul. Why does he reverence this spot? This man was born there. From that experience his entire future was changed.

It is just a small door and you have to bend down to enter through it. Thousands, however, make their way through this small door each year and stand with bowed heads in that little church of the Nativity. Why do they come from all over the world to that place in the little town of Bethlehem? A Man was born there.

All of the true brotherhood, the hope of eternal peace, and the way to eternal life points to that spot. Jesus Christ, who would be the Saviour of the world, if it would let Him, was born there.

Because of Him each of us may point with faith to that occasion and those spots which we may recall as "birthplaces."

O Lord, we thank Thee for those moments of inspiration that are sent from Thee and are born in our hearts. Help us to keep them alive, that we may move forward with them. Through Christ, AMEN.

Conquest Of Fear

"THE ONLY thing we have to fear is fear itself." These were the unforgetable words spoken by Franklin D. Roosevelt at his first inauguration. The nation was in the depths of the worst depression in its history. Those words, and the confidence back of them, helped to give a nation renewed courage in the face of terror and despair. The words are as true today as then.

A certain degree of fear, however, is good for us. It was Lloyd Douglas, author of *The Robe,* who once wrote "When all fear is gone, there may be little remaining that is worthy of respect." The ancient sage wrote, "The fear of the Lord is the beginning of knowledge" (Proverbs 1:7). There must have been some truth in what this wise man said or the ages would have allowed his words to die. Someone has said that it is only the fear of God that can deliver us from the fear of man.

Who of us has not been faced with fear? Fear of failing, fear of tomorrow, fear of death, even fear of life and its problems. When we face these fears we are tempted to panic. Because of the fear of failing the ones we love, or failing in the task which is ours, we give up in despair. Fear is a contagious disease. If left to run its course, it brings death. If not physically, at least mentally and spiritually.

What is the answer to fear? The answer to fear is trust. I paused at the bedside of a man who was to have surgery the following day. One of his limbs had to be amputated just below the knee. As I talked with him and had prayer, I could see that there was a man whose fears had been subdued with trust. He gripped my hand and said, Chaplain, I learned a few years ago to trust God, even though I could not see His complete plan for my life."

Our fears are subdued when we learn to substitute faith for fear. It was Martin Luther, the courageous leader of the reformation, who spoke the sentiments of our hopes in the face of fear. In his hymn, *A Might Fortress is Our God,* he wrote, "We will not fear, for God hath willed His truth to triumph through us . . . " This kind of faith is found throughout this hymn. It is the reflection of a man whose courage never failed. His God was a mighty fortress.

David, the Psalm writer as well as the king, was constantly beset with enemies who sought his life. He said, time after time, that he knew from whence came his help. "What time I am afraid, I will trust in Thee" (Psalm 56:3). Thus did David find consolation in time of distress.

All of us have and do experience fear. Many of us, in those times, have learned that though we may have to face these fears, we need not face them alone. For we know that in all things God works together for good for them who love Him.

Thou hast promised, dear Lord, never to leave us nor forsake us. In this promise we trust Thee to help us overcome our doubts and fears. Through Christ Jesus we pray. AMEN.

Collateral

RECENTLY I went with a friend to the bank to secure a loan. One of the questions the banker asked my friend was, "What collateral have you?" The banker was wanting to know what my friend had to offer, besides his promise, as a guarantee of his ability to repay the loan.

Quite often there comes to my desk a blank requesting my evaluation of an applicant for a position. What are his possibilities? Is he honest? What about his background? In these questions, along with many others, the prospective employer is asking, "What collateral has the applicant to offer?"

Someone has said that character is better collateral than cash. This, really, is what the banker and the prospective employer are concerned about. The question is not alone a man's ability to produce, but his sincere effort to do so.

The wise author of the Book of Proverbs says, "A good name is better to be chosen than great riches, and loving favor rather than silver and gold" (Proverbs 22:1). This wise man is trying to say to us that one may be rich in material possessions but poor in the things that make a life.

A young man was invited back to his home community as guest speaker for a father and son banquet. In the course of the introduction, the Master of Ceremonies who had known the young man from childhood said, "One of the most commendable things I can say about our speaker is that when his name is mentioned you don't have to apologize for him." This is good collateral for anyone. The introduction concerned not only his ability but his honestly.

When Jesus was choosing His disciples His concern was not only their ability but their pliability. He did not choose those, who were to be His followers, from those rich in possessions and education alone. He looked rather for those who were teachable.

The church, the school, the government, and in all places of responsibility there is a need for men and women who place making a life above making a living. Not that making a living is not important. But he who builds a life, which has a foundation on the principles Christ taught, will in the end make a better living.

Lord, Take my life and let it be, Consecrated, Lord to Thee; Take myself, and I will be, Ever, only, all for Thee. AMEN.

Contented Living

WHILE TRYING to locate a family at one of the lakes near where I live I stopped to make inquiry of a couple working in their yard. It was not a stately home but one could see that much loving care had gone into the making of this little home by the side of the lake.

I surveyed the landscape with the green lawn, well planned, beautiful flowers, and their freshly painted house. I also noted a sign fastened to a tree that read, "We're Satisfied." Commenting on the sign, this friendly man in his early seventies said, "Yes, we're satisfied with where we live, but we are never quite satisfied with what we are. We begin and end each day with God."

It is not so much where we live, but how we live that counts toward a sense of contentment. As a nation, we are the best housed, fed, entertained, and best dressed of any nation in the world. Yet, it seems that we are the least satisfied. True satisfaction comes not from the material possessions alone.

Paul, the apostle, writing to the Church at Philippi, said, "I have learned, in whatsoever state I am, therewith to be content" (Philippians 4:11). He had learned to be satisfied, not to worry or be overly concerned with his lot, but to work, worship, and trust God for the present and the future.

One of the reasons Paul was able to do this was that he never lost hope. When hope is gone we quit trying. It was Coleridge, British poet, who wrote, "He is the best physician who is the most ingenious inspirer of hope." Do we inspire hope or encourage despair?

The story is told of a shopkeeper whose building was almost destroyed in the great Chicago fire of 1871. A few days after the fire, someone noted the following sign on the charred door of the store, "All is lost but wife, family and faith. Open for business tomorrow." This is the kind of faith that lives for today and has hope for tomorrow.

Paul, also, learned that contented living comes from living life primarily to give, not alone to get. He kept love alive. He, like Jesus, had a compassion for others. It is not enough to be against hate; we must be for love. When we, with compassion, give of our best for others, the best will come back to us.

Probably the best encourager of contented living is to remember whose we are. As David Livingstone, African explorer and missionary, was leaving his home as a young man, his father's parting words to him were, "David, never forget whose son you are. Live with confidence in God."

Wasn't this why Paul was able to say with faith, "I can do all things through Christ which strengtheneth me" (Philippians 4:13). We too may do the same and know true contented living.

Lord, we believe that wherever we are or whatever our circumstances, that you are with us. Help us truly to believe that all things work together for good, to them who love You. In Thy name we pray. AMEN.

Choosing

ONE OF man's greatest, yet most dangerous powers, is that of choosing. He faces these decisions from his birth to his grave. As a tree is bent so will it grow, are words that are as true of man as a tree.

Some of my first recollections on this subject came to me from one of my first public school teachers. She said, not only once but many times, "What you hope to be you are now becoming. Do not be satisfied to be a second-rater in anything you choose to become."

We spend our lives making choices. None are more important than the ones we make early in life. The story is told of a traveler who came to a road in bad repair. Deep ruts stretched out as far as he could see. A traveler coming from the opposite direction stopped his wagon and said, "Mister, choose which rut you want to travel in before you start, for you will be in it for the next twenty miles."

There are two ways that we may travel through life. We may drift with the current or pick up the oars and row, often against the current. The first will be easy, the latter difficult but more profitable in the end.

I once knew a farmer who gave the following observation, "I may not have the largest farm, but I made up my mind that it would be the best." His crops, livestock, and buildings was a proof of his determined choice. Not only this, but he and his family were examples of the fact that it is not always quantity, but quality that makes for better living.

From the beginning of the history of man, until this day, the Creator has given man freedom of choice. He must, however, give an account of his stewardship.

The wise writer of Proverbs wrote, "The way of the fool is right in his own eyes; but he that hearkeneth unto counsel is wise" (Proverbs 12:15). It is a mark of wisdom to counsel with the wise before making a decision. There is no doubt but what today's youth has more facts, but wisdom is knowing how to use those facts.

In the course of the Sermon on the Mount, Jesus spoke of the two ways when He said, "Enter ye in at the strait gate; for wide is the gate and broad is the way that leadeth to destruction, and many there be that go in thereat; Because strait is the gate, and narrow is the way, which leadeth unto life, and few there be that find it" (Matthew 7:13-14).

There are two ways that stretch out before us. One beckons us to forget caution and get what is coming to us today, for tomorrow we may die. It is the way that says think of yourself, you are not your brother's keeper. Take the easy way out, there is plenty of time.

The other way is the way of peace of mind. On this way will be found opportunities of helping others less fortunate than we. It is the way of sacrifice, but also of eternal benefits. It is the way where one does unto others as you would that they do unto you. It is the way where one finds the will of God and follows it. Jesus exemplified this way. He bids us make it our choice.

O God, give us the wisdom to make right choices and the courage to follow through. This we pray in Jesus' name. AMEN.

"Communication"

WE JUST DON'T seem to be able to communicate." Such are the words of distress that I have been hearing down through the years. It is a condition in which people of all walks, vocations, and ages find themselves.

It is a foregone conclusion that lack of communication endangers family relations. Strained communication is one of the leading causes of wars. It likewise divides nations. It contributes to the lack of unity within the Church.

We hear much, these days, about the generation gap. This is nothing new. I experienced it when I was growing up on the farm. I thought my father and mother didn't understand me. I was like Mark Twain, the philosopher, who once said of his father, "When I was fourteen I thought my father was the most ignorant man I had ever known. When I was twenty-one, it was surprising how much my father had learned in those few short years.

The generation gap, however, is not always found in people of different age groups. It is often found to be of the character and personality, and not age alone.

Even the Master Teacher, Jesus, was not able to reach the minds of many of those whom He contacted. It wasn't that Jesus did not understand them. The difficulty was that they did hear Him, but would not pay the price of discipleship.

The words which seem to describe the condition of the world, in which we find ourselves these days are, confusion, dis-unity, violence, and hate. Put over against these the words that described Jesus and His mission, understanding, compassion, and concern. How much different is the formula of Jesus.

There were those in Jesus' day who thought that He was a revolutionist. But, He "came not to destroy the law, or the prophets; I am come not to destroy but fulfill" (Matthew 5:17). His way was not that of the sword of violence, but through compassion, concern, understanding, and love. His Sermon on the Mount was easy to understand, but not easy to apply. Loving those who despitefully use you; heaping coals of fire on their heads; this was not easy, but it worked, and so it does today.

It is not difficult for us to communicate love to those around us, as long as we do not do it with one hand behind our back. The motive of our concern is often better understood by the one we are trying to win than we think.

Breeding confusion is one of the goals held so important in the plan of our enemies of true democracy. It has always been one of the chief aims of Satan from the beginning of time. Left to run its course, confusion can destroy all that has been contributed to make our beloved Country what it should be.

There is a bit of verse from the wisdom of Proverbs, "Trust in the Lord with all thine heart; and lean not upon thine own understanding" (Proverbs 3:5). Our own decisions and judgements are not without flaws. Praying for understanding of God's wisdon and being able to communicate it to others is the need of our day.

Heavenly Father, give us the wisdom to know the needs of those around us and the understanding that You have had with us, that we may help to lift a dying world to Thee. AMEN.

"Come Before Winter"

THERE ARE many forms of human suffering. Loneliness stands high on the list. It often comes when one is placed in a new situation. When one leaves home for the first time, to go away to college or in the service, when we lose someone dear to us, when it seems that the world is passing us by.

Driving through a town one day I remembered that a faithful radio listener lived there. She had written me many times. She had been told by her doctor that she would never recover from her illness. The last letter from her had said, "I haven't been so good lately. I hope you will get here before it is too late. I, so much, want to see you."

I had never met this good woman, but I felt that there might not be a better time. I stopped. It gave her a lift and I received a far greater one. I learned later that another month would have been too late.

There is a sound of loneliness in the plea of Paul, the apostle, to his good friend Timothy as he says, "Do thy diligence to come before winter . . ." (II Timothy 4:21)

Paul had just written, in this same letter, "The cloke that I left at Troas with Carpus, when thou comest bring with thee and the books, but especially the parchments" (II Timothy 4:13). These were physical and material needs, but there is a tone of urgency in Paul's voice as he says, "Come before winter."

How many times we have neglected to make that call, or write that letter. We knew that we must do it "before winter," but we put it off until it was too late.

I have a little poem in my file, written by D. K. Silverwood, many years ago. Its theme is "Just Tell Him So." The thought in the poem is that if there is someone to whom we can give a little praise, do it now. If you like him, let him know it. A word of encouragement may make her days a little brighter. The poem ends with, "Do not wait till life is over and he's underneath the clover; For he cannot read his tombstone when he's dead."

How often Jesus must have felt a sense of loneliness and forsakenness. How often He must have looked around Himself at those who turned aside with other concerns. "Come before winter," before it is too late. A woman, who felt deeply indebted to Jesus, did come. She came with precious ointment. She did not "wait until winter." Her reward was the word of her Master when He said, ". . . this that she hath done will be spoken as a memorial of her" (Mark 14:9).

Someone is waiting, somewhere, imploring us to "come before winter," before it is too late. This could very well be the voice of God speaking to many of us. Peace of mind is the reward for those who give of themselves to others who plead, "Come before winter."

Father, forgive us for our neglect of those to whom we might have been a blessing. Help us to be diligent in our concern of others. AMEN.

Confidence

THE DAY was perfect. It was the kind of a day in the Fall that made one feel like he was really happy to be alive. I was expressing my appreciation of the perfect fall weather to an old friend of mine. This man, without a smile on his face replied, "Yes, but we'll pay for it before the winter is over."

That little word "but" is often the symbol of those who live by their fears. It is like the dear old lady who used to say to me, "Yes, I'm feeling better today, but tomorrow it will be the same old pain again." The truth is that men and women of God live by their faith and not their doubts.

There are many words that give expression of our attitude toward life. There is one without which our entire future would limp. That one word is "confidence." In early childhood it makes us brave. In youth it gives us courage. As adults it makes the necessary loads easier to bear. On the sunset trail of age it lights our pathway down the valley of uncertainty.

Someone said long ago that confidence is a plant of slow growth and does not ripen in a day. Lack of confidence in ones self has spelled defeat to a most hopeful cause. Overconfidence has shown the same result. The resources of our own are not enough.

God often gives us tasks too hard for us. With those tasks, however, He provides the power with which to accomplish them. It is the partnership of God and man that turns defeat into victory.

Paul, the apostle, experienced many things that tried his faith. In spite of all these things he continued to express his confidence in God's plan for him. One time he wrote, "We are troubled on every side, yet not distressed; we are perplexed, but not in despair; persecuted, but not forsaken; cast down, but not destroyed" (II Corinthians 4:8-9). This faithful apostle possessed the quiet confidence in God that gave him courage to say, and believe, that one may be persecuted, but not forsaken.

Applause is encouraging; however, helpful criticism tempers the muscles of our soul. All of us feel the need of applause, now and then, but we should not be bitter over wise criticism. It was E. Stanley Jones, the well known missionary, who once said, "My critics are the unpaid watchmen of my soul."

When the winds and the storms of life seem as though they would destroy our boat on the sea of life, remember God is near. The writer of the Psalms once said, "God is our refuge and strength, a very present help in trouble . . ." Say, and believe that God is, and the future holds no terror, only triumph. This is the confidence that will never fail us.

O God, without Thee the enemies of our soul would destroy us. Be Thou our ever present help, we pray. AMEN.

Creative Living

THIS IS one of those long winter evenings when it is good to be sitting by our fireside. The snow is silently beating against our window panes and creating miniature drifts on the window ledge outside. We do not need the weatherman to inform us that winter is with us.

As I sit writing, I look across at Thelma, her nimble fingers creating the beauty of another afghan. I wonder at the number of different motions her fingers have made to create this, her eighth piece of art. Why does she do it? Those beautiful spreads make appreciative wedding, Christmas, or birthday gifts. She just plain enjoys making them. This is what one might call one of the creative arts.

Anyone who enjoys trying to make the world, about them, better or more beautiful than before they came on the scene, is practicing creative living.

Joe Louis, world champion heavy weight boxer for many years, donated a vocational school for youth in Detroit. One day he watched some of those young people taking advantage of their opportunities. Joe, watching them said, "I always wished I could do something with my hands, but I never could." This man was talking about creating something worthwhile.

The seamstress, the artist, the farmer, the housewife, the surgeon, scientist, the teacher, and many, many others belong to the great line of creators. Someone has observed that a dog can destroy a flower garden but it takes one with the love of the soil and the beauty of the flower in their heart to produce a garden.

One day, as Jesus walked by the sea of Galilee, He saw Simon and Andrew, casting a net into the sea, for they were fishers. "And Jesus said to them, come ye after me and I will make you to become fishers of men" (Mark 1:17).

I like this verse, found in the Gospel according to Mark. Mark remembers that Jesus said, "I will make you to "BECOME." The creating of any worthwhile endeavor, whether it be the crocheting of afghans, growing more beautiful roses, producing a better strain of corn, or building a more worthwhile life or a more peaceful world, involves a growing, learning, or practicing process. We "become" better by doing.

The disciples of Jesus watched as their Master healed a boy brought by his father.

The disciples had been unable to heal the boy. After the casting out of the demon by Jesus, these humble young men, asked "Why could we not cast the demon out?" Jesus explained to them that it was because of their lack of faith. "This kind goeth out not, but by prayer and fasting" (Matthew 17:21).

Creating is a process that is still going on about us and within us. How much it affects our own lives, and what we may do for others will depend on the amount of faith we have and what we are willing to give up, as well as give over, that God might be able to work through us.

O God, alone we will fail in everything, with Thee we can do all things, that is Thy will. Help us to let Thee guide us. AMEN.

Checking Our Course

THE OFFICE manager's telephone rang one day at noon. On answering the phone the manager heard an inquiring voice ask, "How is your new office boy doing?" The manager replied, "He is doing quite well. Who is this speaking?" The voice responded, "This is your new office boy. I was just checking up on myself." It is good for all of us, at times, to "check up" on ourselves. To review our goals; to test our values.

The twelve-year-old lad, rejoining his uncle after attending Mass at his church, was asked, "John, what did you do in there?" The young man replied, "I was reviewing my conscience." This thoughtful lad said more than he realized.

Regardless of who we are or what our vocation may be, we would do well to "review our conscience" regularly. Have we failed in some of our endeavors? Have we invested our talents to the best of our ability? Have we lived up to all the light that has shown across our pathway?

When we consider how Jesus, facing the aim of His life did so without hesitation, it makes us feel that we need to consider how we can do likewise.

There have been times when most of us have drifted with the currents of life. Times when we lost the urgency of our goals. In such times we need to study seriously the compass and take up the oars and get back on our course.

David, the Psalm writer, was not only a king but a man. He found himself off the course. In his remorse he cried out to God, "Create in me a clean heart, O God; and renew a right spirit within me" (Psalm 51:10). He knew that he must ask forgiveness for his sin of passion. He, also, remembered that in so doing he could say with expectancy, "He restoreth my soul . . ." (Psalm 23:3)

It was Isaiah, the Old Testament prophet, knowing the weakness of human man and the power of his Heavenly Father, who counsels us that, "They that wait upon the Lord shall renew their strength; they shall mount up with wings as eagles; they shall run and not be weary; and they shall walk, and not faint" (Isaiah 40:31).

We have often heard it said that we need to return to the faith of our fathers. This is good counseling, but when we do this we are not really turning back; we are rather going forward with new hope. It is no disgrace to confess that we have failed. By doing this we are confessing our own weakness but reaffirming our faith in God's greatness.

Our Father, renew a right spirit within us and help us that we may measure up to your expectation of us, we pray. AMEN.

Creative Leaping

"ONE SMALL step by a man, one great leap for mankind." Such were the words of Neil Armstrong as he stepped upon the surface of the moon. How much that small step and one great leap may mean to mankind's future, only time will tell.

In the history of civilization there have been many small steps by man, that have proven to be great leaps for the good of humanity. Most of them not as spectacular as the above, but they have contributed more than we may ever know. This, because someone had the courage and the faith to make a creative leap.

Those who see only yesterday, live in the past. Those who think only of today, are not the dreamers for tomorrow. The creative minds of today are working towards the realization of the hopes of tomorrow.

Many years ago, as a young pastor, I sat on the platform and listened to a man speak. He had had faith in the future and courage to take the creative leap. This great industrialist, James LeTourneau, who was known as the "earth mover," did just that. He contributed his success not alone to his ability, but his faith in prayer.

You take a creative leap when you receive and act upon an inspiration. You take a creative leap forward when you turn your back upon a bad habit. But all of his is easier done if you lift your face to God.

The writer of the Book of Acts tells of Peter and John coming to the Temple, at the hour of prayer. There at the gate was a man, lame from his birth, asking alms. Peter said, "Silver and gold have I none; but such as I have give I thee; in the name of Jesus Christ of Nazareth, rise up and walk" (Acts 3:6).

The account says that Peter took him by the hand and lifted him up, "and leaping up he stood and walked . . . leaping and praising God" (Acts 3:8).

There are many incidents of "creative leaping" in the lives of those early Christians. Think of the woman who said to herself that if only she could touch the hem of the garment of Jesus, she could be healed. She took the creative leap in the crowd to Jesus and the result was her being healed by Jesus.

Creative leaping involves many things. One must be willing to follow discipline. One, without a doubt, must be willing to leave some things behind. It certainly involves faith in God's promises as well as courage to make the step. But, all things are possible through prayer.

One could not begin to list those who have taken that one small step that has helped to change, not only their future, but that of countless others. Many of these did it not alone by facing their fears, but trusting their faith.

Grant, O Lord, that the one small step we take in faith, today, may lead us to greater things tomorrow, for Thy glory. AMEN.

Do It Now!

THE TIME is short! Tomorrow may be too late; do it now! Such were the words of an advertisement urging readers to take advantage of a certain opportunity.

As I think of the urgency of showing appreciation, I hear those words again, "Do it now!" How often we have put off the writing of that letter. We know we should make that call on that sick friend. That word of praise to the wife or husband is long due, even though they know how we feel anyway. We expect to do all of this but just haven't gotten around to it. Tomorrow may be too late; do it now!

Charles Hanson Towne, poet, has written a poem about a friend around the corner in this busy world that has no end. He expected to call on him but kept putting it off, for both were busy tired men. Time went by. The poem ends with, "Here's a telegram, sir; Jim died today. And that's what we get and deserve in the end, Around the corner a vanished friend."

A word of appreciation costs so little, but its value to the one receiving it cannot be estimated. I know, for I have been the recipient more times than I have deserved.

I never come to this season of the year but what I ask myself the question; should it be necessary to have a special day to express our thanksgiving? It is good, however, to have special occasions to remind ourselves of other's contributions and God's blessings.

Someone returning from Russia reminds us that a man has to work an hour for a loaf of bread; in America he works six minutes. Of the two billion people in the world eighty-five percent do not have enough to eat. Few in America are in that eighty-five percent, even with the injustice and poverty, which we know exists in many places. I know that I must not put off until tomorrow to show my gratitude.

"Bless the Lord, O my soul, and forget not all His benefits . . ." so said the Psalm writer. This man, long ago, went on to ask, "What shall I render unto the Lord for all His benefits toward me?" The answer to his question was, "I will take the cup of salvation, and call upon the name of the Lord" (Psalm 116:13).

These are not material blessings alone. But in thanking Him for all things, material, physical, and spiritual, we realize how rich we really are.

Many of us, however, believe we are blessed to bless others. Jesus once said, "Inasmuch as ye have done it unto the least of these, my brethern, ye have done it unto me" (Matthew 25:40).

When our cup overflows, the overflow is to be shared with others. As the gospel hymn says, "Look all around you, find someone in need, help somebody today." A kindly word, a neighborly deed, and a sincere prayer. These are some of the needs in our troubled world. The time is short, tomorrow may be too late. Do it now!

Lord, help us not to be weary in well doing, for we shall reap, if we faint not. In Jesus' name. AMEN.

"Determination"

IT WAS the year 1876. A group of men had gathered to watch a young man of twenty-nine make an experiment in his laboratory. He showed them a glass bulb, some wire and batteries. He told them that they were about to witness the first incandescent electric light.

This young man extinguished the light from the candles. He then pressed a switch. There was a small flash of light and all was dark.

The experiment appeared to be a failure, but the young inventor did not panic. He explained to his guests that the filament was not strong enough to carry the current. This determined young man was Thomas A. Edison. His equipment had failed, but not his faith. He continued his venture with determination for three years and succeeded.

Disappointment and failure, like a beast stalking its prey, has followed in the footsteps of man from the beginning of time. Many have hesitated to venture forth with their hopes, for fear of failure. Others, in the very presence of what seemed like defeat, faced their disappointment with determination and faith and succeeded.

William Ernest Henly, English poet and playwright, experienced many disappointments in his youthful career. He faced endless treatments and operations which tested his human courage to its limits. Through all of this he was able to write, "I won't give up, no matter what happens. I thank God for my unconquerable soul." This was why he was able to write his immortal poem, *Invictus*. He concluded this famous poem with the words, "I am the master of my fate. I am the captain of my soul."

The life of Job has brought challenge to many a troubled, suffering soul. The Bible tells us that all that Job possessed of Property, family, and even his own physical body, was being destroyed. Some of his so-called friends thought that the future for him was hopeless. In the face of almost being overcome, by the temptation to give up, he was able to say, "When He hath tried me, I shall come forth as gold" (Job 23:10).

Someone has said that Satan met his match in Job. Here was a man that proved in the end that religion was more than skin deep.

Man's whole future depends on how he faces the disappointments and tragedies each day. Faith and determination are God given, but to put them into practice is our decision.

Jesus, certainly faced disappointments throughout His ministry. It seemed to many that His was an experiment that would fail. It did not fail. He set a Light that has never gone out. The example of His determination has encouraged countless millions, through faith in Him, not to give up.

Help us, Lord, to have that spirit that knows no defeat, but trusts Thee to see us through in every circumstance. In Jesus' Name we pray. AMEN.

Divine Service

ABOVE THE kitchen sink, in the home of a friend of many years, are the words, "Divine services held each day." Most of us would not think that working at the kitchen sink could be a divine service. However, this devoted wife and mother thought differently.

Is what we do each day a task that has to be performed, or do we consider it a service to be rendered for someone else's good? Life's labors take on a different meaning if we can think of them as labors of love.

Recently, we heard Billy Graham introduce his brother. This brother, in response, said that he was not a preacher. He told how that, by God's help, he tried in his everyday life to be a witness to his faith. I say that, in a true sense, he was a preacher. He was performing a divine service each day of his life. In so doing, he was preaching a sermon in service.

I am thinking of many of those that I have known through the years, who have endeavored to serve where they were, with what they could do. These and a host of others have served without fanfare and belong in that long line of splendor. The work of their hands and hearts have been a divine service.

I doubt if the lad who brought his five loaves and two fishes to Jesus realized how great a service he was rendering. This boy did what he could and left the rest to the Master. The lad saw his loaves and fishes increase in the hands of Jesus. As the multitude was fed, this young assistant was amazed at the miracle. No monument, however, has ever been raised to this boy's dedication. His willingness to give what he had was his monument.

Someone has said that a life spent for others needs no monument. What one does, and the spirit in which he does it, is the best monument.

Jesus paid tribute to a woman who came to a home where He was dining. As she anointed Jesus' head the guests complained of the extravagance. The Master responded with "She hath done what she could; she is come aforehand to anoint my body to the burying" (Mark 14:8). This woman, whose life had been changed by the power of Jesus, wanted to do more than sing His praise. What she did was a divine service of love.

Our religion should put a warmth in our hearts and a song on our lips. But, there are those who find this not enough. There are those who are receiving extra dividends out of life. They are the ones whose concern for living is that, what they can do in the Master's name, may give a lift to those about them. This is a divine service.

O Lord God, give us the true spirit of humble service. That we may feel that whatever we can do for others, that we might do it in Your Name. AMEN.

Don't Faint – But Pray

WHEN THE battles of life bring discouragement each day. When almost overcome with the strife, look up — have faith — God cares, don't faint, but pray.

The above words came to me early one morning, recently. I had just been reading in the Gospel according to Luke, the words, "And He (Jesus) spake a parable unto them to this end, that men ought always to pray, and not to faint" (Luke 18:1). A faint heart denotes fear and fear shows the lack of faith. Men of faith do not faint, but they pray. Prayer helps to banish fear.

Don't faint, but find victory over defeat through the prayer of recognition. The prayer, which most of us learned in childhood, begins with, "Our Father . . ."

The unjust judge, of whom Jesus was speaking in the parable Luke gives us, was not concerned for the welfare of the widow who had come to him. But God, to whom we pray, is not only just, but merciful. We can say, "Our Father," and know that He is concerned about our needs. The prayer of recognition helps us to pray as David the Psalm writer, ". . . Thou art with me, Thy rod and Thy staff, they comfort me" (Psalm 24:4).

Don't faint, but find consolation through the prayer of supplication. ". . . Avenge me of mine adversary," pleaded the troubled widow of the judge. The Psalm writer gave solemn declaration when he said, "The Lord hath heard my supplication; the Lord will receive my prayer" (Psalm 6:9).

The prayer of supplication was encouraged by Jesus. He implored His listeners to, "Ask, and it shall be given you; seek, and ye shall find; knock, and it shall be opened unto you" (Matthew 7:7). George Whitefield, English minister and evangelist, prayed long ago, "O God, I pray Thee, give me Scotland or else I die." He did not faint, but prayed the prayer of supplication and a great revival came to Scotland.

Finally, one of the reasons so many have fainted by the wayside, is that they have not been able to pray the most difficult prayer. It is the prayer of relinquishment. Giving up and over to God is not always easy, but only by so doing does peace of mind come. The best example of this kind of prayer is found on that memorable night with Jesus in the Gardent of Gethsemane. Here He relinquished His will to His Father's will by praying, ". . . nevertheless, not my will, but Thine, be done" (Luke 22:42). In that scene of long ago, none of us can picture a fainting Christ in prayer.

Paul the apostle had to learn the prayer of relinquishment. In so doing he found that God's grace was sufficient for each day's needs. The prayer of relinquishment helps us to submit to God's will. It helps us to live each day with faith and with hope for tomorrow.

A fainting faith keeps a life in turmoil. A praying faith spells victory and peace of mind. Look up — have faith, God cares. Don't faint, but pray.

Our Father, help us to have the courage to pray, "Thy will be done." AMEN.

Encouragers

THIRTY YEARS ago we attended one of the national corn husking contests. It was in the days when the husking at the contests was done by hand. Following closely behind one of the young contestants, was his mother. There was no doubt about her identity, for as the ears of corn kept up a steady stream, striking the bang board, this mother kept saying, "That's my boy; he's going to win." Needless to say, that "boy" was one of the first to finish.

Encouragement from someone who has confidence in you makes failure almost impossible. When I think of the long list of those who have encouraged me through the years I wonder what I would have done without them.

Certainly the encouragement from wise and confident parents has given children the assistance that all children need. Teachers, also, have shared in this wise counsel. Husbands and wives have reached many of their treasured goals largely by the encouragement of each other's companionship.

Moses, the leader of the children of Israel in their flight from Egypt, was not permitted to enter the land beyond Jordon. God's instruction to Moses was that he "Charge Joshua, and encourage him, and strengthen him; for he shall go over before his people, and shall cause them to inherit the land which thou shalt see" (Deuteronomy 3:28). Just as Joshua needed the encouragement of Moses for the many difficulties that lay before him, so do those around us need our encouragement.

I was reading again recently the account of the woman who was, according to her accusers, guilty of adultery. These accusers had brought her to Jesus, wanting Him to join them in condemning her to death by stoning, which was the law of Moses. Jesus, knowing the sins of these men, suggested that he that was without sin should cast the first stone.

The Master, writing in the sand, looked up and said to the woman, "Woman, where are those thine accusers, hath no man condemned thee? She said, No man Lord. And Jesus said unto her, Neither do I condemn thee; go, and sin no more" (John 8:10-11). The woman's life was not only saved but her way of living was changed, all because Jesus encouraged her to sin no more rather than to condemn her to death.

Goethe, the German author, once wrote, "Correction does much, but encouragement does more. Encouragement after censure is as the sun after a shower."

The future of many a life has been changed all because someone has been encouraged for what he can be, rather than condemned, alone, for what he has been. Jesus chose this course. We would do well to follow in His footsteps.

O God, our Father, help us to look around us today, and bring a word of encouragement to someone who is discouraged. Help us to feel that we are doing it in Thy name. AMEN.

Evaluating Our Assets

DOWN IN central Indiana where I was born and reared there is a story still being told of the farmer who became dissatisfied with his farm. His discontent grew so strong that his wife suggested that they sell the farm.

The realtor, whom they engaged to be their agent, came to the farm in a few days. He read to them the advertisement he expected to use in the sale of their property. When the farmer heard it he exclaimed, "Wait a minute, Mister; that is the kind of farm I've been looking for all my life. I hadn't realized what a wonderful place this is until I heard your description of it."

There is an old saying that the grass always looks greener on the other side of the fence. We might add that quite often we have to climb the fence before we can evaluate that which we call our own.

There is nothing wrong with trying to better our situation in life. Many times, however, we hold within our hands the best opportunities of improving our situation.

Moses, who led the Israelites out of Egypt, was not sure that he possessed the qualities necessary for the task. God proved to him that all that was necessary he held within his hands. He could not fail providing he recognized the power of God's presence in his daily decisions.

I know a little village church which has served its community well for more than 125 years. In that church was a Sunday School teacher who felt that she had very little to offer except herself. For many years she gave herself to a class of boys and girls. She loved children and they knew it. From that class came boys and girls who became Christian leaders in many vocations. Many of the leaders in that church today are the boys and girls of yesterday who knew this good woman as their teacher. This could be said of many other woman and men in countless places of service.

Edward Rowland Sill, author and poet, in his poem *"Opportunity,"* symbolizes the idea that we are to forget our limitations. We are to make the most of our opportunities and abilities we have and fulfill the promise within us.

John the Baptist, who prepared the way for Jesus, was said by some to be the greatest man who ever took second place. He had very little of the material assets of this world. He did not complain that his lot was to take second place. He was more than willing to fade into the background that Jesus might have first place. He made the most of his opportunities and the world is a better place because of his dedication.

Using what we have for the blessing of others and not complaining that our lot is not richer is one of the secrets of happiness. This is a challenge for each of us. By so doing we may find that God has endowed us with more than we had ever realized.

Lord, help me, this day, to use what I have, where I am, in Your name, that the world might be a better place for my having lived. AMEN.

Evening Glories

"THEY SAY that I am growing old . . . but I'm not growing old. This frail old shell in which I dwell is growing old, I know full well; but I'm not the shell." The above words were spoken by a little lady of more than a hundred winters. The spirit of this silver haired woman and the thoughts in those inspired words is the true picture of so many whose latter years are as evening glories.

It is to those who are older but still growing that I want to dedicate these thoughts.

Someone has said that people are funny, most of us want to live a long while, but we never want to grow old. Many of us think of the days of our youth as the days of our glory. But, God did not intend that it be so. The wise man of Proverbs was inspired by God to write, "The hoary head is a crown of glory, if it be found in the way of righteousness" (Proverbs 16:31).

The fragrant blossoms on the tree in springtime are beautiful. We know, however, that the fruit on the tree is the advancement of the blossoms. We often hear someone say, "I hate to think that I am growing old." But in the wisdom of God, "The hoary head is a crown of glory."

One of the glories of age is a ripened faith. Beneath the red plum tree back on the farm, Mother used to grow the most beautiful hydrangeas in an old tub. Many people, passing by, would stop to admire them. Mother was always ready with some rooted starts of her favorite plant to give them.

In youth we hold our faith much as Mother held those young plants in her hands. Youth holds its faith, but age is held steady by its faith. God knows the hopes of youth and He knows the faith of age. The glories of age is a ripened faith.

Another glory of age is its tolerance. As one grows older he becomes, or should become, more sympathetic with others' failures than when he was younger. I suppose that it might be that we have suffered, somewhat, with our own mistakes. More than this, age has gained much wisdom and wisdom makes for tolerance.

For instance, the disciple John in his youth wanted to call down fire upon some of the enemies of Jesus. In his age, it is said that John's greatest thought was in forgiving those who had despitefully used him.

Throughout the Bible we can find examples of youth's impatience and the tolerance of age. It is true that "The hoary head is a crown of glory, if it be found in the way of righteousness."

Age has it compensations. One compensation is a clearer understanding of God's purpose for our lives. We may not fully understand that purpose in our youthful days. In our youth we think of "What we are, and what we can become." In age we are consoled by "What He is and what He has done." We have confidence in youth. We respect and revere those of declining years and pray that those years may truly be as Evening Glories.

O God, as our years lengthen into the evening time, help us that our faith may grow stronger. AMEN.

"Facing Our Fears"

THE TIME was the 19th of May, 1780. The Connecticut House of Representatives was in session at Hartford. At noon the skies turned from blue to gray. By midafternoon they had blackened so densely that many of the men in session were sure that the end of time was at hand. Some of them, in fear, clamored for immediate adjournment. Colonel Davenport, Speaker of the House, silenced them with the words: "The Day of Judgment is either approaching or it is not. If it is not, there is no cause for adjournment. If it is, I choose to be found doing my duty. I wish, therefore, that candles may be brought."

The enemies of peace have always tried to rule the world by fear. They would have us cry out in despair. But, the cry of despair is not the solution to our troubles. Fear does not solve problems, it only creates greater ones. Living by our fears, instead of our faith, makes us weaker instead of stronger.

"Where are you doing?" asked an Eastern pilgrim on meeting the plague one day. "I am going to Bagdad to kill five thousand people," was the reply. A few days later the same Pilgrim met the plague returning. "You told me you were going to Bagdad to kill five thousand people," said he, "but instead, you killed fifty thousand." "No," said the plague, "I killed only five thousand, as I told you I would, the others died of fright."

Men have been known to die of fear. Doctors tell us that fear can paralyze every muscle in our bodies. Fear can effect the flow of blood to and from our hearts. It can make us powerless to move. What, then, can we do with our fears?

We can run from our fears. Fear in this atomic age would drive us underground. Is this the remedy for our fears? Someone has said that it is better to light a candle than to curse the darkness. It is better, then, to face our fears than to run from them. Experience has taught us that only a small percent of our worries and fears ever materialize. We can best face our fears by turning the spotlight of faith upon them.

At the invitation of Jesus, Peter started to walk toward Him on the water. Matthew tells us that Peter was doing all right, "But when he saw the winds boisterous, he was afraid; and begining to sink, he cried saying, Lord, save me." When Peter took his eyes off of the Master the fear of the waves overcame him. He turned to the only remedy that could save him from his fears. The Master then put out His hand and rescued him.

There is only one fear that is legitimate and necessary; that is the fear of God. It is only the fear of God that can deliver us from the fear of man. The writer of the Psalms said, "The Lord is my light and my salvation; whom shall I fear?"

As we face life's future, it is well that we take precautions. We cannot run from it. We should never blunder into it. We can, and should face it with faith. Faith in a future with Him who said, "Peace I leave with you. My peace I give unto you; not as the world giveth, give I unto you. Let not your heart be troubled, neither let it be afraid." Increasing our faith in Him helps to decrease our fears about us. Trust your faith; it will allay your fears.

O God of Power and Justice, help us when fear would paralyze our faith, to remember that all things are possible with Thee. AMEN.

Fingerprints Or Footprints

THE FOLLOWING words have been credited to Henry Wadsworth Longfellow. The great American poet said that fingerprints are means by which we track our criminals. Footprints are marks by which we follow our heroes. He went on to say that lives of great men remind us that we can make our lives sublime, and departing leave behind us, footprints in the sands of time.

I was reminded of the above words after reading a letter that a young farmer wrote me a few weeks ago. He had just lost his father. To this young lad, who had inherited a great deal of responsibility along with the farm, that father was quite special. The things he said of his father would bring satisfaction to any man and make him feel that his life had not been lived in vain.

This thoughtful son wrote, "My father was not a rich man, as riches are measured by some. He was not a well-educated man, as education is thought of in our day. The greatest heritage my father left me was not the farm, although I am deeply grateful for that. The greatest marks he left behind him were his footprints."

This son proved that the wise counsel of the father had already found a fertile place in his life. He told of his father's influence and respect in the community. He concluded his letter by saying, "It will be difficult to fill my father's shoes, but with God's help I shall do my best."

Some are remembered for great power, fame, or riches. Others, like the father above, are remembered for humble, yet effective lives, lived in their communities in service for others.

Recently, I was reading again the story of Jesus with His disciples in the Upper Room. The beloved disciple John was recounting the act of Jesus washing the feet of the disciples. In so doing, Jesus was proving to them that the greatest of masters can be the humblest of servants.

Some, like Peter, would take the sword. However, Jesus said, "He that taketh the sword shall perish with the sword" (Matthew 26:52. He was saying that he that lives by hate shall parish by hate. Our future survival depends upon our ability to live by our intelligence rather than our emotions.

Some, like the Pharisees, would resort to the stone. It is easy to start throwing stones. It is more difficult to be constructive with them. There are those whose tongues are tuned to criticize while others are more interested in seeking out the virtues in those around them.

We, like Jesus, can take the towel of services and leave footprints in the sands of time. This Master of masters gave such counsel as, "Whosoever would be great among you let him be your minister" (Matthew 20:26). As my young farmer friend wrote, it will be difficult to fill HIS shoes, but by God's help we shall do our best. It is a most worthy endeavor.

O Christ of God, your life's influence can never be measured. Help each of us that our lives may influence someone for good. AMEN.

Forgive And Forget

THE JAPANESE have a proverb which reads: "My skirt with tears is always wet, I have forgotten to forget." Brooding over the past is too often a weakness many of us have. We know that it is useless. Nothing ever comes of it but despair.

Eight-year-old Billy came in from playing, telling his mother between sobs how Jack, his playmate next door, had kicked him on the shins. Billy's mother responded with "Billy, you must forgive Jack in your prayers tonight." Billy exclaimed, "I'll forgive him tonight, but he had better look out tomorrow!" Forgetting to forget or unwilling to forgive dissipates the peace of today and our hopes for tomorrow.

Jesus gave a lesson in forgiveness when He explained to his disciples that they should not only forgive seven times, but seventy times seven. I can hear one of the disciples saying, "Why, that would be 490 times, I'd lose count." That's just it. If we can forgive someone who has wronged us until we lose count, this means we can forgive and forget. This was Jesus' way. By His help it can be ours.

Remorse over past failures comes from forgetting to forget. Remorse seasoned the tears of Peter the disciple after his denial of Jesus. Through the forgiveness of his Master, Peter knew that he too must forget the past or his future witness would fail.

Such was Paul the apostle's decision. "Forgetting those things which are behind," whether pleasant or not, he too had been forgiven. He must now "press on to the mark of the high calling in Christ Jesus."

Cultivating a forgiving and forgetting spirit strengthens ones character. Forgiveness finds its home in the heart of peace. Peace reigns in the heart of one who is too big to carry a grudge.

Paul, writing to the Christians at Rome, admonishes them to practice the spirit of forgiveness. He wrote, "If thine enemy hungers, feed him; if he thirsts, give him to drink; for in so doing thou shalt heap coals of fire on his head."

The past history of the United States when an enemy has been defeated has been to help that former enemy to be rehabilitated. This is as it should be. The best way to destroy an enemy is to make a friend of him. This may not always work, but it is God's way.

It is interesting to read of the many promises of God, concerning His forgiveness. He is not only willing to forgive us but He will not remember our sins against us any more. With His Presence in our hearts we can do likewise.

O God, we know that Thou art all forgiving. Help us to have a forgiving spirit each day, in every way and to everyone. AMEN.

Facing Adversity

"SMOOTH SEAS doth not a sailor make." I was awakened early a few mornings ago. It seemed as if someone was speaking those words to me. The night before, as I retired, I was thinking of a letter I had received from one who follows my column. In the course of her letter my friend wrote, "Many setbacks, physical and otherwise, have come to our family during the past thirty years. Facing them and overcoming them or learning how to live with them, just seems to make one stronger to face the future."

When troubles, discouragements, and heartaches cross our path, what can we do? How do we face adversity? We can give up in despair and go down to defeat; we can worry about it and fight against it with all our might; or, we can accept it, and pray that God will help us to be stronger for having faced our adversities with faith instead of fear.

The Gospel writer Mark tells that one night the disciples of Jesus were in a boat on the sea they loved, but often feared. Jesus, who was on the shore, saw them in distress "for the winds were contrary unto them." They were in despair. They did not recognize Jesus as He walked toward them. When He talked to them and stepped into the boat, the wind ceased and there was a great calm on the waters and in their hearts.

In the face of adversity and trouble Jesus still can and does calm the troubled sea and bring peace to our troubled minds. The writer of Proverbs says, "If thou faint in the day of adversity, thy strength is small" (Proverbs 24:10).

It was said of a man, whose life was such a blessing to others, "He would not have been the man that he was had it not have been for the courageous way he faced the adversities in his life." Some of the most noble people in history have faced the severest adversities and triumphed through them.

None of us are immune to persecution and the opposing forces in life. Paul the apostle writing to Timothy said, "Yea, all that will live Godly in Christ Jesus shall suffer persecution" (II Timothy 3:12).

One of the finest persons I have ever known, and there are many like her, was one who was beset with many physical and mental persecutions and discouragements. However, she never displayed a persecution complex. Her concern was not of herself, but of those around her. She always seemed to act as though there were so many others worse off than she. I am sure that this made her own adversities easier to bear.

Just as God has come to man when life's storms are at their worst, so does He still come to those who call on Him to bring peace to troubled hearts.

O Master of tempest as well as the calm, be especially with that one who is facing the storms of adversity. We know that Thy presence will still the storm and calm the spirit. AMEN.

Facing Change

LIVING LIFE at its best may be determined, to great extent, on how we face the life of change. Needless to say, we live in a world of change. Much of it we welcome; some of it we fear. We welcome the advancements in medical science. We are encouraged by the inventions that make physical labor and living easier. We fear, however, the drifting toward materialism, self-sufficiency, and negative attitudes which are so prevalent today.

As we grow older we like to recall the good old days when life was slower and less complicated. However, some of those experiences of the past are often more enjoyable in recollection than they would be to live over again. But, we are not here to belittle the past, but to extol the present and give hope for the future.

A Jew of many centuries ago loved his country and was concerned about its future welfare. He witnessed the change that was taking place about him. He saw his nation going to pieces and drifting away from God. He saw Rome conquer his beloved Palestine and threaten the destruction of all they had held dear. This faithful, God fearing man remembered that there were some things that would not change, they would abide forever.

Speaking with courage and faith, this man who loves his country and its people says, ". . . . those things which cannot be shaken may remain" (Hebrews 12:27). As we witness some of the changes around us, we could very well be discouraged had we not the faith to say, "There are some things that will not change." God's laws will not be shaken. "Heaven and earth shall pass away, but my words shall not pass away" (Matthew 24:35).

Changes may come and go but the wages of sin will never change. "The wages of sin is death," so wrote Paul to the Roman Christians. Dr. Karl Menninger, the famous psychiatrist, has written a book, *What Ever Became of Sin?* Most of us know that sin is still with us. We may call it an act of uncontrollable behaviorism or a weakness of human action. Regardless by what name it may be called, it is still sin. This fact does not change, for the wages for those who sin are the same.

But the apostle Paul goes on to say, ". . . . but the gift of God is eternal life through Jesus Christ our Lord" (Romans 6:23). God's promise of the gift of eternal life never changes, the decision to accept or reject it is up to each of us.

The Psalm writer of long ago, writing of his confidence in God's unchangeable and eternal presence, said, "But thou art the same, and thy years shall have no end" (Psalm 102:27)

It is good, in times when our country, our world, and even the Church is shaken by man's human weakness, to have something to which we can cling. Something that will hold us steady in a shaky world. Something that will survive the changes about us. That something is Somebody. He is "Jesus, the same yesterday, and today, and forever" (Hebrews 13:8). He will remain with us forever.

O Thou who changest not, abide with me. Help us, O Lord, in the face of changes all about us, to make the right choices. AMEN.

For Goodness' Sake

WE LIVE in a world where it seems that evil, crime, and greed are the powers that predominate. We dwell so much upon the magnitude of these things that we fail to see that there are other influences in the world also.

The longer I live, the more I discover that there is a thousand times more goodness, wisdom, and love in the world than men imagine. It is not my intention to minimize the evil, but rather to magnify the good. A minister of my boyhood days often said, "I am here to speak a word for goodness sake."

There is much goodness in the world today, even though most of it never makes the front page news. Someone has said that evil is contaminating, but goodness is contagious.

We recognize that crime is on the increase. Delinquency was never more prevalent. The F.B.I. has warned us that there have been seven hundred thousand crimes committed by teenagers this past year. We are further warned that this year it may reach one million. This is only one of the many evils that endanger our civilization.

On the other hand, we should never forget the millions of youth that are proving that goodness pays. Their influence is being felt through the 4-H club. Through the Scouts, as well as many other youth groups which have as their goal to build up instead of destroy.

Certainly we cannot forget the great numbers of youth who witness to their faith in God, through the Church, in their efforts for good.

It may not be easy to be good, but it is easy to do a good deed. It was Ralph Waldo Emerson, poet and author, who once said, "He who loves goodness harbors angels, reveres reverence, and lives with God."

Jesus tells of a man that was beaten and robbed as he was traveling on his way to Jericho. Two men who saw his plight passed by without helping him. The third man did a good deed. He stopped to give him assistance. By so doing, he became the good Samaritan. He also proved that not all men fail in the opportunities to do good. That day he cast his vote for goodness sake.

The apostle Paul said of Jesus, what others had noticed about Him, when he spoke of Him "Who went about doing good." A good man doubles the length of his existence; the life he lives and the influence he leaves behind. It may not pay just to go about. Jesus, however, proved that it paid to go about doing good.

The writer of Psalm 33 said, "The earth is full of the goodness of the Lord." Saint Paul, writing to the Christians at Rome, said, "overcome evil with good."

What would happen if we would try each day to look for the good in the world about us? Think what could happen if we would thank someone each day for the good they are doing. If we would, likewise, thank God for His goodness all about us. If we did, we would find that it pays to seek good, do good, and be good. Not alone for Heaven's sake, but for goodness' sake.

Lord, I would be true, for there are those who trust me. I would be pure, for there are those who care. With Thy help we can do so. May Thy Spirit inspire us to live as Thou would have us to live. AMEN.

Facing The Future

I WAS turning the pages of my mother's Bible, the last one of her lifetime. As I did so, I ran across a bit of paper upon which she had written, "I know not what the future holds for me, but I do know who holds the future."

Those words explained the secret of the calm and confident spirit which was always evident in her busy life.

How to face the future is a question that confronts all of us. It has caused mental anguish to millions. It has driven many to suicide. Many others, however, have learned the secret of who holds the future. These live each day without fear.

Of all the poems that through the years have been born in the heart of man, the most familiar one begins with, "The Lord is my Shepherd." More quote it from memory than any other bit of verse. Whether in childhood, youth, age, in joy or sorrow, it seems to give assurance for the present and the future.

This Psalm of David's youth may have been written in manhood after his hair turned to gray. His life had been tempered by hardships, even failures. He had proven it through the years, now he confesses his faith and praise by writing, "The Lord is my Shepherd, I shall not want."

I recall several years ago of discussing this Psalm with my good neighbor, Uncle Orlo Holiday. His words of wisdom are well remembered. In quiet confidence he said, "There have been times when life about me was like a fog, I could not see the road ahead. But I learned to trust God even where I could not trace Him. His restoring power has never failed me."

Fear of what lies ahead in the fog has always caused man to feel his inadequacy. The Psalm writer expresses faith in the Shepherd as he says, "Yea, though I walk through the valley of the shadow of death, I will fear no evil . . . " (Psalm 23:4)

Often, a man who lives by his own self-sufficiency comes to that place in life where he expresses his fear in time of need. It was Robert Louis Stevenson, novelist and poet, who wrote, "Keep your fears to yourself, but share your courage with others." When we learn to trust the good Shepherd, our fears are minimized and we have courage to share with others.

David, in quiet confidence, tells us that he does not fear his enemies. God even prepares a table in their very presence. Even when the enemies of our body, such as the sickness of our physical being and mind comes upon us, God still feeds the spirit and gives secret strength to those who trust Him.

We need not fear the future, for His "goodness and mercy shall follow us all the days of my life . . . " His Presence shall ever be with us and we shall be with Him and those we love, in "the house of the Lord forever."

O Lord, Shepherd of our lives, give us the quiet confidence to trust Thee, even when we cannot see Thy way for us. AMEN.

Fruits Have Roots

THE MOST beautiful, fragrant tuberous begonias grew and blossomed in our yard this past summer. Last fall we dug, dried, and stored the bulbs for the winter. In March we brought the bulbs out. We started them again at a north window. Had we left them stored away they would have been useless, and we would not have enjoyed their fragrance this past summer.

Talents, like bulbs, must be planted. They must be invested where they will grow. In storing them away one finds they, like the bulbs, will not multiply, but rather in the end be of no value. Fruits must have roots.

The parable of the talents, given by Jesus, has always held my interest. The Gospel of Matthew gives the account of the servant who was entrusted by his master with five talents. This diligent servant increased them to ten. Likewise, the servant who received two. He gained other two. However, the servant that received one talent, for fear, hid it.

It is not how much, or little, talent we have; but rather the use we make of it that counts.

What is talent? Someone has said that it is the gift of God. It is something to be used for good. It is seed to be sown, to be increased. Buried seeds will grow; buried talents never.

There is a little gem of practical wisdom, written by a wise man of long ago that says, "Cast thy bread upon the waters: for thou shalt find it after many days" (Ecclesiastes 11:1). Many times it is the quiet every day good deeds, done without expecting a reward, that really does more good than we realize. From these come our greatest rewards.

There is a little song we learned as children in the Sunday School. It was written by Ina Duley Ogdon. This young woman wanted to be a missionary but, due to physical handicaps, was unable to do so. The thought in the song was that we should not wait to shed our light afar, but to the many duties near at hand be true. Brighten the corner where you are.

Most of us will never be famous for great deeds, but all of us can be worthy of letting our light shine in the corner where we are by giving ourselves to those around us and doing what we can where we are.

The great Master, Jesus, taught that we are our brother's keeper. Millions still need to realize this. All around us there are those who are saying, "Let me serve where I can, with what I have." These are increasing their talents, not alone to the blessing of others, but to their own joy of living.

Father in Heaven, help us to use what you have given us, that our talents may increase and others be made better for our having given our all for Thee. AMEN.

Friendship

FRIENDSHIPS are somewhat like bank accounts, the more you accumulate the greater the interest. Mrs. Jennings and I have been made to realize anew, around the time of our golden wedding anniversary, how rich we are in friends.

So many cards and letters have come from new friends who have followed this column through the years. We wonder if we will ever be able to answer them all. We, likewise, have been made to realize the value of old friends who do not forget you. Although we feel most unworthy, we are grateful.

There is a poem, though the author is unknown, that says, "Since I have no gold to give/And love alone must make amends/Lord, make me worthy of my friends."

A friend is one who knows all about you but still loves you. It is someone who comes in when the world goes out. A friend listens to your innermost longings, shares your hopes, rejoices with you when you rejoice, and comforts you in your sorrows.

One of the warmest and most human accounts of friendship in the Bible is the friendship of David and Jonathan. This friendship was not only a mutual regard for each other, but even when Jonathan's father, Saul the king, due to his jealousy, tried to kill David, Jonathan's friendship helped to save his life.

At least three times we read that, "Jonathan loved David as he loved his own soul" (I Samuel 20:17). This true friendship lasted as long as they lived. This kind of friendship is eternal.

Away back in the days when we read that so and so begat so and so, we come upon a man by the name of Enoch. One of the exciting, yet wholesome, things that was said of Enoch was, "And Enoch walked with God; and he was not; for God took him" (Genesis 5:24).

Enoch took walks with God. It was a mutual friendship. No doubt Enoch was a radiant personality. The kind of folk you love to know and have around. What was the secret of his radiancy? He had a friendship with God.

Someone asked Charles Kingsley, inspiring English clergyman and author, the secret of his radiant life. His answer was, "I have a Friend." It was through this experience of "having a Friend" that caused Joseph Scrivan to write, "What a Friend we have in Jesus/All our sins and griefs to bear./What a privilege to carry,/Everything to God in prayer."

We cannot place a price or value upon human friendships, they are not for sale; we need every one of them. If this be true, how much more so is the fact that we need that eternal friendship with God.

Would that those whose lives we touch might be able to say of each of us as they said of Enoch, "He walked with God." This is the kind of friendship that makes life worth the living.

O God, help us to so live that we can feel Thy presence with us day by day as a faithful Friend. AMEN.

Fishermen

HERE IN northeastern Indiana the summer residents have returned and the vacationers are coming and going. The main purpose of most of them is to get away from the hurry of life and relax. Others have come to fish. I see boats out there this morning. They may catch more fish but they will not have any more fun than I did as a boy. With my old fishing pole and a can of worms, a day spent along the little Whitewater River down in central Indiana was a time to remember.

My father had, at least, three rules for fishing. Those three rules were, go where they are; use the right bait; and stay out of sight. As I think about it now, those rules were taught and exemplified by Jesus. When He called Peter, James and John, He said to them, " . . . Come ye after me and I will make you to become fishers of men" (Mark 1:17). These young fishermen left their nets and followed Him. They learned from their Master how to reach others for Him and likewise learned better how to catch fish.

These humble men learned from Jesus to cast their nets where the fish were. Jesus came upon them early one morning. The disciples had been fishing all night but had caught nothing. They heard a voice from the shore but did not know that it was Jesus. He had called out asking them if they had caught any fish. Their answer was no. Jesus said to them, "Cast the net on the right side of the boat and ye shall find" (John 21:6). The catch was more than they could have ever dreamed.

Many of us have found that to reach people, we have to go where they are and not always wait for them to come to us.

Most successful fishermen have discovered that they must use the right kind of bait to catch different kinds of fish. Learning people's interests and being able to converse with them in that field, helps in winning them. However, the most important thing is to be able to provide for their needs and the longing of those who are discouraged and dissatisfied with life.

The needs of man have always been met in Jesus Christ. His promise, made long ago, is as true today as when He said, "Come unto me, all ye that labor and are heavy laden and I will give you rest" (Matthew 11:28). We may use many ways to try and get people into the church, but unless Christ comes into their hearts, their needs will never be fully met.

The third rule of a good fisherman, so taught my father, is to stay of out of sight. John the Baptist was a courageous man. He stirred the people of his day. But his humility was one of his most noble attributes. One day he said of Jesus, whom he represented, "He must increase, but I must decrease" (John 3:30). If we are to become fruitful fishers of men, no better aim could be ours than that they might see more of the Master and less of us.

Lord, keep us humble that our lives may be more fruitful for you. Through Christ we pray. AMEN.

Feminine Influence

MANY OBSERVATIONS have been made concerning woman's place in the world. Long before the Women's Liberation Movement, women have made their impact upon the world.

We have long recognized woman's influence in the home, the school, in public affairs, and in government. We recognize her contribution in the field of entertainment and the arts, as well as the inspiration she has brought through writing and many other avenues of service.

The first one to whom I reached my infant hands, who guided me in those childhood years, and encouraged me throughout her life, was a woman, my mother.

The one who taught me first to write my name was a woman, my first public school teacher. Yes, there is the one who has endured my weaknesses and has encouraged me in my efforts. This one is a woman, my wife and companion for fifty years.

Feminine influence has probably been felt as much or more in the field of religion. The Church has, from its beginning, felt the impact of woman's sincere concern.

Paul the apostle advised, "Let the woman learn in silence . . . but suffer not a woman to teach . . . (I Timothy 2:11-12). Even though he mentioned this at other times, he was most grateful for the leadership and association of the women in the early Church.

There was Lydia, of Philippi. Her house became a center of this new Christian movement. Who could forget Dorcas? She was the president of the first women's society in the early Church. It was said that, "she was full of good works and alms deeds which she did" (Acts 9:36). At her untimely death, those whose lives had been influenced by her spirit and deeds of mercy, sent for Peter. Peter came to their aid and through his prayer and faith, God raised Dorcas up to life again.

During Christ's ministry on earth He often encouraged the sincere efforts of the women with whom He came in contact. We, today, are deeply indebted to Jesus and His concern that woman might have her rightful place in life.

Space, time, and memory would not permit us to give an account of all of those whose lives and talents have influenced the growth of the Church.

We could not begin to name those who are serving today, without fanfare, in the many fields of endeavor. Most of those faithful women may never be named in the Hall of Fame or in the book of Who's Who. But, with their dedication to Christ and His Church, the world today is a better place in which to live. Tomorrow will be a better age because they have shared their concern and talents today. God has blessed womanhood from the beginning of time. May we be worthy of His continued blessings.

Lord, we pray that you would continue to speak through the voice and influence of those we are pleased to call our mothers and our sisters. AMEN.

Faith

GRANDPA'S BIG bank barn with its great haymows and vast stables below was an exciting place for the grandchildren.

Late one evening Grandpa had thrown hay down for the stock and had gone below to do the feeding. Grandson Jimmy had tarried to play in the haymow. On discovering that Grandpa was below, he looked down into the darkness and cried, "Grandpa, I want to come down." Grandpa called out, "Jump, Jimmy, I'll catch you." "But it's dark down there, Grandpa, I can't see you," Jimmy anxiously replied.

Grandpa, endeavoring to relieve his grandson's fears called out, "Jimmy, I can see you even though you can't see me; jump, I'll catch you." With uneasy fear of the darkness below, but quiet confidence in Grandfather, Jimmy jumped out into the darkness and was safe in the arms of the one who would not fail him.

Someone has said that faith is a jump in the dark. But, faith is more than this. It is quiet confidence in the one out there in the darkness. Recently, I talked with a man who was to have surgery that day. This man confided in me that he had no fears. "I have known my surgeon for several years," he said, "and his success in this type of surgery gives me confidence in him." Then he concluded by saying, "I also know the great Physician above will be with and will guide the hands of my surgeon."

Man has his limitations, but faith turns defeat into victory. A wise man once said that fear knocked on the door, but courage answered the door, and there was no one there.

The eleventh chapter of Hebrews has been called the faith chapter. It begins with, "Now faith is the substance of things hoped for, the evidence of things not seen" (Hebrews 11:1). This chapter is filled with the examples of those who trusted God, without whom they would have failed. One example was the faith of Abraham, of whom it was said, "By faith Abraham, when he was called to go out into a place which he should after receive for an inheritance, obeyed; and he went out, not knowing whither he went" (Hebrews 11:8).

Paul the apostle once said that faith without works is dead. We know that this is true, but some of us have found, just as did Paul, Peter and many others, that works without faith in God leads to failure. It is our faith in Him that gives us the power to act. Only His presence within us can give the victory we need and hope for.

Recently, I found on my desk a little tract. I have not found its author. It began with the words, "Doctor, how long will I have to stay in bed?" The doctor answered the anxious patient with, "Just one day at a time."

It is true we only live a day at a time. To each day we must give a heart of faith and courage. God has promised to sustain us. The writer of the Psalms has written, "Cast thy burden upon the Lord, and He will sustain thee" (Psalm 55:22).

What tomorrow has in store for us we do not know, but we walk by faith, not by sight. Yesterday's mercy and tomorrow's promise should inspire today's trust and tomorrow's confidence in Him who said, "I will never leave thee nor forsake thee."

Dear Lord, increase our faith each day, that no doubts can find a place in our lives. AMEN.

Greatness

THE MEASURE of greatness is often greatly exaggerated. To say that one is great because they have become famous, may not always be true. Riches, talent, popularity, or anything one possesses does not always make one great.

My Quaker grandmother had a saying, "Pretty is as pretty does." It is the same, I believe, with greatness, "Greatness is as greatness does." It is not just having a very high I.Q. Nor is it having a noble opinion of oneself. It is rather how we use what God has given us that really counts.

The disciples of Jesus were discussing among themselves who was the greatest in the Kingdom of Heaven. Matthew tells us that Jesus called a little child to Him and said, "Whosoever shall humble himself as a little child, the same is the greatest in the Kingdom of Heaven" (Matthew 18:4). He was saying that greatness comes from a repentent heart, a spirit of humility, and a dedication of service.

It seemed that the young men Jesus chose to be His disciples were plagued with the temptation of the position of greatness. In the midst of another debate on this subject, Jesus informed them, "But he that is the greatest among you shall be your servant" (Matthew 23:11).

The Master, Himself, was the true example of greatness. He came to be the servant of all, even unto the cross.

The greatest of men and women that the world has ever known have been the most humble. Abraham Lincoln was made fun of and even insulted by those who should have honored him. But, in those dark days of the Civil War, he showed the true spirit of greatness when he said of one of his generals who had insulted him, "I would gladly hold his horse if he would bring us victories."

One of the true marks of greatness is not lording it over someone else. It is rather displaying a true spirit of humble service.

Phillips Brooks, famous pastor and author of another era, once observed, "No man has come to true greatness who has not felt in some degree that his life belongs to his race, and that what God gives him he gives him for mankind."

Most of us will never become great as far as the world measures greatness. We can, however, give ourselves in humble service to those around us and to the age in which we live. Doing this in the Master's name we can leave the rest to the greatness and goodness of God.

We pray, O God, that humility of spirit may dwell in our lives that Thy Holy Spirit may better use us in Thy service. AMEN.

Getting The Most From Life

THE PARADE was coming down the street. A boy, approximately six or seven, yet small for his age, had arrived late and was standing tiptoe trying to get a glimpse of the action.

A stalwart young man, at least six feet tall, was standing nearby and saw the boy's predicament. The man bent over, said something to the boy, then lifted the smiling lad to his shoulders. The parade continued on. From his special seat on the man's shoulder, the small boy witnessed it all.

As the man lowered the boy to the ground, I heard the lad exclaim, "Thank you, Mister." The boy disappeared into the dispersing crowd. The man, with a smile, went on his way. Two people had been made happy. One who had given aid and the other who had received it.

Getting the most out of life comes from giving as well as receiving. To live life on tiptoe we need, at times, someone who can give us that extra lift.

Jesus, trying to explain His coming as the Good Shepherd, to give and not to get, said, "The thief cometh not, but for to steal and to kill and destroy; I am come that they might have life, and that they might have it more abundantly" (John 10:10).

Get all that you can out of life. Get it honestly if you can, but get it. This is the philosophy of the thief.

Some invest in the soil, others waste it. All too soon they discover that the soil is depleted, the forests fast disappearing, and scarce, wildlife destroyed. This is a parable of how the thief of life, and its opportunities, operates, leaving us in a state of despair.

To help mankind live life to the fullest was the Master's mission. Not to steal or destroy, but to give power to make the most of life. Those whose lives He touched were changed. Life before had been spent in despair and defeat. Now for the first time, they were able to face the world with new hope and a victorious faith.

The master artist at the close of the day was asked by one of his students if he might borrow his tools that evening. The eager student, with the master's tools, worked on into the night. Finally, gazing on his unfinished picture, he sat down discouraged.

The master teacher came into the room, took the brushes and with expert, yet kindly hands, corrected the student's mistakes. The picture became all, and more than the inexperienced student had hoped for.

The young student, tired and weary, but now full of hope, thanked his teacher, then said, "Now, I know I needed not so much the tools as I did the master's spirit."

Jesus comes, as the Master Artist. Life's picture is incomplete without Him. The abundant life comes from the Spirit of the Master. We fail without Him. We cannot fail with Him.

Help us, Lord, to lift someone's burden today, in Thy name, for in so doing our own will be much lighter. AMEN.

God's Way

"GOD'S WAY, even though it is not easy to understand and often difficult to explain, is the best way." Those were the words of a young businessman who had experienced some trying times. He went on to tell how that he and his wife had become highly successful in their early years of married life. So much so that their home life and their spiritual lives had suffered.

An accident in which they lost one of their children and a business recession in which they lost practically all that they possessed "brought us to our senses." Following his story of those sad experiences this man, still in his early forties said, "I have learned that the proverb is true, "In all thy ways acknowledge him and he shall direct thy paths" (Proverbs 3:6).

God's way is not always easy to understand or explain, but His way is the key to true happiness, lasting inward peace, and eternal values.

George C. Biggar III, of North Augusta, North Carolina at the age of twelve, expressed his thoughts on "God's Way" in the following: "God's expression is in such a way/God is a word rather hard to say/He is a bluebird, a sparrow, or a wren/God is the sky the birds fly in/God holds the key to Heaven above/God holds the key to hope, peace and love/God knows the way to the skyway of trust/God is not a maybe—God is a must." The above words though written by a lad of twelve could well be the philosophy of an adult.

I had to learn, long ago, that I could not honestly turn to God just in time of trouble and forget Him when all was going well. I too, discovered that "God is a must." I needed Him not only to protect and deliver, but to direct all my ways.

The disciples, that evening in the Upper Room long ago, were fearful and doubtful of the future. As they sat there listening to their Master, they heard Jesus say, "I am the way, the truth, and the life: no one cometh to the Father, but by me" (John 14:6). This young Man who, in a few hours, would be bearing His cross as well as dying on it, had not only pointed out the way but was that way in deed as well as precept.

Abraham Lincoln stood on the observation platform of the train that was to carry him to Washington and the presidency. As he bade his friends and neighbors farewell there in Springfield, he concluded his remarks by saying, "Without the assistance of that Divine Being, I cannot succeed, with that assistance I cannot fail."

Many of us have discovered in our own personal lives how true those words are. We, likewise, have found that when we, "acknowledge Him in all our ways," He directs our paths.

Gracious Lord, we still pray; with Thee with us all things are possible, without Thee we fail. AMEN.

God Is

EIGHT-YEAR-old Jimmy was busy drawing a picture. His mother, looking over his shoulder asked, "Jimmy, what are you drawing?" "I'm drawing a picture of God," responded the enthusiastic artist. "But nobody has ever seen God," his mother replied. "They will when I have finished!" exclaimed Jimmy.

What kind of a picture of God are we drawing? How big is our God? Is He still alive? One of our astronauts, flying far out in space, said that he could not help from believing in a great God, who he believed created and organized such an indescribable universe.

It is good, at times, to ask ourselves some questions like, is God really necessary in my life? We live in a day of self-sufficiency. Many have called it a materialistic age. We recognize and are grateful for the great discoveries of science. Man is a marvelous creature, but he has his limitations.

Many of us have grown weary of those "God is dead" and "the Church has served its day" articles. Much of this that we have read has been coming from those who are not willing to pay the price of letting God really live in their lives.

What do these heralds of a new way offer in the place of God and the faith that the Church has contributed through the centuries?

In the rear window of a car ahead, I recently read, "My God is alive, I'm sorry if yours is dead." He is. I saw Him, a few mornings ago, as I entered a hospital room.

A woman, having had eye surgery the day before, was in darkness. Sitting beside her bed was a student nurse reading from the Book that was so necessary for this woman each day.

What is the temperature of our religious practice? Paul the apostle was in Athens. Following a tour of their city, he stood at Mars Hill and said, "Ye men of Athens, I perceive that in all things ye are too superstitious. For as I passed by and beheld your devotions, I found an altar with this inscription, TO THE UNKNOWN GOD" (Acts 17:22-23).

These men of Athens were not the only ones who worshipped many gods but were faithful to none. This has been true of many in every generation.

Jesus said, "Ye are the light of the world." He also said, "Ye are the salt of the earth." We are not only to light the way but we are, likewise, to have compassion on those less fortunate than we.

Religion is not a robe to set us apart from those we call sinners. Rather, it is a spirit that dwells within us that draws us to those in need of the love that Christ has for all people.

We do not need to defend God, but proclaim Him. When man awakens to the fact that he cannot destroy the One who created him, man will then discover that God is far ahead of us still creating. He will, likewise, find that God is very near to those who need Him most.

O Living God, we know that you live today, for we see you in others and we feel you in our own hearts. Help us ever to keep that freshness of Thy presence ever. AMEN.

Honoring Father

THE POETS have, with a great deal of feeling and dexterity, paid honor to mother, and well they should. Without a mother's presence in the home, it often falls apart. But, the world has never become too enthused over Father's Day.

Mrs. Bruce Dodd, whose father had been a Civil War veteran, had felt for some time that there should be a special day set aside to pay honor to fathers. She, with the assistance of others, was able to get that day proclaimed in 1909. Since that year, the third Sunday in June has been set aside as Father's Day.

One of the Ten Commandments, given to the Israelites as they made their journey to the Promised Land, was a commandment with promise. "Honor thy father and thy mother: that thy days may be long upon the land which the Lord thy God giveth thee" (Exodus 20:12).

Several years ago, I wrote a column on the subject of "Fingerprints." The subject concerned the influence of a father upon his family. I mentioned the fact that our children, more than we realize, are influenced for years to come by our fingerprints and footprints upon their lives.

A few weeks later a letter came from a son telling what his father had meant to him. He wrote, "My father left me 160 acres of good land, but far more valuable than the land was the influence of his life." The son concluded by saying, "I have tried to follow in his footprints because he followed the footprints of One far greater than either of us."

It is well that we should honor our fathers, even though some of us know that we, as fathers, are not perfect. Being a father is a great challenge and an opportunity.

The teacher was telling her class about God. Without mentioning God, the wise teacher was saying earnestly, "I want to tell you about one who is kind, strong, is unafraid in the dark and one who supplies our every need."

She then asked, "Of whom does this remind you?"

A boy of eight, who had been listening closely replied, "That's my Pop."

When the Psalm writer wanted to describe the Heavenly Father's compassion, he compared Him to the earthly father by saying, "Like as a father pitieth his children, so the Lord pitieth them that fear Him" (Psalm 103:13). This is a challenge to every father.

We pause to·pay memory to our fathers whose influence is still with us. As we do, may we as fathers, accept the challenge to be, by God's help, the kind of a father whose children will hold him in loving memory and proud esteem in the years to come.

Almighty God and Father of us all, bless the memory we have of those earthly fathers, who through the inspiration they received from Thee, were good examples of Thy love for us. In His name we pray. AMEN.

Help!

THERE IS one word which we use daily at every age of our life. It is one of the first words a child makes use of as he or she learns to talk. We avail ourselves of this word, as youth or adults, in times of trouble or our inability to cope with life's situations. That one word is HELP!

As a child we soon realized that we needed only to cry out, "Mama, Daddy, help me!" In so doing we obtained the assistance we needed or wanted. As adults, we often learn how really helpless we are within ourselves.

Think how often we use the word HELP in prayer. In the Bible, the word HELP is found many, many times. The Psalm writer says, "I will life up my eyes to the hills. From whence cometh my help? My help cometh from the Lord who made heaven and earth" (Psalm 121:1-2).

The Psalm writer knew that there were those, in his day, who believed that their gods lived in the hills but he, even though he loved the hills, knew that his real help came from God who made those hills.

In times of need, physically, materially, or spiritually, it is a consolation to know that help is available.

One of the axioms of a public school teacher of my youth was, "The Lord helps those who helps themselves." Even though those exact words are not found in the Bible, Jesus often asked those, whom He healed, to help themselves. As He healed the man with the withered hand, Jesus commanded, "Stretch forth thy hand" (Matthew 12:13). On another occasion, as He was in the process of restoring sight to a blind man, He placed clay on his eyes and said to him, "Go wash in the pool of Siloam" (John 9:7). Each of these men received healing by obeying Jesus and helping themselves.

The resources of God are endless, but we must "stretch forth our hand" of faith and avail ourselves of that help. God's help is available but he does not force it upon us. In the Sermon on the Mount, Jesus points out the two ways but informs His listeners that the choice of one or the other is theirs. Our prayer should be that we might make the right decision.

One of the most rewarding things about HELP is that it is something we can share with others. One of the most beautiful compensations of life is that no one can sincerely try to help another without helping himself.

We used to sing a song that said, "Look all around you/ Find someone in need/ Help somebody today./ Tho' it be little/ a neighborly deed/ Help somebody today!" This is one of the proofs of our religious belief. It was one of the finest things they said of Jesus, "who went about doing good." The help we often need is found when we, in the spirit of the Master, turn to help another.

Help us, Lord, that we might follow in Thy footsteps and go about doing good from day to day. In Thy Name we ask this. AMEN.

His Presence

A YOUNG man was leaving home to go into an experience for which he had no desire. There was dread and fear in his mind as the time drew near for him to go. In the early morning hour, just as he was leaving, his father put his arm around him and said, "Son, I can't go with you but remember, I'll be with you in spirit."

What one of us has not dreaded a task that seemed greater than ourselves. Many of us have had someone in whom we had confidence reassure us by letting us know that they would not forget us.

Recently, I was reading again the experiences of Moses. Especially his call from God to lead the Israelites from slavery to Egypt. Moses felt that he needed reassurance many times that God was still with him. On one occasion God spoke to Moses and said, "My presence shall go with thee, and I will give thee rest" (Exodus 33:14).

It was this confidence that Moses had in his God that gave him courage in hours when he needed it most. There were times when he felt that he stood all alone. Times when it seemed that everybody had turned against him. In those hours he could once again hear, "My presence shall go with thee."

Recently, my son sent me a piece of paper on which were nine words, "Living without faith is like driving in a fog." All of us have had the experience of the fog closing in upon us. So dense was the fog that the lights of our car could not penetrate it. Danger lurked ahead and behind us.

Life's experiences are so often such that without faith it is like driving in the fog. It is good, in times like this, to know that we can trust Him whose Presence is with us.

In one of our well known clinics, a famous surgeon broke the news to a patient that she must have surgery that morning. The patient, in fear, said, "Dr. Mayo, my family will not be here, I'll be all alone." This surgeon laid his hand on hers and reassured her with, "Don't worry, you won't be alone, I'll be with you." The patient grew calm and faced her surgery unafraid because she was confident that her surgeon would be with her through it all.

The Great Physician's presence has calmed our fears many times because of our confidence in Him. The author of Hebrews wrote, ". . . for he hath said, I will never leave thee nor forsake thee." He goes on to say, "The Lord is my helper, and I will not fear what man shall do to me" (Hebrews 13:5-6).

It is true that we need His Presence in time of trouble; and we have it. It is good to know, however, that His Presence can be our daily companion in health and happiness. His Presence makes the good life better.

A. H. Ackley, the author of many gospel hymns, wrote "When God is near, with light my path is glowing; And all the world's a paradise when God is near." This can be the experience of us all.

O Lord, although unworthy of your Presence we need you every hour. Without you we fail, with you we cannot fail. AMEN.

He Restoreth My Soul

HE WAS a farm boy of ten. He was full of the adventure that can be found by any boy whose life is spent in the country. That hot summer day he lazily trudged up the lane from the woods. In one hand he carried a straw hat, battered and torn from doing battle at a bumble bee nest. The day was hot and his thirst had driven him to the house.

As he pumped cool, clear water from the well in the yard, he lifted the cup and drank eagerly. He felt refreshed, his thirst was quenched. He lay down upon the grass nearby in peaceful reverie. Little did he know of the many times in his life ahead when he would be driven to seek out that which would quench the thirst of his soul as well as his body.

It is a wise man who, knowing the source of supply, seeketh out the restoring power for both body and soul. It has been said that a pocket full of gold is of little value to a man dying of thirst.

It is not work that kills so many these days, but rather the strain of trying to reach the next rung in the ladder of success. Someone in my presence recently said that some of us spend half our lives trying to keep up with the Joneses and the other half paying for it. The terrific pace of these days can rob us of the soul restoring moments. These we all need.

David, the Psalm writer, sought out that sanctuary of restoring power many times. He found it in the symbol of the still waters when he said, "He leadeth me beside the still waters, He restoreth my soul." You may find it as you look upon a waterfall, a mountain, or a spring of cool water. You may find this restoring power if you take time to think of Him who created all of these natural and physical blessings for man.

Recently, with a group of fifty young people, we visited the Chapel of the Sky at Chicago Temple. There, high above the busy streets of Chicago, we found a place of quietness and devotion. Any vacation that does not include some time for quiet meditation has failed to do all that a vacation is supposed to do for one.

I know a busy mother of five children. She confessed to me that there were times when the cares of the family and household would drive her to the brink of distraction. "When those times come," she confided, "I go to my room and shut the door. There I spend some moments in quietness with Him who has never failed to restore that calmness of soul that every mother needs at times."

Our Lord set the example. Countless times He felt the need of the solitary hours alone in the mountains with His Heavenly Father.

When we face problems too great to solve alone, we may rest assured that we can find that restoring power with Him. As Jesus said while He walked on earth, He says to us today, "Come unto me all ye that labour and are heavy laden, and I will give you rest."

Thank you Lord, for the way that you restore our strength, faith, and courage, when we call upon Thee. We need this assistance each day. Be near to us we pray. AMEN.

Heroes

WHAT IS THE definition of a hero? Webster's Dictionary says that a hero is a man of distinguished courage, moral or physical. A boy extolling the virtues of his father to a playmate one day said, "My dad is the greatest, the tallest, and the wisest. He is a hero."

History records the greatness of our heroes. However, if we should tell the simple truth of some of our neighbors, we would discover that there are heroes all about us. Heroism is being courageous in the face of what seems like sure defeat, for heroism knows no defeat.

On the bulletin board of a small village church I once read, "We believe the power behind us is greater than the task before us." The above affirmation is what heroes are made of.

Abraham Lincoln, in a dark hour of his life, spoke courageously when he said, "I believe that the will of God prevails. Without it I cannot succeed. With Divine assistance I cannot fail." Lincoln, like many of our heroes, was no less remarkable for what he suffered, than for what he achieved. Through hardship and ridicule he rose to true greatness because he would not accept defeat as final. He felt, no doubt, that he like Queen Esther of Old Testament days, had come to the kingdom "for such a time as this" (Esther 4:14).

Faith begets courage and courage produces heroism. In the Book of Hebrews there is a chapter telling of a long line of splendor. Here is listed many of those who believed that the will of God prevailed. Their courage, that knew no defeat, has had an influence on countless lives.

Chapter eleven of Hebrews could not begin to tell of all those whose courageous faith in God gave them a place in religious history. The chapter concludes with the words, "And all of these, having obtained a good report through faith, received not the promise. God having provided some better thing for us, that they without us should not be made perfect" (Hebrews 11:39-40).

History has produced its men and women of heroism but they are not enough. We too have a place to fill. We have a part in the history of today and tomorrow.

All about us are unsung heroes whose courageous faith in God has held them steady. Most of us will never be listed in the Hall of Fame. We can, however, by God's help exemplify the truest and most courageous of all, Jesus, of whom it was said, "He went about doing good."

Come, Spirit of God, dwell within us that we may have the courage and wisdom to face what we must and be victorious. AMEN.

Healing Wounds

A FAMILY DOCTOR, whose philosophy was worth as much as his medicine, once said that the worst way to heal a wound was to keep picking at it. The good doctor did not realize how much real truth, about life, he had said in those few words. There are many wounds, not alone of the body, but of the mind and society that would have healed long ago if we had not kept picking at them.

It seems to be a weakness of human nature that we are willing to bury the hatchet as long as we can leave the handle sticking out. We can forgive but it is difficult to forget.

In counseling with young couples who are making plans for marriage, I never fail to pass along to them one of the tried and true rules. That rule is, if you can agree to disagree without becoming disagreeable, your marriage will stand a good chance of being a success.

There will never be a time when two people will see eye to eye in everything. There will, likewise, never come a time when the people of the world will agree without reservations. Someone has prayed, "O Lord, help us to make the world safe for our differences."

Man's wounds will not be healed by dwelling upon each other's differences, but rather by amplifying our likenesses. God has given us certain basic hungers. There is the hunger for physical sustenance. The longing for peace of mind and the pursuit of happiness is basic in all our hungers. In all of these and more, man has a God given right to pursue. The road we travel to obtain these necessities can either heal wounds or make them worse.

In the twelfth chapter of Romans, Paul the apostle gives us some of the basic attitudes of one who would be a healer of wounds. He writes, "Recompense no man evil for evil . . . therefore, if thine enemy hunger, feed him; if he thirst, give him to drink; for in so doing thou shalt heap coals of fire on his head."

Heaping coals of fire upon your enemy's head mean returning good for evil. This is not easy, but Paul found that God's grace was sufficient to help him to do so. It works for us also.

Recently I heard a world traveler say that the people of the world could come nearer living in peace if everyone spoke the same language. But, have you ever thought that there is an international language of hope and longing in the world. The trouble is how to break down the barrier of the lack of trust for one another and the senseless greed and fear. We are all creations of God, yet plagued by imperfections.

I suppose that it seems a far off dream, that the many wounds that separate man from his brother will ever be healed. The great Master had this dream. He gave His life for it. He gave us the formula and the secret of the power that can bring it to pass. We would do well to continue His plan and hope and ask for His wisdom and grace.

God grant us courage and wisdom, and the power of Thy Spirit, to pour on the oil of love that the wounds of the world may be healed. AMEN.

Hasten Slowly

TAKE YOUR time and not your life. Those words on a sign by the side of a busy highway caught my attention. During the past twenty years, at least, speed and power have motivated almost every action of our generation. They have, likewise, been the means of increasing the physical death rate and the moral decay we witness on all sides. "Take time for all things for great haste makes great waste," so cautioned Benjamin Franklin, one of the founders of our country.

As we approached an old covered bridge one day, I read the words, "Slow to a walk." The ancient bridge could not continue to stand the rush of the modern day vehicles.

Thus, the words of the horse and wagon days were still the rule for today. In slowing to a walk we are not only protecting the material things but we have time to see and meditate.

Since slowing down on the highway to fifty-five miles per hour, we have had time to witness many of the beauties along the way. In my state there are 189 less deaths, at this date, than a year ago. The answer could be that we are taking our time and not our lives.

Slow down and live! This is true in every avenue of life. Take time to read, it inspires and lifts one's vision. Take time to meditate, it strengthens the heart and gives new hope for tomorrow. Take time to pray, it quiets our fears and is an anchor for the soul.

James, the brother of Jesus, and the author of the book that bears his name, gave wise counsel when he wrote, ". . . let every man be swift to hear but slow to speak, slow to wrath" (James 1:19). Think how many friendships might be strengthened if we would practice being, "slow to speak and slow to wrath." How much more temperate the answer to that harsh note that came today, if we would only sleep on it and wait until tomorrow to write that letter. Thinking before you speak is still good advice.

Being anxious is the haste that wastes. The hastening of our minds into the worries of tomorrow dissipates the joys of today. Jesus, talking with His disciples, asked them, "Which of you by taking thought (by being anxious) can add to his stature one cubit?" (Luke 12:25) To me, Jesus was trying to get us to see that the developing of the physical as well as the spiritual takes time. Anxious hastening will not ripen the fruit, but rather bring frustration.

The wave of the sea does not become a cloud by its anxious rising and falling. It eventually reaches that orbit by its quiet willingness to be the best wave in the sea. In due time it is drawn by the sun to become one of God's clouds in the sky. Live not in haste and anxious thought, but in quiet faith. Give God and the world your best and each day will develop into a richer tomorrow.

O Lord of wisdom, impart a portion of that divine wisdom to us that we may make right choices and know how to use those choices. AMEN.

House Cleaning

HOUSE CLEANING is a necessity, if not a joy, to the conscientious homemaker. It is the occasion of renewal of dedication to the task of keeping the house in order. It is a good time to get rid of some of those non-essentials that have accumulated through the years. It takes courage as well as wisdom to decide what is worth keeping and what is no more than chaff.

Down on the farm we used to thrash with the steam engine and the separator. When the thrasher pulled out it was a signal for the chickens to come to the feast. They would dive in and the chaff would fly. I noticed this, however, the chickens ate the wheat but left the chaff.

This is a parable of life. We need to pray for wisdom to learn the difference between the chaff and the wheat, and the courage to separate the one from the other.

We become like that with which we associate. We will not love those things that are pure if our minds dwell upon those things that are impure. Dr. Smiley Blanton, noted psychiatrist, once wrote, "What we shall love is the key problem of human existence, because we tend to become the reflection of what we love."

Jesus in His teaching reminded His listeners, that, "Where your treasure is, there will your heart be also." We do become the reflection of what we love.

House cleaning is not only a time to discard the chaff. It is, likewise, a good time to evaluate the things that bless and sustain us.

It seems that we are living in an age when the main word is "destruction." Riots, vandalism, and other acts of subversion, are the order of the day. It is not enough to destroy the material and physical, but there are those who would also do away with the God who created them.

Most of us who think seriously about the affairs of life realize that our house is not in perfect order. But, what are those who are set only on destruction offering in the place of what they would destroy?

We have only to look around us to realize the many blessings and opportunities that are ours. We have been blessed with so much in America that we have forgotten to be thankful. We cannot forget, however, that the good things of life have come to us that we might share them.

Paul the apostle writing to the Christians at Rome, urged them to remember that "We then that are strong ought to bear the infirmities of the weak . . . " (Romans 15:1)

It is not alone our responsibility, but our opportunity to strengthen and encourage those less fortunate than we. In so doing we help them to know the joy that comes to those who place their confidence in God.

Truly, the time of spiritual house cleaning is the renewal of the dedication of keeping our house in order. It is then that the Spirit cleanses and gives direction to all our efforts to fruitful living.

Cleanse me, O Lord, and help me to keep my house in order for Thy daily Presence. AMEN.

It Is Later Than You Think

"ENJOY YOURSELF — it is later than you think." Those words were seen originally on a brass plate in a beautiful Chinese garden in Peking. These thought provoking words became the theme for a most interesting book written by Dr. Frederick Loomis several years ago.

The words, "Enjoy yourself — it is later than you think," are not to be taken lightly. I am sure that they might mean, "get a lot of fun out of life while you can." But, there are many ways of getting fun out of life.

Far too many of us let life slip by and find that we are on the sunset trail, and we haven't really taken time to live. There are those who live out the summertime of their lives and discover that they have not lain aside, in life's storehouse, those necessary things against the winter storms of life. One cannot expect to make withdrawals without first making deposits.

It is later than you think. We could take the pessimistic side and say that is possible that the bomb may already be made that could destroy us. Our enemies are slowly sapping our material strength. It seems that we only get out of one trouble spot in the world until we get into another. Our people's will to continue to give of themselves to help the world has been broken. All of this could be true to a certain extent.

It is later than you think. We know that the spirit of America has never known defeat. We, likewise, have discovered, in times gone by, that we have only known true, and lasting peace when it has come by that greater Power than our own.

Above the door of an auto body repair shop I read, "Making the best of a bad mess is our business." Have we ever thought about making the best of a bad mess?

Enjoy yourself — it is later than you think. Start living positively. Believe and live like there is hope ahead. There is nothing impossible with God. Do not worry about tomorrow. Live the best you can, by God's help, and the years ahead will be happier.

Look around you. Enjoy your work as though it is a part of God's plan for your life. Enjoy yourself — give life your best and the best will come back to you. It is later than you think.

Jesus urged His disciples to note that the fields were white unto the harvest. He sent them out to invest their lives in helping to make a better world. This is what really brings joy to life. This Master of true values said that a man's ife consisteth not in the abundance of the things which he possesseth.

God has given us the canvas, paint, and brushes. He will help us to complete the picture. Let us take up the brush and enjoy ourselves in our tasks and opportunities, for it is later than we think.

O God, how desperately we need Thee that we do not fail in life's living, giving and serving. Guide our hands, soul and mind. AMEN.

Involvement

"I DIDN'T want to get involved." Such was the statement made by one who stood by with a group of witnesses to a crime being committed. The witness concluded by saying, "I didn't think that it was any of my business.'

Charles Jackson, author, once wrote a novel which he called, "The Outer Edges." It was a story of brutal crime committed by an adolescent delinquent boy. The import of the story was its effect on a group of people in the New York area. Indirectly, they were all involved in the crime. The spectators, the boy's school teacher, the minister, the Sunday School teacher, as well as the police in the neighborhood where the boy resided.

The bypasser, the onlooker or the so called sidewalk judge, we are all involved, indirectly, in the movements about us, good or bad. To a certain extent we are responsible for the conditions in our world.

Jeremiah, one of the early Biblical prophets, lamenting on the conditions of his nation, cried out, "Is it nothing to you, all ye that pass by?" (Lamentations 1:12) Centuries later, a young lawyer questioned Jesus, "Who is my neighbor?" Jesus then gave the parable of the Good Samaritan. In this parable the priest and the Levite did not care to get involved so they "passed by on the other side." The Samaritan, thinking not of his own safety, but rather the need of the traveler who had been beaten and robbed, turned aside to give him aid. The Samaritan showed this mercy not because he was obligated to do so, but rather because here was a need and he could not pass by.

On the day of the crucifixion of Jesus there were those who passed by. Some to ridicule, others to lament, while others openly avowed their loyalty to the end.

The movements and changes that have made the world a better place in which to live have come about largely because those who saw the need made it their business to get invovled.

The list is endless of those who have dedicated their lives and talent in the field of medical science, education for the underprivileged, the national and world needs, and in spiritual welfare.

Some have been martyrs to the causes in which they believed. Others, like many of us, have felt the need of doing what little we could do to hold up the hands of those who have done so much. Someone has said that we will not be held accountable for that which we cannot do, only for those things which, by God's help, we can do but fail to do.

O Christ of God, we know that you were continually involved with others' needs. Help me this day that I shall be willing to do likewise. AMEN.

Joy

LIVING LIFE at its best may be determined by the way we interpret joy. Joy is not always an audible exuberance but more often an inward experience that expresses itself in our actions.

We were visitors one Sunday morning in a worship service. The first three pews at the front of the church were reserved for a special group. Those who sat in those pews were deaf and mute worshipers. As the service progressed an interpreter, the minister's wife, stood before them.

Even though these people could not hear the audible service they "heard" it through their interpreter. During that service, I observed the expressions of joy on their faces. They were enjoying the service as much as we who were hearing with our ears.

Joy is not a selfish experience. It is like the favorite Psalm, "My cup runneth over." Joy is something you can't hide. It is something you share. Joy is something you spill on yourself when you share it with others. Joy, like happiness, to pursue it, for the sake of possession, is to lose it.

The highest joy often comes through suffering or sorrow. It often comes to us when we have given ourselves to others in their times of sorrow. Someone has observed that no flower can bloom in paradise which is not transplanted from Gethsemane.

The author of Hebrews, speaking of Jesus as the Author of our faith and the example of courage in suffering, wrote, " . . . Who for the joy that was set before Him, endured the cross . . . " (Hebrews 12:2) Our Lord knew the victory that was to follow His cross.

The joy is not the experience of enduring our crosses but rather the joy is in the victory that we experience after we have faithfully done that which had to be done. The Psalm writer once said, "They that sow in tears shall reap in joy" (Psalm 126:5)

The route to real joy is marked by milestones, such as light, repentance, forgiveness, and acceptance. The outcome is joy.

Jesus, talking with His disciples concerning the cost or formula for joyful living, concluded by saying, "These things have I spoken unto you, that my joy might remain in you, and that your joy might be full" (John 15:11). Joy to the fullest does not come through material or physical things alone, but rather in love. The kind of love that does not ask for favors but gives itself instead.

Lord and Master, we thank Thee for the joy of living. Help us that we might so share this joy with others that they too might know the joy of Thy daily presence with them too. AMEN.

Judge Not

"IT IS always easier to spot a vice than it is to recognize a virtue," so expressed Mort Crim, news commentator, recently. How true it is. We are often too prone to point out flaws and defects in others.

A speaker at a P.T.A. meeting held up a white sheet of paper with a black dot on it. He than asked his audience what they saw. The first comment was, "I see a black dot." This observer never mentioned the white sheet of paper.

I wonder why my neighbor, looking at our beautiful flower garden remarked, "Don you have a few weeds amongst your flowers." Might it be that we expect perfection in others but are inclined to see first their imperfections. Someone has observed that there is so much bad in the best of us and so much good in the worst of us that it ill behooves any of us to speak ill of the rest of us.

Jesus had a few things to say along this line. In the midst of His Sermon on the Mount He cautioned, "Judge not that ye be not judged. For with what judgment ye judge, ye shall be judged; and with what measure ye mete it shall be measured to you. And why beholdest thou the mote that is in thy brother's eye, but considerest not the beam that is in thine own eye?" (Matthew 7:1-3)

This admonition by Jesus was not to excuse the evil in anyone's life. It was, rather, that no one was so perfect that he should condemn the imperfections of others.

It is said that many years ago there was a custom among some Indian tribes of appointing judges who went from village to village to try the unlawful. One young brave, upon being chosen for this important position, sought guidance of Him who judgeth righteousness. With hands uplifted this young Indian judge prayed, "O Great Spirit, forbid that I judge any man until I have walked for two moons in his moccasins."

This young man, like Solomon of old, was asking for an "understanding heart." It is often easy to pass judgment upon someone of whom we know little. But, after we have stood only briefly in another's moccasins, our judgments become merciful.

John, the Gospel writer, tells us that Jesus urged His listeners to, "Judge not according to the appearance, judge righteous judgment" (John 7:24). "Righteous judgment" is not given until after we have tried to understand the motive of another's action.

I once learned a bit of verse. A part of it said, "Could we but draw back the curtains/That surround each other's lives/See the thought and motives/Less prone we'd be to criticize/More inclined we'd be to see the good/If we only understood."

Praying for an understanding heart, with compassion for those whose imperfections we are prone to judge, helps us to be less inclined to judge and more charitable to love.

O merciful God, help me to be less prone to judge others but rather to face my own sins and shortcomings. AMEN.

Keep Pitching

CARL HUBBLE, famous pitcher of my youthful generation, was being complimented on his past achievements. His response was, "No one can rest on past laurels. He has to keep pitching." This is true not alone in baseball, but in all walks of life.

It is amazing how quickly a tool rusts without use. A musician once said that if he failed to practice one day, he could tell it. If he missed two days, his audience noticed it. What does it mean? It means that if we expect to continue to win the battles of life, we have to keep alert and in practice.

As a young man being ordained to the ministry, I, along with my fellow classmen, was asked some questions. Among the questions asked by the Bishop who was leading in the ordination was, "Are you going on to perfection?" Our answer was, "God being my helper, I will."

The older I grew the more I realize what that answer entailed. Even though I shall never reach that goal of perfection in this life, I know that I must, by God's help, keep ever striving for it.

To be at our best we have to keep in practice. Yesterday's achievements will not suffice for tomorrow's needs. A wise man, long ago, said that when we cease growing we begin to die. This is true intellectually, as well as spiritually.

"Pray without ceasing," implored the apostle Paul. "Watch and pray that ye enter not into temptation: the spirit indeed is willing but the flesh is weak," so instructed Jesus (Matthew 26:41).

Being watchful and praying without ceasing means tht we can never lay down the oars and expect to drift forward. If anything is worth striving for, it is worth endeavoring to keep ever before us.

Timothy, the spiritual son of Paul, was urged to "study to show thyself approved of God, a workman that needeth not to be ashamed . . . " The victories of life do not come by chance. They come through vision, dedication, faith, and determination. If we would be "approved of God," as well as have the satisfaction of work well done, we must keep learning and practicing.

I have always had a feeling of sadness when I read in Bible history of Saul, the king who failed and Samson who played with life. Both began as men of promise but dissipated their God given talents and came to a tragic end. How much different with men like Paul who was able to say, "I have fought a good fight, I have finished my course, I have kept the faith" (II Timothy 4:7).

There will always be those whose past is worth remembering because they kept the present alive with faith in the future. We too, by God's help, may join this line of splendor if we "keep pitching."

O God, we pray for the power of Thy Holy Presence in our lives that we may never give up, but finish the course that is before us. We shall praise Thee. AMEN.

Living Life At Its Best

"THE TIME of life is short. To live it basely 'twere too long," thus wrote Shakespeare many years ago. This truth still has meaning for us today.

Too often man spends his life reasoning on the past, complaining of the present, and trembling for the future.

The number of years we put into life is not as important as how well we invest in those years. The law of life at its best is to use wisely or lose it. This is true of the physical, the intellectual, as well as the spiritual.

Sometime ago we visited the Linville Caverns in Virginia. There we saw, swimming in the water, fish that were blind. They were not without eyes. We were told that because these fish did not use their eyes in these dark caverns that the optic nerves were dead.

In the realm of the physical, our talents and abilities are improved by exercise. They are likewise weakened by disuse. This is just as true inthe intellectual and spiritual.

Phillips Brooks, famous preacher of years ago said, "Do not pray for easy lives; pray to be strong men. Do not pray for tasks equal to your powers, but pray for powers equal to your tasks."

I have always admired those straight A students. The secret of the success of any-one's life, however, is not being afraid of trying again and again until he has reached the goal. A well known writer was once asked how he wrote such successful stories. He answered, "It was not so much how I wrote them, but rather how I rewrote them that counted."

In the Book of Matthew, Jesus gives the parable of the talents. This parable is not so much a formula on how to make a fortune in life, but rather how to keep from making life a misfortune.

In the parable the lesson of the law of talents is clearly stated. Unto everyone who hath the will to exercise the capacities which are his, there shall be given greater capacities. He who does not use what has been given him, it shall be taken away.

Bible history contains many experiences of those who lived life at its best because they exercised their faith and invested their talents.

To live life at its best, one's own ability is not enough. Those who have succeeded in life's endeavor have done so because they have made their life and talent a dedication to something greater than themselves.

I once attended a funeral of a man who, for many years, had been a great physician. The storms were never too severe or the night too dark for him to go to the aid of someone in need. I heard the minister say that this able physician had become a great doctor because he not alone knew how to use his hands but he, likewise, knew how to use his heart.

The time of life is short. To live life at its best we will do well to invest both our hands and our hearts. Give of your best to God and man, and God's best will come back to you.

The time of life is short. To live life at its best we will do well to invest both our hands and our hearts. Give of your best to God and man, and God's best will come back to you.

Life's Greatest Reward

RECENTLY, A very capable young lady came to interview me. At the close of the interview she said, "Now, I have one more question I would like to ask you. What do you consider the greatest reward of your life's work?"

Without hesitation I replied, "To have the feeling that I have helped someone."

There are many rewards that come to us, regardless in what field or vocation our lives have been spent. I am sure that I have more than my share of those rewards. I have been grateful for the opportunities to use what talent God has given me.

There is often the temptation to be mercenary. That is to ask, "What is there in it materially for me?" The material gain is important but not at the expense of those rewards that are more lasting and that bring peace of mind.

Recently, I visited with a retired nurse. She related some of her experiences of these fifty-four years. "My most satisfying rewards," she said, "came from the feeling that I had helped to make life easier for someone."

Each of the three Gospel writers, Matthew, Mark, and Luke, give an account of the young man who seemed to have almost everything except peace of mind. This man noted that Jesus had something that he did not possess. On coming to Jesus, he asked. ". . . Good Master, what shall I do that I may inherit eternal life?" (Mark 10:17).

This man who was rich in things had been inheriting material possessions all his life but was not pleased with what he was. He had kept all of the commandments but lacked one thing — his concern for others.

He forfeited the most rewarding experiences of his life by refusing to follow the formula Jesus gave him, to sell what he had, give to the poor and take up his cross and follow the Master. In so doing he would be giving his life to others and would have had treasure in heaven.

Life's greatest benefits are not found alone in getting, but in giving. Jesus once asked His disciples, "What is a man profited, if he shall gain the whole world and lose his soul . . .?" (Matthew 16:26) One of the finest things they said about Jesus was that He went about doing good.

I had the opportunity recently of speaking to a group of retired teachers. They called themselves, "The Young at Heart." One teacher, with a record of fifty years in the school room, said to me, "Mr. Jennings, it is like you said, our teaching never ends. What we have tried to do in our active years, goes on in the lives of others. This is my greatest reward.

My sincere prayer for many years has been, "Lord, grant that what I say, write or do, may help someone along the way, to a more fruitful and satisfying life. That at the close of life's day the good I have tried by God's help, to do may continue on in the lives of others." This, I believe, is the greatest reward. AMEN.

Love Never Fails

ANY WORTHY cause guided by an honest motive and propelled by sincere love will always succeed in the end. There may be many obstacles in the way, but love never fails.

Thomas Carlyle, British philosopher, once said that the block of granite which was an obstacle in the path of the weak becomes a stepping stone in the pathway of the strong. Life's highways are strewn with hazards and blessed with opportunities. Our whole future depends upon what we do with these hazards and opportunities. Courage and determination propelled by love will never fail.

The poet Shelley, referring to love as the most misused word, wrote "It is one word too often profaned." Love is too often expressed to get what we want, but not to give. Someone has said that cheap love is soft soap, and soft soap is eighty-five percent lye. This is the kind of love that is always asking but never giving.

One of the most familiar chapters in the New Testament is the thirteenth chapter of First Corinthians. From this choice piece of gospel we learn that charity, or love, never fails.

Paul, the apostle who wrote the words, says that material things, alone, fail. We may give all that we have but only when the gift is shared in the spirit of love does it profit the giver as well as the one who receives it. The gift without the giver is bare.

We learn from this chapter on love that knowledge shall fail, for knowledge is folly unless it is guided by wisdom. Wisdom is understanding, and understanding produces love.

I look back to my first days, as a child, in public school. I am sure that the reason that first teacher of mine succeeded with her pupils was not that she had the knowledge alone, but that she possessed wisdom and loved her children. She taught the child and not just the lesson alone.

The great movements from whence humanity has really benefited have been those movements whose leaders and champions have put their hearts and themselves into the cause.

Jesus, meeting with His disciples in the Upper Room, said many things to them as His parting words, before His trial and death. Love was foremost in all that He said and did. At one point He said, "Greater love hath no man than this, that a man lay down his life for his friends" (John 15:13). The love motive had ruled His life from the beginning of His teachings, through all of the miracles He had performed, and now in the supreme test, love would not fail.

There is not greater need in our world today than that all of our actions might be controlled by the love motive. Problems unsurmountable by other means would be solved, for love never fails.

Lord of Love, help us that our lives may be guided by the love motive, in all our decisions and actions. Through Christ we pray. AMEN.

Lamplighters

ROBERT LOUIS STEVENSON, British novelist, loved to reflect a childhood memory. On winter evenings as a child, he enjoyed sitting at the window at dusk, watching the lamplighter making his way up the hill. This humble workman would stop at each lamp post. A taper glowed, the lamp was lighted, and another circle of light reached out to pierce the gloom.

In later years Robert Louis Stevenson writes of this childhood experience in "The Lamplighter." His greatest resolve, as a child, was that when he grew stronger he might go about with the lamplighter helping to light the lamps.

Being a lamplighter is a pretty important business in this world. There is plenty of darkness to trouble and confuse our vision, to cause men to stumble and lose their way.

There are more people involved in this business of lamplighting than we realize. Life has been made richer, the life span longer, and the eternal hope stronger, because of the faithful lamplighters.

From that night the great Heavenly Lamplighter set the Light aglow in the little town of Bethlehem, down to this day, the lights from that Lamplighter has continued to grow. Harry Lauder, beloved Scottish singer, speaking of the lamplighter, once said, "You can always tell where the lamplighter has been by the trail of light left behind him."

The great Master Lamplighter once said, "Let your light so shine before men that they may see your good works, and glorify your Father which is in heaven" (Matthew 5:16). It is better that men see where the lamplighter has been by the trail he has left behind him than it is that he be seen. As Jesus said, we should let our light shine that men might see the works that we leave behind us and give glory to God.

There are many avenues of life in which we can be lamplighters. Wherever we are there is someone who is waiting for a word of cheer or encouragement.

It has been said that we are conductors. Just as the electric light line is conductor of power and light and warmth, so are we conductors through which God may send His message of hope to a discouraged soul.

"Make me an instrument of Thy peace," said a consecrated young man of long ago. This young man through word and deed went about as an instrument in God's hand. His name became famous as one of the Master's lamplighters, Saint Francis of Assisi.

We may never become famous, but if we let our light shine, where we are, now, there will surely be those who will thank God for the trail of light that has helped them to better find their way on life's journey.

O Lord, grant that the small light of my life may, by Thy help, guide someone along life's road this day. Through Christ I pray. AMEN.

Like A Tree

AS I WORK at my desk by the window, I can't help from looking out upon an entrancing scene. Parallel with our white board fence around the back yard are beautiful Norway Spruce. The first snow of the season has settled upon our trees. The birds that spend the winter with us hide in their branches, coming out only to snatch a bite from the bird feeder on a post nearby.

Those trees, that are now so much a part of us, have not always been so. It seems only yesterday that I received through the mail a small package no larger than a bunch of celery. Those were our trees. What has happened? Through God's eternal nature and our tender loving care, they are growing.

How like the development of a life. My thoughts, this winter evening, recall some other "trees" that have grown up through the years. Those young men and women were, only yesterday, little children. I have seen them develop into able bodied men and women, responsible Christian citizens of their communities.

I once heard a man speaking to youth. He used as his theme the words, "Alive in the middle, Dead on both ends." He was speaking of appetite versus mind and body. One of the things this wise man said was that an appetite that gets the best of a person produces a mind that is stunned and feet that stumble.

One of the finest things they said about Jesus in His youth was, "And Jesus increased in wisdom and stature, and in favor with God and man" (Luke 2:52). This did not just happen. It came to pass through His obedience to His Heavenly Father and the tender loving care of parents who were concerned.

Growing to a maturity that brings the favour of God and man does not just happen. Sometimes we are made to wonder what is happening to the growing process of the youth of our country. I still have confidence to believe that the majority of youth are not all bad. However, one bad potato in a basket can make one think the whole lot is rotten. Unless something is done about it, in the end the whole lot will be contaminated.

Most of us know that it is not easy to grow and produce a good harvest year after year. The kind of a world we would leave to our children is not grown in one generation, but each generation must contribute its part.

The Psalm writer speaks words of wisdom when, in the first Psalm he speaks of the man whose "delight is in the law of the Lord . . . He shall be like a tree planted by the rivers of water, that bringeth forth his fruit in season." Deep down in each ones heart, this is the kind of tree one longs to be. This kind is grown only through prayer, labor, and concern.

God of all creation, help us to grow in wisdom that we might become what you would have us to be, and what we hope to become. AMEN.

Living Under Pressure

I AM NOT quite sure what happened. But the little lady who has cooked my meals, and has kept me straight for many years, had an accident with the pressure cooker. It blew the safety plug. Thelma almost lost an eye and in her fright lost confidence in the pressure cooker. An expert informed us that the relief valve became plugged causing the accident.

This is a parable of our time. In this busy, rushing age there are all kinds of gadgets to help make life easier, but less time to enjoy it. In our hurry and worry, pressure builds up within us, then before we know it the safety plug blows and our whole day is ruined.

Many of the pressures of life are not of our own choosing. Many others are due to the fact that we let ourselves become involved in too many things.

A young housewife concerned about this matter asked me this question a few days ago, "Is blowing your top once in a while the only way to relieve the pressure of tension?" She went on to say, "It relieves me for the time being, but it hurts those around me."

I am sure that this young mother is not alone in this problem. Frustrations and resentments must find relief or release. If they don't find it one way they will another. Is "blowing your top" the only way?

My mother lived in another age, but I am sure that she had her days of frustration and anxiety. You don't bear nine children and rear eight of them and not experience some days of pressure.

Mother loved to sing and I am sure as I look back, that when those difficult times came that she relieved the tension somewhat by singing instead of complaining. By the way she lived she must have had a prescription like a mother of many years who said, "In times of stress I pray for a right attitude. Not that I might run away from my troubles, but rather face them sensibly, without being anxious."

Jesus knew that the frustrations and pressure would engulf His disciples. He tried to prepare them for those days. He exemplified His teaching by going aside to a quiet place to rest and pray when there were trying times ahead. At the very close of His ministry He consoled them with the words, "Peace I leave with you, my peace I give unto you; not as the world giveth, give I unto you. Let not your heart be troubled, neither let it be afraid" (John 14:27).

What is a good prescription for relief of the pressures of life? Live a day at a time and trust God for tomorrow. Take time out during the day for some quiet moments to rest the body and replenish the soul. This break is just as essential as the coffee break and more lasting. Invest more time in relief for others; this will bring strength to your own spirit. The peace that comes will be a relief valve and a satisfaction in a time when it is needed.

Forgive us, Lord, for not turning to you when the pressures of life would overcome us. We know that you have the peace we need. Thank you, Lord, for having the answer through Christ Thy Son. AMEN.

Life's Benefits

I STOPPED, recently, to congratulate a good woman on her one hundredth birthday. I had visited with her many times. On each occasion I have been impressed by her faith, her courage, and her joy of living. On this special day of celebrating her reaching the century mark, I asked, "Grandma Wert, to what do you attribute such a long and happy life?" She smiled, thought a moment, then answered, "I was born on the farm. I worked hard, married young, reared nine children, and thanked God every day for good health."

Life's values are not always found in the number of years we live. It is not how many years we put into life, but what we put into those years that counts. It has been proven many times that the happiest person is not always the one who has the most of the material things in life. More often it is the one who is grateful for that which he has. Being thankful for a beautiful sunrise makes the entire day more meaningful.

Gratitude in action is worth more than many words of praise. I would rather see a sermon walking than to hear one any day. What we are trying to say is, that life's benefits are doubly so when we not only express our gratitude but let our actions prove it.

We have read, many times, of the healing of the ten lepers by Jesus. We noted the ingratitude of the nine who failed to return to show thanks. We have often thought of what the nine missed by not turning back to their benefactor.

The one leper had been healed by Jesus, just as the other nine. He had gone on his way just as they, but when he realized that he was healed he turned back to show his gratitude to Jesus. It was through this act that he received the extra blessing from the Master. "And he (Jesus) said unto him, arise, go thy way; thy faith hath made thee whole" (Luke 17:19). This sincere act brought benefit to the physical but, likewise, to the mind and spirit.

"Thank the nice lady for the apple," urged the young mother of her son. The lady who had given the young child the apple smiled, then replied, "He doesn't have to thank me." "He may not have to thank you," replied the mother, "but the apple will taste better if he does."

Days come and go and we often accept God's blessings as a matter of course. We do not have to show gratitude but life will "taste" better if we do.

One who cultivates the spirit of gratitude may not live longer, but he will live better. Is not this one of the reasons why our Pilgrim fathers began their sojourn on this continent with a period of thanksgiving? They were thankful for not alone what they had received, but for what they had escaped and hoped for in the future.

As a nation of people, we have prospered in many ways. God has been good to us. We have much for which to be thankful. We would do well to remember the Psalm writer who said, "Bless the Lord, O my soul, and forget not all His benefits" (Psalm 103:2).

O God, we have so much to thank Thee for. Help us to not forget the daily blessings. We do thank Thee for them all. AMEN.

Living Alone

"THE FARMER'S life is the most independent yet helpless life in the world," so said my father many years ago. He then went on to paint a word picture of the farmer's kingdom in which he was pretty much his own boss. He concluded, however, by explaining to his sons that we are dependent upon the elements above us and about us over which we have very little control.

I have often thought of those words of wisdom. I once heard a well known scientist say that the farmer may own the land four thousand miles beneath him, but he has no control over the elements one mile above him.

Man has made many exciting scientific discoveries. He has learned how to lengthen the span of life. He is able to control or increase production. He is now on the verge of conquering outer space. But with all of this, he discovers now and then he still has his limitations. He finds that he is still dependent upon his fellow men, and above all the Creator who controls man's final destiny. He cannot live alone.

Paul, the apostle, writing to the Roman Christians once said, "None of us liveth unto himself, and no one dieth unto himself" (Romans 14:7). To me, he was saying that our lives are tied up pretty closely to those of our fellowmen. We are influencing and being influenced by those whose lives we touch. Man does not live alone, nor in his death does he leave this world without his influence being felt in the lives of those about him.

John Donnie, poet of the sixteenth century, once wrote, "No man is an Island, entire of himself, every man is a part of the mainland. Any man's death diminishes me, because I am involved in mankind." We need one another not alone for self preservation, but for the future existence of all mankind.

This philosophy of the mutual need of one for another was taught and practiced by Jesus of Nazareth. He taught that we should bear one another's burdens. He illustrated this in many ways but especially in the parable of the Good Samaritan.

The philosophy of the robber was, what is yours is mine. The philosophy of the one who passed by was, what is mine is my own. The innkeeper's idea was, what is mine is yours if you pay for it. The Good Samaritan practiced the philosophy of what is mine is yours, we'll share together.

The true Christian philosophy is that no man is an island, no man walks alone. We need one another. Life's problems are better solved together. Man's burdens are made easier to bear when we see one another as brothers. This the Master taught. This is one of the urgent needs of our world today.

Help us, O Lord of compassion, to better understand that we are in this world to share one another's burdens in love. AMEN.

Life's Motives

THE COLOR in the leaves was at its best in south central Illinois, on a beautiful day this past fall. With anticipation, we climbed the hill that led to New Salem State Park. Anyone who loves and reveres the life of Abraham Lincoln is sure to be impressed by the humble surroundings and beauty of New Salem, where Lincoln spent those few years of his youth.

One could only imagine, as we lingered in those rustic buildings, what ideas and ideals were formed in the mind of this young man. This backwoods, but sincere lad who was destined to be the great President of this country during those discouraging Civil War days.

Many times I had read the words spoken by this sad faced man, "With malice toward none." As we stood there and looked again at the bronze statue of this rugged young man, with his ax in hand, I saw not a sad faced man, but a sincere, determined youth. Here was one who had a single motive in his life. That motive was to give himself to the opportunities that lay before him. This he would do without malice in his heart toward anyone who would disagree with him.

It reminded me that Abraham Lincoln must have had within him the Spirit of One who, also, faced the world very much alone, centuries before. Jesus was that man. He faced a world that thought that the gospel He preached was not practical. They ridiculed Him. They made fun of Him. They passed judgment on Him and at the very height of His ministry they took His life.

Through all of this persecution there was no malice in the Master's heart toward anyone. As He was dying he cried, "Father, forgive them, they know not what they do" (Luke 23:34).

One whose disappointments are saturated with malice suffers a malady that strickens the mind, ages the body, and destroys life's hopes. One who lets ill feelings, toward those who disagree with him, rule his life defeats his own cause.

The synonym of malice is charity. These two cannot live, in harmony, together in the same heart. Paul, the apostle, never gave better philosophy than when he said, "Charity suffereth long, and is kind, charity envieth not . . ." (I Corinthians 13:4)

Man's motives in life have been many. The life, however, that is motivated with malice toward none but with charity and justice for all, will be a life that shall live on long after his earthly sojourn has ended.

Lord, help us that our hearts may be filled with a charitable spirit at all times, that the influence of our lives may live on, for good, after we are gone. AMEN.

Life's Investment

RECENTLY A man, from that long line of unfortunates called transients, stopped at my office. He came to ask for a handout but tarried to pour out his heart. He, like most unfortunates, had known better days. He recalled how that he had a good, respectful family background. An uncle of his had been an influence for good in his childhood and youth. In spite of all these influences he knew that he had failed. This young man in his remorse of a wasted life confessed, "I have made a mess of my life when it might have been a message."

Life has gone sour for many. It is not alone the down and out. There are many who have plenty to live on but seem to have little to live for.

Matthew, a disciple of Jesus, records the account of the rich young man who came to the Master. Even though he had much to live on, life had grown stale. He saw something in the life of Jesus that his money had never been able to buy.

This young man asked the Master, "What good thing shall I do that I may have eternal life?" (Matthew 19:16). The formula that Jesus gave him was too costly. On discovering that the young man had kept all the commandments from his youth up,

Jesus said unto him, "If thou wilt be perfect, go sell that thou hast and give to the poor and thou shalt have treasure in heaven; and come and follow me" (Matthew 19:21). This young man, however, was not willing to become poor that he might be rich.

In planning our life we must decide what we really want. One wonders if we, in this modern day, really want. One wonders if we, in this modern day, really know what we want. Someone has said that with a magnitude of gadgets we are not really happier than before. With the decline in the death rate we have not really learned what to do with our lives.

This young man was not a waster, nor was Jesus. He merely was asked by the Master to invest what he had in those who were needy. "The greatest use of life, said Harvard professor William James, "is to invest it in something that will outlast you."

E. Stanley Jones, long-time missionary and author, once said about life, "Life is like an egg; its future depends on how you handle it; either you give it up or give it away." If we would have peace of mind and live a full, free and useful life, invest it, give it away for something that will outlast you.

This young man was asking, "Master, what can I do to make my life worthwhile?" As Jesus said to that young man He no doubt would say to us; Look to the needs about you; Honesty in the market place; Integrity in government; True religion in the temple.

Life need not be a mess. We need not throw it away. Life can be a message. We can give ourselves away, that inasmuch as we do it unto the least of these we do it unto Him. Just as surely as there can be no interest without investment, or a harvest without a seeding time, so can there be no eternal returns of life without investing what we are and have in Christ's Name.

Eternal God and Father of us all, help us not to withhold anything we have, are, or can be, for we know that in letting go and letting you control our lives, all shall be well. AMEN.

Labor And Wait

HENRY WADSWORTH LONGFELLOW, American poet, left a rich heritage of poetry of moral elevation as well as fine artistic sense. His life was not all roses. He lost his young wife in his youth. He felt that he could not go on with his work.

Early one morning, as the sun streamed through his study window, the words came to him, "Let us then be up and doing, with a heart for any fate; still achieving, still pursuing. Learn to labor and to wait."

There is a saying, "All things come to those who wait; but when they come they are out of date." This was not Longfellow's philosophy in his poem he called, "A Psalm of Life." In the last verse are the above words, we must "learn to labor and to wait." Waiting upon God surely means to pray, but it also means to trust Him and keep going on.

It is not always easy to take up the load when, in sorrow and disappointment, life seems so hopeless.

Paul, the apostle, writing to the Christians at Corinth said, "We walk by faith not by sight" (II Corinthians 5:17). There are many experiences in life that we cannot understand. There is the loss of a loved one in the very prime of life; a sudden sickness that means the changing of many plans; or the disappointment in our life's work that changes our entire future hopes. What can we do?

The attitude of the weak, in the face of these situations is to display impatience, worry, and deep frustration. Those who have a profound faith in God have built up a strong wall of trust. They have learned to "walk by faith not by sight." They have learned to "labor and to wait."

There is a familiar verse given us by the prophet Isaiah of long ago. He says that even the strongest may faint by the wayside and give up. But, says Isaiah, "They that wait upon the Lord shall renew their strength; they shall mount up with wings as eagles; they shall run and not be weary; and they shall walk and not faint" (Isaiah 40:31).

A most able and fruitful pastor had an invalid wife. Many thought that she was a handicap to his work. Instead of being a hindrance, she was a power of strength to her companion. In times of greatest difficulties, this pastor and husband went to his devoted wife and through her strong faith, and their counsel together with God, he came away equal to the task. This is like waiting upon God.

Longfellow was right, through faith in God, we have "a heart for any fate," we learn "to labor and to wait."

Lord, help us to have the kind of faith that gives the patience of waiting, knowing that in Thine own good time Thy will shall work out in our lives, for our good and Thy glory. AMEN.

Loneliness

A SONG, popular some years ago, asked the question, "Have you ever been lonely? Have you ever been blue?" Most of us could answer in the affirmative, to the above question. Loneliness is experienced by all ages, rich or poor, under all circumstances of life. No one is exempt.

One need not be alone on the highest mountain or in the deepest valley to know loneliness. It is not always a feeling that comes to us when we are literally alone. Oftentimes the most extreme sense of loneliness comes to us when we are in a crowd. People are all around us, yet we have a feeling that no one cares about our problems.

The Psalm writer expressed the human cry of many of us when he said, "I looked on my right hand, and beheld, but there was no man that would know me; refuge failed me; no man cared for my soul" (Psalm 142:4).

There may be consolation in the fact that, as we experience loneliness in the crowd, there are those around us who are feeling it likewise.

What is the remedy for loneliness? Is there no relief? Many have found that loneliness is overcome when they begin to think of others. One of the most lonely persons is one who lives within himself.

I once heard a lovely girl, with a pleasing personality and voice, sing, "Let me live for others, in a self-forgetful way." I know that she must have experienced loneliness at times, for she was blind. She had, however, in her darkness, learned to know the joy of life by living for others.

There are some things in life that we seem to have to face alone. But, if in facing them, we can have the feeling that we are helping others, this makes our burdens easier to bear.

Even Jesus must have experienced loneliness many times. The most vivid example was in those final hours on the cross. In that hour He must have felt that even His own Heavenly Father had deserted Him. In His suffering and loneliness, the Saviour cried out, "My God, My God, why hast Thou forsaken me?" (Matthew 27:46)

This plea from the cross was the cry of the human side of the divine Master. Even though He had known that He could not make provision for the salvation of the world without His suffering and death, He felt forsaken in that lonely hour.

When life's darkest hours of loneliness comes and you feel that you have been forsaken, remember Jesus. When it seemed that the whole world had forsaken Him, He continued to go about doing good, even to the cross. Trusting in Him we can do likewise. By so doing, the joy of living will be restored.

Our Father in Heaven, we know that you are not far from us when we feel that we are all alone. Help us ever to be mindful of Thy presence, regardless of the circumstances in which we find ourselves. AMEN.

Light A Candle

"IT IS better to light a candle than to curse the darkness." Those words, though most familiar, have inspired many people to make use of their opportunities regardless of how great or small they might be.

Such words as opportunity, ability, fear, and decision have blessed or plagued man from the beginning of time. It is not what one has or is, but rather what he will use or become that counts in his future. James A. Garfield, twentieth president of these United States, once said, "I cannot do much, but I will not let what I cannot do interfere with what I can do."

I read, with a great deal of interest, of the work Edgar Buell has done over in Laos. Edgar Buell, self-styled agriculture missionary to the unfortunate people of Laos, comes from a fine farming community in northeastern Indiana. I had the happy privilege of serving the little country church where Edgar attended in his youth. I knew him as a quiet, friendly, hardworking, and cooperative lad.

The story of his years in Laos is an extremely interesting one. He has been helping those unfortunate people to help themselves. He is literally sowing seeds that are sure to grow. He is one of those who believes it is better to light a candle than to curse the darkness. Edgar Buell decided to use the talent he had to light a candle in Laos.

In His parable of the talents, Jesus tells of the man who, going away on a journey, delivered his goods to his servants to invest for him. "To one he gave five talents, to another two and to another one; to every man according to his several ability; and straightway took his journey" (Matthew 25:15).

Two of the servants lit a candle. They invested the talents that had been entrusted to them. The other, in fear, cursed the darkness. He hid what he had. The law of life, however, proved to be true. Those who had invested, received abundance. The one who also had, but failed to use it, and hid it, lost what he had. The law of life is use it or lose it.

Very few of us are five talent folk. Most of us are like the man who was given two talents. We are not famous or obscure. Of most of us, the world will little note or long remember what we do or say here. We can, however, by God's help, use what we have, where we are now. As in farming, so in life, it is not alone the number of acres we have but how well we use them, that counts.

Henry Wadsworth Longfellow, American poet, once wrote, "The heights by great men reached and kept were not attained by sudden flight. But they, while their companions slept, were toiling in the night."

Jesus summed up His lesson on the talents by saying, ". . . Inasmuch as ye have done it unto the least of these, my brethren, ye have done it unto me" (Matthew 25:40).

When the great Score Keeper comes to judge our life's work, it will not be how many times we have won or lost, but whether we have, by God's help given life our best. It is not alone our ability, but our dedication that counts. Light a candle and help someone's darkness turn to light. It will be a good investment.

Lord, help us to let our light so shine that others may see our good works and glorify Thee. AMEN.

Life's Springtime

AS I WRITE this I am thinking of two of my loved ones who slipped away from us recently. One was my sister, Ruby, only fifty-nine; the other my father in-law, ninety years of age. Each of them faced life to the end with the courage and outlook of Springtime in their hearts. This attitude was observed by all who knew them. As I think of them now, I think of how true are the words, it is not how long we live, but how well, that counts.

Springtime is a season, but it is also a spirit. There are those who exemplify this season in their lives continuously. There are those who are young in spirit at eighty, while others are old at twenty-five. It is the outlook, or the lack of it, that makes the difference.

Springtime is eternal. It comes, it goes, but comes again and with each coming it is as fresh and new as ever. It is like Whittier, the poet, said of his old apple tree, "It grows a little new wood each year." Growing a little new wood makes each Spring-time come alive with new hope. It does the same for the physical and spiritual. Those who live only in the past have but their memories. Those who keep hope alive, have both their memories of the past, their joys of the present and their goals for the future.

There is a bit of wisdom found in the Old Testament that has always meant much to me. You may read it in the first six verses of the eleventh chapter of Ecclesiastes. We often think that we will wait for the right time to do a good deed. The bit of wisdom, to which I refer, has a wise man saying, "Cast your bread upon the waters: for thou shalt find it after many days." Do not wait for a better day to sow a bit of kindness. "In the morning sow thy seed and in the evening withhold not thine hand: for thou knowest not whether shall prosper, either this or that, or whether they both shall be alike good."

Charles Hanson Town, American poet, once wrote a poem which he titled, "Around the Corner." It concerned a friend "around the corner," whom he expected to call on but kept putting it off. One day a telegram came that said, "Jim died today," and Towne concluded his poem by saying, "And that's what we get, and deserve in the end; Around the corner, a vanished friend."

Those who keep life's Springtime eternally in their hearts do not wait for a better day. Their guideline is, "This is the day which the Lord hath made; we will rejoice and be glad in it" (Psalm 118:24).

One of the memories I shall ever treasure of my sister Ruby, was her ever present and contagious smile, even in the presence of pain and discouragement. Her concern for others' needs helped to lighten her own burdens. Attributes like these help us to exemplify the Springtime of life.

The concern of Jesus, in His last hour on the cross, was for others. Such a life as His, living in us, empowers us to do likewise.

Father, we thank Thee for those who kept the Springtime of the Spirit in their lives as long as they lived. Give us grace to do likewise. AMEN.

Like A Tree

I HAVE many friends. Many more than I deserve. These friends have made many contributions to my life. I often get quite sentimental about some of those faithful friends. All of them seem human although they are not all two-legged friends.

John Burroughs, poet and naturalist, in his book, *Wake-Robin,* writes, "Trees are among my dearest friends." As the years come and go and my life becomes seasoned by the experiences of life, I think that I know what John Burroughs meant.

As I look out of my study window, I see many of these friends. I had a hand in planting most of them. They have repaid me many times over. The crimson maple, the evergreens, and all of the other varieties. Each of them have found a warm spot in my affection. But, after all of the other trees have shed their blossoms, fruit and leaves, the evergreen, like a faithful friend, keeps plodding away winter and summer. Each of these faithful trees, however, yield their fruit in season.

God has spoken to man many times through the parable of the trees. There was the tree in the center of the Garden of Eden—it spoke to us of discipline. Through the barren fig tree, by the wayside, Jesus gives us the lesson of fruitfulness. The tree that was hewn down and made into a cross, spoke to us of sacrifice. The Bible closes with the parable of "The leaves of the tree of life were for the healing of the nations."

There are many other comparisons but this one more will suffice. The Psalm writer begins his book by saying that blessed is the righteous man, "He shall be like a tree planted by the rivers of water, that bringeth forth his fruit in season; his leaf shall not wither; and whatsoever he doeth shall prosper" (Psalm 1:3).

There are many varieties of trees but there are really only two kinds; fruitful and barren. Jesus counseled His listeners many times about fruitfulness. To His disciples he said, "Herein is my Father glorified, that ye bear much fruit; so shall ye be my disciples" (John 15:8).

There is nothing more distressing than a barren tree, unless it be a barren life. The Adam in man, in the Garden of Eden, rebelled and became a fruitless soul. The God in man was never satisfied or at peace until he found his way back to his Creator.

In the early Springtime the earth appears to be defeated and dead, but it only appears to be so. It is only waiting for nature to stir it to new life. Man's future welfare often seems hopeless, but God, in His wisdom and mercy, reaches down and brings new life out of despair. By God's help and power, man becomes again, "like a tree planted by the rivers of water."

O God, Great Keeper of the vineyard, help us to bear fruit that we might be worthy of our place in the orchard of life. AMEN.

Life's Struggle

THE HISTORY of mankind is a story of man's struggle between right and wrong. The goal of Satan from the beginning of time has been to prove that evil is stronger than good. God has designed that man can overcome evil with good.

Recently, a hospital patient said to me, "Sometimes it seems that life doesn't make sense. We see the righteous suffering and evil flourishing. I often feel like saying, 'God, which side are you on?'"

Most of us at times in our lives have been overwhelmed by the force of evil. It is difficult at times to see God's design in the presence of evil. One of the best examples of this is the moving story of Joseph who was sold by his jealous brothers into slavery in Egypt.

The story of Joseph in Egypt is an example of noble character in the presence of evil. The climax of the story is reached when Joseph, in the presence of his brothers, reveals himself to them. He might have said, "What you did to me was meant for evil but God meant it for good." He did say, "Therefore be not grieved, that ye sold me hither; for God did send me before you to preserve life" (Genesis 45:5).

Evil too often operates behind a disguise. However, as someone has said, whitewashing the pump does not purify the water. Evil is like a fifth column, it often works behind the scenes. It is not nearly as interested in making one evil as it is in keeping one from doing good.

There were certain laws of conduct which had been implanted in the life of Joseph. His reliance upon God and His unfailing laws held him steady. ". . . whatsoever a man soweth, that shall he also reap," (Galatians 6:7) was not only a code of ethics, but Joseph's way of life.

We are living in a strange age. We see a struggle for intellectualism without wisdom; culture without conscious; liberty and freedom without discipline.

Evil's disguise tempts us to "do our own thing" without respect for law and order. God's design is that man shall not live by his appetitie or his own will alone, but by the guidelines of divine direction and his respect for his fellowmen.

The Psalm writer's advice is still relevant to this day, "Commit thy way unto the Lord, trust also in Him and He shall bring it to pass" (Psalm 37:5). Bring what to pass? What is best? He did for Joseph. He was tempted but did not fall. It has been the same for many of us.

The battle between good and evil is an endless one. Evil tempts with getting all one can out of life. Good designs that by giving ourselves to the best, the best will be ours eternally.

Give us wisdom, O God, to know right from wrong and the courage to make the right decision. AMEN.

Making A Will

I, JAMESON JONES, being of sound mind, do will and bequeath . . . Thus begins a form whereby we may "will" certain of our possessions to those we love.

Bequeathing possessions is not new. There were wills in the Bible. Elisha begged Elijah for a "double portion of thy spirit to be upon me" (II Kings 2:9). The request was granted.

Jesus, in His concern for those He loved, made certain bequests. He willed His mother to His close friend, John, the son of Zebedee. He willed His spirit, as He was hanging on the cross, back to His Heavenly Father.

The will, of which I am thinking this morning, is when He said, "Peace I leave with you, my peace I give unto you: not as the world giveth, give I unto you. Let not your heart be troubled, neither let it be afraid" (John 14:27).

Peace is a wonderful word and a valuable one. It calms the spirit and strengthens the soul. It is like a rainbow of hope after a destructive storm. It is the enfolding arms of a loving mother around her little one. Homes are broken without it and the world is given new hope where it prevails.

Peace cannot be purchased. One cannot buy lasting friendships. Someone has observed that our generation knows the price of everything but the value of nothing. We know that we cannot purchase peace of mind or health of body.

John D. Rockefeller, American capitalist, by the time he was fifty years of age, had become one of the richest men of his day. He tells how that, with all of his money, he could buy all of the food he wanted but couldn't enjoy it. He could not purchase health. He began thinking of others and with this concern his health began to improve and he lived to be one of the greatest philanthropists of our time.

Peace may be undeserved. Most of us husbands need more love than we deserve, and most of us receive it.

When the prodigal son, Jesus tells of, decided to arise and return to his father, he confessed within himself that he was not worthy to be called a son, but was willing to become a servant. With this confession, peace came to him; he returned home and was received by a forgiving father.

Last, but not least, peace is given as a reward of our faith. "My peace I give," Jesus said. It cannot be purchased. It may not be deserved. It is a gift. Isaiah, the prophet, once wrote, "Thou wilt keep him in perfect peace, whose mind is stayed on thee; because he trusteth in thee" (Isaiah 26:3). Peace is not found within ourselves. When we recognize our inability to make peace and accept God's offer, that "peace which passeth all understanding," can be ours.

We know, Lord, that we cannot have peace around us, until we have peace within. We pray that this peace within may be ours from day to day, that we might help to bring peace to others. AMEN.

My Business

AN ARTIST friend of mine had just completed a picture. He was surveying the finished project. As I stood beside him I asked, "Fred, how do you paint such life-like beech trees?" His answer was, "This is my business."

It was not with a tone of sarcasm but rather with pride that he spoke. I happened to know that he had made painting his business for many years.

It makes no difference what our vocation may be. If we gain the praise of others and satisfaction for ourselves, it will be because we really make it our business.

One day I met a man who impressed me with his sincere personality. I asked him what business he was in. He smiled, then answered, "My business is being a Christian. I sell gasoline for a living."

Luke, the gospel writer, tells us that Jesus, as a boy of twelve, recognized that His real business was that He might "be about His Father's business." He worked with His earthly father to make a living by carpentering. He labored with His Heavenly Father to make a life.

Someone has said that if we make Christianity our business, God will make it our blessedness.

Weeding corn, on a hot summer day on the farm, was never considered recreation to a boy of twelve in my day. However, I recall as we paused in the shade one day, that my father said, "Boys, it is hard work, but I never thought it made sense to plant corn and then let the weeds take over."

This is what can and does happen in life unless we make being a Christian our real business.

Making a living is big business. Making a life is greater still. The business of making a living brings sweat to the brow. Making a life brings concern to the heart.

It was Paul the apostle who felt that one could not separate the business of making a living from the concern of making a life. In writing to the Roman Christians he once said, "Be not slothful in business; fervent in spirit; serving the Lord" (Romans 12:11).

If America is to continue to enjoy freedom of worship, it will be because we have not forgotten that it is our business to keep alive our religious fervor.

The athiest's business is to destroy all that we, who believe in God, have held dear. We who have this faith in God must be just as determined to keep it alive. The need was never greater. This is our business.

O God, give us strength and courage to make Your business our business that others may profit by our dedication. AMEN.

Mountain Top Experiences

WE HAD just left Estes Park, Colorado, and were climbing the road that leads to the Rocky Mountain National Park. The grandeur of the mountain above, the beauty around us, and the scenes below were breathtaking. It was then that I thought of the words that I had found in a vacation folder, "A real vacation should inspire, not tire."

The inspiration of the mountain top can be for all of us, but most of us must return to the valley to live. Mountain top experiences come to us that we might face the valley of life with greater courage.

Many of us have had uplifting experiences that we wished might not end. James and John, disciples of Jesus, experienced an occasion like this. They had gone with Jesus to a mountain top. There they had witnessed the transfiguration of Jesus talking with Moses and Elias.

This was such an impressive experience that Peter spoke with enthusiasm, ". . . Lord, it is good for us to be here; if thou wilt, let us make here three tabernacles; one for Thee and one for Moses and one for Elias" (Matthew 17:4). The occasion, however, was more than a sight to behold, it was to be another proof of who Jesus was.

But there was work to be done in the valley. Had they stayed on the mountain top, as inspiring as it was, the boy who was brought by his father, would not have received healing from Jesus. We too, must not miss the opportunities in the valley, and the strength for that service.

Recently, a young mother told me of a moving experience that had come to her spiritually. Several months after this experience she lost an infant son. "There is no doubt," she said, "but what God was preparing me for that sad experience." Her heart was heavy but her spirit was warm. She knew not why her loss, but she could better face it now than she could have three months before.

There is a legend concerning Zacchaeus who, the Scripture says, climbed a sycamore tree that he might better see Jesus. As the legend goes, each morning the wife of Zacchaeus noticed her husband leaving the house early. He would be gone for some time. On returning his face was aglow and his voice full of love.

One day she followed Zacchaeus at a distance. He went to the spring, got a pail of water. He then took it to the tree from whence he had witnessed Jesus' passing. He poured the water at the base of the tree. He knelt a few moments and returned refreshed. The experience of that day with Jesus was kept fresh in his mind.

Oftentimes God gives us a glimpse of heaven that we might help to make earth better. We too, come from those moments refreshed in spirit.

O Lord, may we so live that each day may be a mountain experience, that we may carry down into the valley of need. AMEN.

Making The Best Of Life

"IT IS NOT so much where you live but how you live that counts." Those were the words of a retired farmer whose hair had turned to silver, but whose eyes still had the twinkle of youth.

This man with the spirit of adventure still in his voice went on to say, "Ma and I have had our troubles. There has been a lot of sickness and we haven't been able to accumulate much of this world's goods, but I have always believed in making the best of life wherever you are."

Making the best of life was the philosophy of George Washington Carver, negro scientist, who was born in poverty but lived to bring riches to others. It was the wisdom of John Bunyan, English writer, who wrote his famous Pilgrim's Progress under adverse circumstances. This could be said of many, many more.

If there is to be any happiness or peace of mind in our lives we must come to terms with our habitation. That is, if we cannot find the ideal place in life, we must learn to make where we are our ideal habitation.

There is an art to living where you are. Contentment is something we have to learn. It is right that we should be content with what we have but not with what we are.

There is an old saying of long ago that reads, "I complained because I had no shoes until I met a man with no feet."

Complete contentment may be dangerous, especially if it has an element of indifference in it. Indifference is not thought of as a virtue, but rather a vice.

The art of living where you are comes by keeping in step with your surroundings. It is not so much what those unhappy occasions do to us, but rather how we face them that counts for our future welfare. Who knows but what that undesirable situation, in which we find ourselves, is God's way of helping to make us strong.

There is an old hymn that says, "To serve this present age, my calling to fulfill. O may it all my powers engage to do my Master's will."

In the art of living where we are we learn that we are here primarily to give and not to get.

Paul, the apostle, learned to live where he was. He learned that in, "Whatsoever state I am therewith to be content" (Philippians 4:11). He learned that to be happy one must learn to do without. Paul learned to do without his health, as well as without his youth. In all of this he was able to say, "I can do all things through Christ which strengtheneth me" (Philippians 4:13).

What we have been trying to say is not, how can we make life an existence, but rather how we can live life to the fullest. This we can do by giving it our very best in the Master's name, and the best will be ours.

O God, Giver of life, help us that we will not be satisfied with a life of existence, but lead us into the fullness of living. AMEN.

Moving Day

AS I WRITE THIS, "moving day" is upon us. We have moved before, but after forty years one accumulates things that seem to become a part of you. It is not easy to cast them aside. We have been busy sorting. There are certain possessions that we are selling, others we are giving away and most of our belongings we will take with us. Both Mrs. Jennings and I find ourselves retrieving some little keepsake that the other had decided to get rid of. In short, our decision must be on what to take along and what to leave behind.

Last night, as I was surveying the situation, I thought that, in life, every day is moving day. As we move along through life there are certain things we want to carry with us.

We will carry with us into tomorrow the inspiration and memories of friends. Not that there will be no new friends, for Weir Mitchell, author, has said, "He alone has lost the art to live who cannot win new friends." There are those friends, however, that have made a contribution to our lives that we can never seem to forget. It seems that God sent them our way when we needed them most.

As one moves from one experience to another he should take along the memories of his mistakes. Not that he should dwell upon those mistakes in remorse and frustration, but that he might not forget to profit by those errors of the past.

As we move from the present to the future, we must not discard our hopes. The candle of hope is the afterglow of the past and the beam that lights the future.

Paul the apostle, writing to the Roman Christians said, "We are saved by hope . . ." (Romans 8:24) The only way that we can ever become the person we have always wanted to be is by keeping that hope ever alive within us.

In moving from one situation to another, there are some things that we cannot take with us. There is no room to carry an unforgiving spirit with us. Nothing depresses the future like being unwilling to forgive and forget. Many of us were taught to pray, "forgive us our debts, as we forgive our debtors." We receive in return that which we are willing to give to others. Take along a generous supply of forgiveness, there will always be a place for it.

As a young minister was moving he was making a final call on a faithful little lady of his congregation. He informed her that everything was packed. The little lady, who had seen many pastors come and go, responded, "Pastor, there is one thing you cannot pack. Your influence you must leave behind."

It is true that our influence is something that we cannot take with us. It is like the fragrance of the flower in the air about it.

So was the life of the great Master who moved from day to day. Among the lives He touched He left an influence that could never be destroyed. Are you moving? If so, be careful what you take along and leave behind.

We pray, Lord, that as we move from day to day that we might be led to know what to cling to and what to leave behind. AMEN.

Making The Best Of The Worst

FOR SEVERAL months I had been making my way to the bedside of a good woman who had, what was said to be, an incurable disease. The last visit I had with her before leaving her community, she said, with a smile on her face and courage in her voice, "I have been trying to make the best of the worst."

There are many folk in the world who belong to this long line of splendor, who try to make the best of the worst.

On going to a new field and place of labor, I received a card from a friend. On the card were the words, "May you experience enough success to keep you encouraged; and suffer enough disappointments to keep you humble." I think that this has been true throughout the years of my life. It is as it should be.

This has been true of those of all walks of life. The disappointments that keep us humble are tempered with enough success to encourage us to fight on.

A beautiful stone fence stands in front of the farm house where I grew up. It is there not alone because the fields on our farm in those days were covered with rocks, but because my father decided he would turn a thing of discouragement into a thing of beauty. We wore blisters on our hands building the fence, but got rid of a lot of stones that had plagued us. We literally made the best of the worst.

In the Book of Ruth there is the beautiful story of Naomi who married and went to Moab. The story is beautiful, but sad, for death took her husband and her two sons, leaving her only poverty, grief, and two widowed daughters-in-law. Courageously, she started back to her own people. "You stay with yours," she bids the widows, Ruth and Orpha. They would find no husbands among the foreigners in Naomi's Bethlehem; in Moab they would re-wed.

Orpha, weeping, stayed in Moab. Ruth went with crushed Naomi to glean in the fields of a rich kinsman. Naomi, making the best of the worst, became a match-maker; she managed the marriage of Ruth and Boaz, the rich kinsman.

One day Naomi clutched Ruth's baby to her heart. The baby was Obed, the child that was to be the grandsire of King David. No, this grandmother was not a schemer, for she had wanted to go alone to Bethlehem. But, now that she had the opportunity to reward Ruth for her loyalty, she did so and in the end was, herself, rewarded.

God, in His own way and time, has always made provision in one way or another for those who place their trust in Him. We may be called upon to make the best of the worst. However, through it all we are made stronger and better able to meet the opportunities or problems of the future.

Dear Lord, Thou hast promised never to leave us nor forsake us. Help us that we may stand the tests that face us each day. In the name of Him who truly made the best of the worst. AMEN.

Measuring Time

WE OFTEN measure time by recalling the events of the past. Some measure time by remembering the unpleasant experiences of the past, such as, it was the year I had the mumps. It was the summer that the chinch bugs destroyed our crops. It was the year I broke my leg. There are those of us who seem to find satisfaction from looking for the worm in the apple and miss the fragrance of the fruit.

There are many, however, who find that there are remembrances of the past that help to make the present more fruitful and the future more blessed. Recently, I visited with a farmer who had been in a bad accident five years before. The year of the accident, he had not been able to be out of the house the entire season. With mixed emotions he said, "My crops, that year, were the best that I can remember. My good neighbors took over from planting to harvest time." He then added, "It also gave me an opportunity to get better acquainted with my family."

It is not always easy to see a calamity as a good fortune. Measuring time by recalling the blessings that came in spite of tragedy makes the victories of life more meaningful.

I once heard E. Stanley Jones, the missionary say, "I remember the year of my greatest decision. It was the time when I got out of the driver's seat and turned it over to God."

I can imagine Paul the apostle relating many times his experience on the road to Damascus. "That was the day of the turning point in my life," Paul, no doubt, recalled. It was the day that he was struck blind by the light from God. His mission of destruction and hate came to an end. His real mission for Jesus Christ began.

Most of us can look back and mark the day that was a turning point in our lives. That day may have had its disappointments at the time but, in years to come, we recall that the events of that day changed our whole future for good.

I once had a good friend who gave me this bit of philosophy. "Don," he said, "the worst thing that can happen to you may be the best thing that can happen to you if you don't let it get the best of you."

Was this what Paul, writing to the Roman Christians, meant when he said, "We know that all things work together for good to them that love God, to them who are called according to His purpose" (Romans 8:28). Many of us have found that God is able to salvage some good from the worst experiences for our benefit and His glory.

God always has the last word. If we live with trust in Him each day, we shall look back remembering that, with each experience, God is preparing us for something better in the future. If God be for us who can be against us?

Our Father, we remember that you have promised never to leave us nor forsake us. Help us to believe this promise and trust Thy providence for each day. AMEN.

No Roses Without Thorns

HAY MAKING and berry picking time go hand in hand. The scent of new mown hay to a farm boy has an aroma unsurpassed by any other. But that aroma also meant sweat and aching backs.

Rich, black raspberries hanging lush and fresh, deep in the woods reminds one of luscious pies and jam. But it also is a reminder of the prickly briers and chiggers.

As a boy of ten, many years ago, sweat, aching backs, briers, and chiggers were not uncommon. How well I remember those days. A barn filled with new hay. A table spread with the fruit of the vine and bush. My conclusion now is that the benefits far outweighed the thorns and the hardships.

Anything worth striving for presents hardships. The poet has said that your roses may have thorns but don't forget, your thorns may have some roses too.

Life's hopes seem to be continually beset with discouragements. However, where determination prevails, our hopes are realized and the hardships are minimized. Our hands may be pricked by the thorns and our hearts ache from some disappointments, but the fruits of our labor are recompense enough for all these things.

Fanny J. Crosby, the gospel hymn writer, had much for which to be discouraged. She was blind and had been so from her childhood. This remarkable woman lived to the golden age of ninety-four years and wrote many hymns of faith. This writer of hymns had three rules by which she lived. She said, "I never worry. I never find fault with anyone. I trust God for all things."

This courageous woman knew something of the thorns of life, but her songs proved that the thorns in ones life were small compared to God's grace. Someone had said that the truly happy are not those persons who carry no hurt or burden, but those who overcome them.

Jesus proved that life with all of its troubles can be lived victoriously. He not only gave us an example in living but He said, "I am come that they might have life, and that they might have it more abundantly."

God has a purpose for every life. It does not mean that life with Him is without trials. Spiritual muscles, like physical muscles, are developed through some of the so-called impossibles.

At the base of a sundial were the words, "Without a shadow, nothing." Trying times develop tried and true men and women. Those who learn how to bear their own burdens, understand better how to help others bear theirs.

With the help of Him who knew the hurt of the thorns and the joy of the crown we can say as David the Psalm writer said, "The Lord is my Shepherd, I shall not want." His grace is sufficient for all our needs.

Through the grace and courage you have given us, Lord, we have found that the roses of life have far outweighed the thorns. For this we give Thee thanks. AMEN.

On Being Honest

"HONEST TO God, cross my heart, I hope to die." Those were the words used, years ago as a youth in my teens, by some of us to emphasize that we were telling the truth or making an honest promise.

Honesty, integrity, and sincerity represent a state of character, of which we have never had an over supply. A public school teacher, of my early school days, had a maxim that she impressed upon us many times. It was, "Always tell the truth and you will not need to remember what you say."

The wise man of Proverbs once wrote, "Buy the truth and sell it not" (Proverbs 23:23). Yes, honesty is a valuable possession. The more it is practiced the greater its value.

Honesty is not only the best policy, but it is the only way to a peaceful conscience. It is a far better aid to restful slumber than any tranquilizer.

Being honest with our fellow men causes those with whom we deal to say, "His word is as good as his note."

Luke, the writer of the third Gospel, tells us that Jesus warned His disciples many times against accepting and practicing the hypocrisy of the Pharisees. ". . . Beware ye, of the leaven of the Pharisees, which is hypocrisy" (Luke 12:1). Paul the apostle added his admonition by saying that Christians should keep the feast, ". . . with the unleavened bread of sincerity and truth" (I Corinthians 5:8).

We can best be honest with God by being honest with our fellow men, as well as ourselves. We can do this only as we do it with, "sincerity and truth."

Hippocrates, who was known as the greatest of ancient Greek physicians, was interested in making the best physicians of the young men who studied under him. He, also, wanted these young men to be sincere in their life and practice.

Hippocrates was the author of an oath that he asked each of his graduating medical students to take. One sentence of that oath was, "I will lead my life and practice my art in uprightness and honor."

Although the above oath was written for physicians, it sets an enduring pattern of duty for all professions. The practice of truth was foremost in the life of the greatest Physician, Jesus; it could well be ours.

Lord, I would be true, for there are those who trust me. So, help us Lord, to strive for uprightness of character in all our ways. AMEN.

Only Believe

"FAITH ALONE never helped anyone. It is what we do with faith that makes the difference." These words were the words of John Redhead, well known minister. I have thought of those words many times, since I heard them many years ago. I have discovered that when I put my faith to work it comes alive, for "faith without works is dead" (James 2:20).

As a lad at home on the farm, I was helping my father paint our house one summer. My father had made a roof ladder. This ladder was nothing more than two boards with cleats, or nails, that it might stay on the porch roof so that we might paint the gable end of the house. I was fearful of it until my father said, "Get up there and step on the ladder. The more of your weight you put on it the safer it will be. He was right. I had to act on it. This is, likewise, true with our faith in everyday life.

Mark, the Gospel writer, tells of an incident in which a father brings his young son to Jesus. This father, no doubt, had tried many so-called remedies but his son still had the seizures. This father was desperate.

Mark reports that Jesus said unto this concerned father, "If thou canst believe, all things are possible to him that believeth" (Mark 9:23). Mark said that the father of the boy cried out and answered with tears, "Lord, I believe, help thou mine unbelief" (Mark 9:24). How often, we too, have cried out in our weakness, "Lord, I have faith, but not enough, help me."

One of the most devastating hindrances to our faith is our fear and anxiety. Fear and anxiety smothers our faith and jeopardizes our present and future welfare.

A young housewife confided in me recently. With concern in her voice she said, "One day I feel like I could conquer the world, the next day a worm could not be lower." Most of us do not live on a mountain top experience continually. The mountain top is good for us, but it may be preparing us for the drought in the valley. I have often observed that Heaven calls us that we might make earth better.

There is nothing wrong in confessing our weaknesses. When we recognize our own inadequacy it is then that we accept God's strength. "Help me in my doubts," cries the father of the young child. It has often been said that our extremity is God's opportunity. Jesus healed the son and the father's faith was made strong.

Many years ago Paul Rader, the famous Chicago minister, wrote a song. The chorus says, "Only believe, only believe, all things are possible, only believe." Those words are as true today as then, for they were first the words of the Master. When we take that step in the direction of believing Him, the rest of the way grows easier. We then have His strength added to ours.

Lord, we do believe. Help us in our weakness to trust Thee fully. AMEN.

One Day At A Time

"ALL WE ever have is today. If we can't live today, we probably won't live any day," so observed Minton Jonston, popular Canadian pastor.

Learning to live one day at a time takes courage, faith, and purpose. One can think of this day as the last day of ones life or we can look at it as the first day of the rest of our life. Despair is the attitude of the first, faith is the outlook of the second.

"Life, regardless of how short or long, is worthwhile as long as I have you to live it with," said a young husband, who was fighting for his life in a discouraging illness.

His faithful companion of ten years, laid her hand on his and responded with, "We'll fight it through, dear, a day at a time and trust God for the future."

A will to live; a purpose for living and God's promise to be with us, and give us peace of mind. It helps us not to be overly anxious about tomorrow, but thankful for this day.

The wise man of Proverbs, who has given us so many words of wisdom, has something to say about living a day at a time. "Boast not thyself of tomorrow," he says, "for thou knowest not what a day may bring forth" (Proverbs 27:1). To me, he is saying that we should make the most of this day. Do all the good you can. Sow all the good seed you can. Build up a confidence in God today and tomorrow will take care of itself.

Someone has observed that we should live as though we might die tonight, but work as though we expected to live forever.

No one has enough strength, physically, mentally, and spiritually to bear today's burdens and tomorrow's worries all in one day. Only as we face them a day at a time can we do so.

In these days of uncertainties, when we are wondering what the future has in store for us, we have to cling to those things of which we are certain.

Jesus was speaking about those who become overly concerned about tomorrow and its needs. He counseled, "Seek ye first the kingdom of God and his righteousness; and all these things shall be added unto you" (Matthew 6:33). Following this wise counsel, we discover this day goes better and tomorrow's needs are left with God whose supply is never limited.

My dear mother's philosophy, by which she lived was, "I know not what the future hath in store for me, but I know who holds the future." This is good enough for me; I'll go on living one day at a time and trusting God for tomorrow.

Help me, Lord, to have faith to live this day and trust You for tomorrow, and we shall praise You each day. AMEN.

Pruning Shears

AS I SIT at my desk, writing, I look out upon a snow covered yard and garden. It is January and I am reminded that this is the month that I prune our grape vines.

How well I remember my father's use of the pruning shears and the saw in our orchard on the farm. Dead branches in the apple trees, in those days, were of short duration. My father's philosophy was, "Dead branches never produce fruit and they are a detriment to the rest of the tree. Get rid of them." We did just that. Some of those trees that bore fruit in that orchard sixty years ago are still there.

Jesus was well acquainted with the care of orchards and vineyards. He likened the lives of His followers to the trees and vines. He said, "I am the true vine, and my Father is the husbandman. Every branch in me that beareth not fruit he taketh away: and every branch that beareth fruit, he purgeth it, that it may bring forth more fruit" (John 15:1-2).

None of us are perfect specimens of fruit bearing. We all need the pruning shears at times. My grape vines did exceptionally well for three-year-olds, but I must "purge" the vines that they may do even better this year.

As children we didn't always like to be corrected. But, later in life, we realized it was for our own good. The writer of Hebrews says, "For whom the Lord loveth he chasteneth, and scourgeth every son whom he receiveth" (Hebrews 12:6).

We often think when we are chastised, that we are being punished and we either rebel or cry out in despair. But God is really using the "pruning shears" on us that we may be purged that we might bear more fruit. We realize later that it was for our good.

I love the oak tree but, unlike the maple, in the winter many of its brown leaves continue to cling to its branches. When spring comes the oak tree must release its old leaves before it can send out the new leaves.

Life is so much like this. We grow and produce Christian character by elimination and propagation. To do this requires relinquishing our will to God's will. It is not always easy but it is always best.

There is a poem by Harold Lillines, a part of it speaking of those difficult times and unexplainable experiences, he writes, "The Maker of your destiny is striving, To fit your heart to be His royal throne."

So then, look up, take heart; remember God loves you. He wants for you the best and He wants us at our best.

Dear Father in Heaven, whatever is needed in our lives to make them worthy of Thy daily presence, come and cleanse, forgive and fill us with Thy Holy Spirit. AMEN.

Perseverance

THE SPIDER wove its web between our mountain ash and our front porch. We brushed it aside. The next morning it was there again. We were impressed by the persistence of this small creature of God's creation.

I watched the obstinacy of that small, yet determined spider for a few days. I thought, how like this spider is the perseverance of many people I have known. A familiar proverb, which I had known from childhood, came to my mind, "If at first you don't succeed, try, try again."

It was Shakespeare who said, "An enterprise, when fairly once begun, should not be left till all that ought is won." Success in any enterprise comes only through determined perseverance.

We made our way one day to the Lincoln Boyhood National Memorial in southern Indiana. Amongst the many sayings of Lincoln, I read, "And having thus chosen our course, without guile, and with pure purpose, let us renew our trust in God." Our country was founded and nurtured by men and women who had this kind of faith and perseverance. If it is to continue it will do so only by the same kind of courage and determination.

One whose belief causes him to go forward with determination is often called obstinate by those who disagree with him. However, in all honesty, you cannot help from honoring his perseverance.

Paul, the apostle, was writing to the early Christians concerning life and death. He concluded by saying, "Therefore, my beloved brethren, be ye steadfast, unmoveable, always abounding in the work of the Lord" (I Corinthians 15:58). This man had learned from experience, the victory that comes from pressing on. He knew that God's work prevailed only through determined, active faith.

A child does not learn to walk by falling down, but rather by getting up. Each and every undertaking in the life of an individual, group or nation, is accomplished by not acknowledging defeat because of one failure.

In times when it seems as though all is to no avail, it is good to remember that one person and God is a majority.

A disciple of Jesus, called Peter, stumbled many times. This man, so human yet determined, would not give up. By God's help he persevered and became a rock of faith. This we can do by God's help and our own persistent courage and faith.

We thank Thee, O Lord, for those back through the years who did not give up, but kept the faith. Help us that we may have the courage to follow Thee as they have followed Thee. AMEN.

Prayer – The Lifeline

IT SEEMED that Martha Bryan had more than her share of tragedies. Her eight-and ten-year-old daughters were killed in an auto accident while riding with a neighbor. After an illness of two years, her husband died. In spite of these and other tragedies, Martha did not give up. In witnessing to her faith, one day, she courageously said, "Prayer was my lifeline through it all. I prayed as though everything depended upon God. I worked as though everything depended upon me."

Many of us have found that prayer is the lifeline. Prayer does not keep trouble from us, but it gives us strength in the midst of disaster. Prayer is not a vaccination against calamity, it is rather a lifeline between man and God. It is not alone a refuge for the weak but a weapon for the strong.

The disciples of Jesus saw how their Master was able to face each challenge of the day after He had prayed. These honest young men came to Him one day and said, ". . . Lord, teach us to pray, as John also taught his disciples" (Luke 11:1). He answered their request by teaching them the Lord's Prayer. This prayer has become a guide and a power to millions down through the centuries.

Dwight L. Moody, American evangelist of another generation, entreated his listeners to remember, "When you pray be serious, be honest. Decide whether you want your will or God's will." It was said that Saint Augustine, in a period of perplexity before he became a Christian prayed, "O God, make me pure, but not yet." Sincere prayer changes things. It is not so much how it changes God, but how it changes us.

One of the most significant parts of the prayer Jesus taught His disciples was, ". . . Thy will be done in earth, as it is in heaven" (Matthew 6:10). Surrendering our will to God's will is not always easy, but in the end, it is the best and only way to peace of mind. Even Jesus, in the Garden of Gethsemane prayed, ". . . not my will, but Thine be done" (Luke 22:42).

Down through the years, men and women whose lives have been a blessing to so many, have learned that we walk by faith, not by sight. It was often said of a woman most dear to me, "When mother prayed she seemed to bring heaven down to earth." This has been said of many; would that it might be said of all of us. How often I have been driven to pray, "Without Thee, Lord, I shall fail, with Thee I cannot fail."

Someone has observed, that we need men and women of science, government, industry, agriculture, all walks of life, but we need more men and women of prayer. Civilization will be lost without them, for prayer is the lifeline.

Forgive us, Lord, when we fail to pray that Thy will might be done in our lives. May Thy will truly be done in earth as it is in Heaven. AMEN.

Press On

A VISIT to Mayflower II, replica of the rugged ship of the Pilgrim's crossing, taught us many things. One of the things we learned was that the average speed, during much of the voyage across the Atlantic, was only two miles an hour. What an example of pushing ahead under discouragement.

This is a good thing to remember when it seems that our progress toward some goals in life seems so slow. But, we are not to give up, and we are to encourage others to press on likewise.

All explorers, inventors, and leaders of every walk of life had their discouraging times. Each attained his goal by finding and clinging to a guiding principle.

George Washington Carver was born in a slave cabin. Through sacrifice, study, and courage he made many scientific discoveries in his laboratory. He once said that his guiding principle was the promise, "In all thy ways acknowledge Him and He shall direct thy paths" (Proverbs 3:6).

With all the discoveries in his laboratory, Dr. Carver tells us, "I didn't do it. God has only used me to reveal some of His wonderful providences."

The conscious knowledge that we are being directed is enough to give us confidence, even though our progress is slow.

The most confident person I know is the one who keeps a joyous outlook in his journey through life. Joy encourages health; likewise, with worry and misery comes disease.

Certainly Jesus could have had reason for discouragement. Consider the lack of sincere concern for His way of life. However, He went about His Father's business with joy. He kept the goals ever before Him of doing good for others. He knew that He was doing right, not wrong. He was confident of His Father's approval.

Whenever I become anxious that what I am doing is moving too slowly, I like to think of the words of the Psalm writer when he said, "This is the day which the Lord hath made; we will rejoice and be glad in it" (Psalm 118:24).

It was Carlyle, the author, who said, "Our main business is not to see what lies dimly at a distance, but to do what lies clearly at hand." He was saying, "This is the day, get on with it, rejoice in it."

We cannot live without hope, no more than we can live without the air we breathe. It is the hope of a better tomorrow that keeps us going today.

How far we shall advance along life's way this day is not important. The significant thing is that we "acknowledge Him in all thy ways and He shall direct thy paths." Then, spread the sails of faith. Keep your eye on the compass of hope. All shall be well.

Help us, Lord, that we may ever keep the sails of our spiritual barque unfurled, that we may catch the breeze of Thy mercy. AMEN.

"Quiet Zone"

IT IS SAID that when one of the great generals of a past generation became a Christian he changed his daily schedule. Early in the morning following breakfast he reserved an hour from his busy program of the day. During this time he was not to be disturbed. Everyone knew that the Generalissimo was spending that hour in prayer and Bible reading. One of his body guards set up a sign near the general's tent which read, "Quiet Zone, do not disturb."

Many of us have learned that the day goes better if we, too, set up a quiet zone at the beginning of each day.

In these times when success seems to be measured by hurry, noise, and whirling machinery, it seems wasteful to many to take time out to "be still."

When David, the Psalm writer, wanted to witness to his faith in the quiet hour he gave us the Twenty-third Psalm. He spoke of the Lord as his Shepherd who "leadeth me beside the still waters." Not the rushing waterfall, nor the singing of the brook as it tumbles over the rocks; but the still waters that run deep. David had already spoken of being led to "lie down in green pastures," not places of frustration but rather peace of mind.

In the Forty-sixth Psalm David says that, "God is our refuge and strength," and then he seems to hear God saying, "Be still, and know that I am God."

Isaiah, one of the great prophets of Old Testament days, believed that the success or failure of a man's life depended upon his dedication to God.

He once wrote, "But they that wait upon the Lord shall renew their strength; they shall mount up with wings as eagles; they shall run and not be weary; and they shall walk and not faint" (Isaiah 40:31).

Frustration seems to be the lot of far too many these days. To some, giving up in despair seems to be the only way out. This need not be so.

A very dear friend of mine was about to give up. There seemed to be no way out. There was a broken engagement and a nervous breakdown. All of the things she had always hoped for appeared to be gone. Amongst other things, I suggested that she keep my favorite Bible verse before her, "For we know that all things work together for good to them who love God, to them who are called according to His purpose" (Romans 8:28).

Through prayer, waiting and trusting that God would make possible, "that all things might work together for good" for her, the life of this friend was changed. In the end she has found that "things" have worked out for her good.

When the winds of adversity blow the strongest we often feel the weakest. However, if we will but turn aside in quiet, simple faith, we will find our trust in Him not to be in vain. The quiet time is time well spent.

O God, grant me the serenity to accept those things that I cannot change, courage to change the things I can change and the wisdom to know the one from the other. AMEN.

Restoring The Soul

THE BATTERY in a young motorist's car was weak and would scarcely start the motor. I stood by as the wise garageman informed the young man that this would continually be his trouble as long as he tried to operate so many extras on his car. "We can recharge your batter," said the mechanic, "but you will have to use common sense to keep it up."

This, I thought, was a parable of life. Most of us, in these modern times, find that our lives are encumbered with too many extras. We recognize the need of the recharging of our physical as well as our spiritual batteries.

This recharging must be more than a yearly vacation or annual spiritual retreat. There must be a regular, daily refreshing if we would be at our best.

When David, the writer of many of the Psalms, composed the familiar Twenty-third Psalm he said of the great Shepherd, "He restoreth my soul." The great Shepherd is able to do this only if we are willing to "Lie down in green pastures," and to be led by Him, "beside the still waters."

Rest and relaxation seem such a waste of time to those who are enslaved by the many material concerns of life. Only when they are forced to slow down do these unfortunate folk, find that restoring power which they have needed and hungered for so long.

A faithful old negro had, for many years, held the respect of his neighbors because of his continued cheerful attitude. Someone asked him for the secret of such an outlook on life. The man without hesitation replied, "When I works, I works hard. When I rests, I sets loose, and I trusts the Lord in both work and rest."

Life is too short not to recogize that we jeopardize our whole future if we become so busy sawing wood that we can't take time out to sharpen the saw.

As busy as God must have been in His creation, the Bible says that He "rested on the seventh day from all his work which he had made" (Genesis 2:3).

Jesus, with only three years to complete His ministry, turned aside regularly to pray and meditate. There in the mountain, away from the world, He received that strength to complete His task on earth.

In a busy city in the very heart of the business district there stands a small church. Office buildings have risen about it, but still it stands guard as a sentinel of peace and light in a troubled world. On the small lawn is a sign, "Come in, rest and pray awhile."

Like many others, I have entered its doors and, with the busy world shut out, have spent a few moments and come away refreshed in soul and body.

Before we go back to the tasks of the day could I say: Take time to relax, it eases the tensions; Take time to meditate, it quiets the fears; Take time to pray, it strengthens our faith.

O Giver of the quiet and peaceful mind, restore unto us, O Lord, that strength which is needed for another day. In Christ's name. AMEN.

"Reflection"

I STOPPED, one day, at a farm home of some old friends. I had not been to see them since they had moved to this new location. As they greeted me, I responded with "I could tell that this was where you live, it reflects your tastes and your personalities."

We reflect what we are, where we live, and what we think. We cannot separate mind and thought from action and deed. Thinking is the talk of the soul to itself. We are the reflectors of our inner self. Someone has observed that the mind is like a setting hen; it is sure to hatch what it broods over.

As a man thinketh in his heart, so is he, said the wise man of Proverbs. A physician once said to me, "Having a right attitude in illness hastens healing." A positive faith reflects in our lives. A compassionate heart reflects in our kindness and mercy toward others. A mind at peace reflects in a cheerful countenance.

In His Sermon on the Mount, Jesus said, "Ye are the light of the world. A city that is set on a hill cannot be hid" (Matthew 5:4).

The leader in a small group of worshipers, had used the above text in his evening devotions. He then suggested that they choose the various lights on the automobile and apply them to their lives. One said, "I'd like to be the headlights that I might help people along life's dark road." Another exclaimed that she would be happy if she could be the fog lights, for there are so many who are lost in the fog these days. Still another was ready to be the tail lights to warn people of the danger ahead of them. Finally, a young man in the group spoke up, "Just let me be the reflector in the lamps that I might help to make someone's light shine a little brighter."

What could be a better choice than to be a reflector of Him who said, ". . . I am the light of the world . . ." (John 8:12) The brightness of our light of compassion and love is in proportion to the reflection of the light of Christ in our hearts. We are the channels of His blessings.

Those who have influenced my life the most through the years have been the most humble. I think of Uncle Orlo. It was not so much what he said, but how he lived. When he spoke you knew that his words were the reflection of his thoughts and dedication. There have been many others like him. Each seemed to radiate a personality that drew you to them. There was a sincerity about them that made you feel that their's was a reflection of a greater Power than their own.

Yes, we are reflectors of a power within us that will influence someone for good or evil. It will depend upon that source of power to which we give our allegiance. The prayer of David could well be our prayer ". . . Lord, lift up the light of Thy countenance upon us" (Psalm 4:5)

O Lord, help us each day that what we say may be the reflection of what we are, and that both may be the reflection of your life in us. AMEN.

Remembering To Forget

A LITTLE couplet from the poem, *Forget the Past,* by Tom McDonald reads: "Some folk eyes behind them cast, Seem to want to make their troubles last." Troubles, worries, and wrongs of the past seem to have a way of wanting to hold our attention. Someone has observed that we cannot keep the birds from flying over our heads, but we can keep them from nesting in our hair.

A letter, signed "a reader" from somewhere in Minnesota, reached me recently. It is a letter filled with remorse, yet a feeling of forgiveness from God. Peace of mind and remorse cannot live in the same heart.

Remorseful living makes one ill, physically, mentally, and spiritually. It solves none of the problems of the present nor can it change the past mistakes. In the end it makes for a miserable future. We all have failed in the past. As this "reader" wrote, "regret and remorse are the cancers of the soul."

Think how many times Paul the apostle could have looked back with anguish of mind, on that day that he sanctioned the stoning of Stephen. He would have been miserable had he kept looking back. He now could do nothing to bring Stephen back to life. He could, however, by God's grace do much to bring new life to others along the way. Life, for Paul, was different after that day that he met his Lord on the Damascus Road.

He now writes, "Brethren, I count not myself to have apprehended, but this one thing I do, forgetting those things which are behind, and reaching forth unto those things which are before, I press toward the mark for the prize of the high calling of God in Christ Jesus" (Philippians 3:13-14). This does not mean that we do not profit by the wrongs of the past. But, it does mean that we need not let them fester in our hearts.

What a comfort it is to remember that we have a God who forgives and does not remember our sins of the past against us, "I, even I, am He that blotteth out thy transgressions, for my own sake, and will not remember thy sins" (Isaiah 43:25). We believe that God does not remember forgiven sins against us, but rather remembers to forget.

A young athlete friend of mine, who had many difficulties along his way to success, had this motto: "Always do your very best, and leave to God the rest."

There is a song we used to sing that kept using the phrase, "Take your burden to the Lord and leave it there." We may still have our crosses, all followers of God do, but we no longer need to carry the old burdens of the past. As we carry our cross with a smile of faith, we make or help to make others' crosses easier to bear and thus lighten our own. In doing this, with renewed courage and faith in God, we discover that we too have remembered to forget the remorse of the past.

God of mercy, who forgives and does not remember our sins against us, help us that we may forgive and forget other's sins. AMEN.

Such As I Have

RECENTLY, I was a Lenten speaker in a church where I had served many years before. At the time of my pastorate there, the church building had burned. I had been there only three months when the disaster occurred.

The membership at that time was small but the people had a mind and a spirit to work. Three days after the destruction of the church by fire, a ten-year-old boy, a faithful member of our Sunday school, knocked at our door. When I opened the door there stood Junior Barkley, all smiles. He greeted me with, "My mother baked cookies this morning and I've sold some of them. Here is sixty cents to start rebuilding the church."

Needless to say, Junior's donation led all the rest. Today, there stands a beautiful little church on that spot. All because this boy and many others gave such as they had.

The Acts of the Apostles relates that Peter and John, two of the original twelve, were going to the temple at the hour of prayer. A man, lame from birth, was sitting at the gate of the temple. He begged for help. Peter paused, looked on the lame and said, "Silver and gold have I none; but such as I have give I thee: In the name of Jesus Christ of Nazareth rise up and walk" (Acts 3:6). The lame man's greatest need was not alms. No one, however, had ever offered him more than this. Peter's gift was such as he had. This meant the difference between a day's existence and a future full of hope.

Someone has said that to give a man a fish you feed him for a day; teach him to fish and you feed him for a lifetime. By giving what he had, Peter encouraged this lame man, not only for a day, but gave him hope for his entire future.

God has not time to make nobodys. History has given us many examples of those who seemed to have few talents, but were willing to use what they had. Man's entire future welfare depends upon those who, through sincere dedication, are willing to give such as they have to lift the hopes of the hopeless.

The richest legacy anyone can leave behind is to so live, give and serve, with what they have, that the world will be a better place for their having lived.

Lord, we have very little to give, but we come to Thee with what we have and what we are. Use us for Thy glory. AMEN.

Signs

THE FARMERS' ALMANAC is a little book that I look forward to receiving each year. As usual, during the past 150 consecutive years of its publication, it is filled with "signs" and wonders. If you believe in signs you may read in this little book what your birth month, according to the Zodiac, has in store for you.

According to the Almanac, if you were born the first part of October, as I was, you were born under the sign of Libra. You are well balanced, handsome, graceful, tasteful, gifted, and peace lovers. You dislike hard work and are careless in money matters. Monday is your lucky day and your unlucky day is Thursday. If there is any truth in the "sings," and many say there are, we must be willing to take the bitter with the sweet.

I have, also, become pretty well acquainted with another Book through the years. This Book says that if you are born of the Spirit, under the date of any month, your life will be filled with joy, peace, gentleness, goodness, and you shall reap life everlasting. Under this sign, every day of the week is a day of opportunity for making a life as well as a living. This sign never fails.

Seldom, if ever, was my father's potato crop a failure. When the sign was right he planted his potatoes. I think it had something to do with the moon. Understand, I am not making light of this; all I know is that those potatoes grew and I, along with my brothers and sisters, spent many a weary hour getting rid of the potato bugs.

Someone commented to my father on his success with his potatoes. Dad replied with the words coined by Henry Ford, a man he admired. This mechanical genius said that success was five percent inspiration and ninety-five percent perspiration.

In God's Book are many signs and wonders; how we believe, accept and practice them determines our future success or failure. One of the most familiar might be, "Be not deceived; God is not mocked; for whatsoever a man soweth, that shall he also reap" (Galations 6:7).

The wise man who wrote Ecclesiastes, musing over some of the signs of life's highways wrote, "In the morning sow thy seed, and in the evening withhold not thy hand . . . " (Ecclesiastes 11:6). This man of wisdom believed that all signs pointed to our day of destiny as now and he concludes his book by saying, "Remember now thy Creator in the days of thy youth . . . " (Ecclesiastes 12:1) He then goes on with the changing signs of life and concludes his words of wisdom by writing, "Let us hear the conclusion of the whole matter; Fear God, and keep His commandments, for this is the whole duty of man" (Ecclesiastes 12:13).

There are many signs found along the highway of life, from the cradle to the grave. These God given signs are either for a warning or our enlightenment; they are all for our good. Happy is the man that heedeth them.

The great Master once said, "Therefore, whosoever heareth these sayings of mine, and doeth them, I will liken him unto a wise man which built his house upon a rock" (Matthew 7:24). Accepting this challenge, we, likewise, shall be able to weather all the storms of life.

We thank Thee, Lord, for the wise counsel we receive from Thy Word, which is a lamp unto our feet and a light unto our pathway. AMEN

Sowing And Harvesting

I LEFT the farm many years ago, in body only, not in spirit. The old saying has been true in my life as it has in the lives of other farm boys, "You can take the boy off the farm, but you can't take the farm out of the boy."

I have kept in close contact with life on the farm. Through the years I have served with many rural people, and with many others whose roots of interest are still with the soil.

As Spring comes to the countryside I find myself eager to get out in the soil. I love to see things grow and to feel that I have had a small part in the harvest.

My good neighbor, Uncle Orlo, and I used to enjoy gardening together. He had a little piece of philosophy that I have never forgotten. "The harvest," said Orlo, "can be no better than the seed. The seed can be no better than the soil. The harvest, seed, and soil all depend upon the sower."

The Great Teacher, Jesus, stood by the seaside one beautiful spring day. He saw the farmer in the distance preparing the soil and sowing his seed. The Master Sower turned to the multitude that had gathered. He pointed, no doubt, to the farmer and said, "Hearken; behold, there went out a sower to sow." Then Jesus followed with the parable of the sower and the seed (Matthew 13:3-9).

Whether we recognize it or not we are all sowers. Consciously or unconsciously we are sowing our seeds of influence. Some of the seed may fall, as in the parable, by they wayside or on stony ground or even among thorns. It may seem, at times, that the increase is small or short lived. However, in years to come, we discover that some has fallen in good soil and has brought forth a good harvest making all efforts worthwhile.

I know that all of us have, at some time in our lives, wondered if we were any good to anyone. I once, long ago, had that feeling. I asked myself if a life, thinking of others and doing for others, was really worthwhile. In that darkest hour a voice seemed to speak to me. I discovered that I had been thinking too much about myself. That Voice, speaking through a very dear friend, suggested that I read the eleventh chapter of Ecclesiastes, especially dwelling on the sixth verse, "In the morning sow thy seed, and in the evening withhold not thy hand . . ." (Ecclesiastes 11:6)

I long ago decided that one should do what he can, with what he has, where he is now, and leave the rest with God who knows the intent of our hearts. In so doing, someone may reap because we have been willing to sow with faith and courage.

O God, help us to sow the good seed of life each day and do all we can to grow a good harvest, but to leave the future outcome to Thee. In Jesus' Name we ask. AMEN.

Solitude

ON A PLAQUE, at Florida's Singing Tower, I read these words: "I come here to find myself. It is so easy to get lost in the world." As I stood there in meditation, I thought how true are those words. It is so easy, due to the pressures of life, to lose sight of the way. We need a place of solitude to "find ourselves."

So often the noise and the rush of the world deafens our ears to the still small voice that would be our guide and stay. There are so many voices trying to gain our attention. We need to take ourselves from the mad stream that would force us into conforming to all that is around us.

There are those who argue against solitude. Someone has said that solitude is selfishness. Another contends that it is retreat from duty. A good friend of mine confessed that she could not stand to be alone.

Some of our greatest leaders increased their wisdom for leadership by occasions of solitude. They too needed a place where they might "find themselves." Solitude shows us what we should be; society shows us what we are.

Jeremy Taylor, English divine of the seventeenth century, once wrote, "Solitude hath the advantage of discipline, and society opportunities of perfection." Solitude is not shrinking from duty, but rather preparing us for the tasks before us.

Many times during the ministry of Jesus, He found it necessary to seek a solitary place. According to the Gospel of Mark, Jesus had spent a busy day teaching and healing. "And in the morning, rising up a great while before day, He went out and departed into a solitary place, and there prayed" (Mark 1:35). If the Master of Life needed the solitary time, surely each of us do also.

To some, solitude is found in taking a walk out into God's great world. To others, it is leaning back, closing ones eyes and ears for a few moments in quiet contemplation. To another, it may be turning aside and finding oneself in the reading of a good book. The Bible leads them all in this field. Many of us, like Jesus, have found the solitude in prayer the answer to life's problems.

The richest of all solitude can be found when we, like David the Psalm writer, remember that ". . . He leadeth me in the paths of righteousness . . ." (Psalm 23:3) In these paths we find ourselves, and from them we return prepared for the tasks that are ours.

O Lord, from whom cometh all inward strength, help us that in solitude, we may know the strength for the tasks before us. AMEN.

Stir Up What You Have

MANY OF you may recall that during World War II, there were words that were common only to that day. Such words as synthetics, rationing, priority, and many others came into use because of shortages due to the war effort.

During the War, a man sitting at a restaurant counter asked a waitress, "May I have a little more sugar for my coffee?" The replay was, "Stir up what you have."

At least, during those days, we learned to stir up what we had. We have learned that in any emergency we grow stronger by using what we have.

Using what we have increases its value. He who waits to invest what he has of time, talent, or material possessions, until they increase, will find there will be no increase.

The twelve disciples witnessed many of the miracles of Jesus. They felt a sense of frustration because they could not perform such miracles. Luke tells us that they came to Jesus and said, "Lord, increase our faith." And the Lord said, "If ye had faith as a grain of mustard seed, ye might say unto this sycamine tree, Be thou plucked up by the root and be thou planted in the sea; and it should obey you" (Luke 17:6).

He was saying to them, stir up what faith you have, and it will increase. It is not how much land, seed, or talent we have, but how we invest it, that determines its real value. So it is with our faith, using what we have increases its value also.

Someone has said that God does not make nobodys. A case worker was trying to appeal to a young lad in a children's home to really make something out of himself in spite of his background. The boy responded with, "Shucks, I guess you are right, I ain't nobody's nuthin."

We should never fail to encourage the discouraged, with the fact that there is no one to whom God has not entrusted a precious gift.

Using what we have strengthens our faith. James Russell Lowell, American author, once wrote, "No man is born into the world whose work is not born with him; there is always work and tools to work with, all for those who will."

Learn to believe that God has a purpose for you. That you are significant in His eyes. Remember that He does not give us tools with which to fly until we have learned how to walk. If we are willing to use what faith we have today, we will be prepared for greater tasks tomorrow.

It was George Elliott, the philosopher, who spoke words of wisdom when he said, " 'Tis God who gives the skill but not without men's hands." He could not make Antonio Stradivarius violins without Antonio.

If we stir up what we have, God will give the increase. Our faith will grow stronger and our lives will be richer.

Keep us ever mindful, dear Lord, that what we have comes from Thee and is to be used for good and for Thy glory. Through Christ we pray. AMEN.

Speedometer Or Compass?

UNCLE ORLO and I were working in our gardens one day. We were talking about the speed of our modern day. My wise philosopher made the comment, "Some folks are known more by their speedometer than their compass." He concluded with, "It isn't nearly as important how fast you are going as it is the direction you are traveling."

It is quite often true, when a new family car is being purchased that mother notes the upholstering and the ease of riding. Father is concerned about how economical the car is on gas and oil. The son, however, is convinced that it is the car they should buy for it has cruising speed of eighty miles an hour.

Is it true that we have become so interested in the speedometer that we have forgotten the compass?

There was a time when our grandparents thought nothing of waiting two days for the next stage coach. Now, we become frustrated waiting our turn to use the revolving door.

I heard a judge say, a few days ago, that one of the main causes of crime and the high accident rate was speed. "We need a return," he commented, "to the days when our fathers kept their eyes more on the guideposts and less on the mileposts."

I am not so much against speed as I am that we not forget the compass. A man's destiny in life is not determined so much by the speed with which he travels, as it is by his decision of direction.

Recently I visited with a man in the hospital. This man knew that he was quite seriously ill. He confided in me that he had spent the last twenty years trying to do one thing. His goal was to make one hundred thousand dollars.

Broken in body and weakened in spirit he wept as he confessed, "What a fool I have been. I've been so busy making money I've forgotten all about the things that make a life."

This man's eye had been so concerned with the speedometer he failed to follow the compass. The consequence had overwhelmed him.

Luke, the gospel writer, tells of a parable by Jesus of the rich man whose ground produced more than he had room for. In his nearsightedness he was blinded by the things he possessed, and lost sight of the real purpose of life.

The wise Master, who never lost sight of the compass, also said, "What shall it profit a man if he shall gain the whole world and lose his own soul?" (Matthew 16:26)

While traveling through the hills of southern Indiana, I recently read on a church bulletin board these words, "Make haste slowly." No better advice could be given. The Word of God is our compass. We would do well to make haste only as we follow its direction. The writer of Proverbs has said, "He that is slow to wrath is of great understanding; but he that is hasty of spirit exalteth folly."

O God, help us not to be foolish in our haste, but wise in our direction, ever looking to You as our Guide from day to day. AMEN.

Salvaging

WHILE WORKING at my desk I look out upon our flower garden and lawn. A blue jay is cracking sunflower seeds at the bird feeder. Down on the ground hungry sparrows are salvaging what is wasted by the greedy blue jay.

How like life is the scene which greets my eyes. How much in life seems worthless to one, yet valuable to others. As someone once said, "One man's junk is another man's treasure." The blue jay would not waste his time salvaging the pieces, but not so with the sparrows.

A man's wasted life may often seem worthless in the sight of human values. But, in the sight of God there is a treasure too valuable to be lost.

Jesus fed the five thousand using the young lad's lunch of five loaves and two fishes. This Master of true values did not stop here but commanded the disciples to gather up the fragments that nothing be lost. He salvaged twelve baskets full.

Peter, one of the disciples, was seen by many in his early life as a poor, blundering, wavering failure. Jesus saw in him the possibilities of a rock of faith and courage. Jesus proved that there was something in Peter that was worth salvaging.

We could well be pessimistic concerning the conditions we see all about us in the world today. The lack of respect for law and order. The blasphemy of God and the Church and against all decency. This is the plan of evil minds that would destroy our beloved country and all that it stands for.

What can we salvage for good out of all of this? Can we remember that prayer is a greater force for good than all the evil that would destroy? Can we, like the Master on the cross, pray "Father, forgive them for they know not what they do"?

If we are to survive and the future endure, there must be a greater faith in what God can do with the remnant of those who would not give up to evil but would be faithful to God.

Billy Graham has said many times that no nation is ever taller than when on its knees. Sometimes we may feel that we are very much alone in our praying and in our battle for good in a troubled world. But, as God spoke to Elijah, when he felt that he was the only one left, God speaks to us saying that there are many whose, "knees have not bowed to Baal" (I Kings 19:18).

In the end, if we do not give up, God will help us to gather up the pieces. Our world can, in spite of the testing fires of adversity, be a better place in which to live and serve.

Dear Christ of God, we know your concern for gathering of the pieces. It is because of your concern that we have come to know Thy forgiveness. Help us to have that concern, likewise. AMEN.

Small Game Hunters

G. CAMPBELL MORGAN, noted preacher and teacher of another era, once used the following words in his prayer, "Lord, help us to control the ants, we can take care of the lions."

Often in the most unlikely places we find the most vigorous bits of practical wisdom. In the romantic poem, the Songs of Solomon, in the midst of the fair maiden's confession of love, we read the words, "Take us the foxes, the little foxes, that spoil the vines" (Solomon's Song 2:15).

Everything we treasure or hold dear, health of body, peace of mind, happiness in our homes, success in our life's work; all of these and many more are in danger of attacks of little foxes. We need ever to be alert. We must be small game hunters.

It is the little things that annoy. If we let them grow in our minds, they will destroy us. Little imaginations, bickerings, insignificant differences, these little trouble makers like the slip of the tongue, an unkind word, or a small bit of gossip. These are the things that in the end destroy a friendship or break up a home.

The indifference and lack of concern in our beloved Country is one of the grave tragedies of our day. We recognize the danger of Communism thousands of miles away, and we do not belittle this sly enemy. But, too often one of the real dangers of this day is the softening attitude toward the evils about us. These little, crafty foxes are destroying our true freedoms one by one.

It is not by open warfare that most evils triumph, but rather by infiltration in government, schools, churches, and society in general. It is like the little foxes and the ants that we fail to notice until it is too late.

It is true that we can never destroy all of our enemies. The greater challenge may be to rise above many of them. John Wesley, religious pioneer, once said, "I have learned to live above trifles." However, this does not make them any less dangerous. We will continue to need to fortify ourselves with the faith that lifts us out of our littleness.

Paul, the apostle, once wrote, ". . . whatsoever things are true, whatsoever things are honest, whatsoever things are just, whatsoever things are pure, whatsoever things are lovely, whatsoever things are of good report; if there be any virtue, if there be any praise, think on these things" (Philippians 4:8).

Someone once said that there are two ways to get rid of an enemy; either shoot them or befriend them. I like to think what Jesus did about it. He did not say that we were to return evil for evil. Rather, He said, "Love your enemies, bless them that curse you, and do good to them that hate you . . . " (Matthew 5:44)

Most destructive fires have started with a small spark. Most defeats of life have had small beginnings. We can, by faith in God, turn defeat into victory by emphasizing the good and eliminating the evil.

Heavenly Father, keep us alert and ever mindful of the little things that could destroy us and awaken us to the blessings that can strengthen our lives. Through Christ we pray. AMEN.

"Sorgenfrei"

NAMES AND their meaning have always held my interest. Sometime back, I met a man who said that his name was Sorgenfrei. I responded with, "Yes, I know, and they tell me that the name, Sorgenfrei, means free of worry." The man's wife, with her cheerful personality, spoke up with, "That is right, Max never worries."

That brief incident caused me to think. What do people think of when they hear your name or mine? Most of us do not have such interesting names. To those who know, however, our names suggest something.

Does our name suggest a complainer, a trouble maker, a worrier, or does it suggest a cooperator or a cheerful personality? It may be that it is sorgenfrei, one who never worries.

Sorgenfrei, free from worry, means faith in the present and hope for the future. Free from worry means to let go and let God, when we have done the best we know.

A physician once told me that health and worry cannot sleep in the same bed. No more can fear and faith live in the same heart.

The Psalm writer brought hope to our hearts and life to our days when he said, "This is the day which the Lord hath made; we will rejoice and be glad in it."

Sir William Osler, physician and author, speaking to the students at Yale University, quoted Carlyle with the words, "Our main business is not to see what lies dimly at a distance, but to do what lies clearly at hand." He was saying, "This is the day, get on with it; rejoice in it."

One cannot rejoice in this day, which we believe the Lord hath made, and worry about the tomorrow that God has planned. We cannot live without hope no more than we live without the air we breathe. It is the hope of a better tomorrow that keeps us going today.

Recently, I received a letter from a young woman who had experienced serious surgery in the hospital. At the conclusion of her letter she included what, she said, was her philosophy of life; "Look not forward to the changes of this life in fear; rather look forward with hope. God, whose you are, will deliver you out of them. It is He who has kept you heretofore; He will lead you through all things."

The same everlasting Father who cares for you today will take care of you tomorrow and every day. Either He will shield you from suffering or He will give you unfailing strength to bear it. Be at peace then, put aside all anxious thought. By His grace, we too, can be called sorgenfrei, "free from worry."

Dear Lord and Father, we believe that you are concerned about the future of our lives, as Thou hast been with us in the past and are with us now. Give us an unworried and trusting faith. AMEN.

Smile, God Loves You

"SMILE, GOD loves you." Those words, on a little card, greeted me each time I visited with a good woman in her hospital room. I had known this woman for more than forty-five years. She practiced the words on that little card. I should know, for she was my mother-in-law.

For many years, this faithful woman taught a Sunday School class of children. In fact, on her ninetieth birthday she retired from formal teaching. Her interest, however, in children and youth never ceased. There was no generation gap with mother Inez Wright.

There is more than meets the eye in those words, "Smile, God loves you." A beautiful smile to the countenance is as the sunbeam on the landscape; it changes drabness to beauty. It was Mark Twain who once observed, "Wrinkles should merely indicate where smiles have been." A smile that lasts comes from the heart. Like the sun that shines through the rain, so often do smiles shine through tears.

The secret of a contagious smile is found in the confidence that God loves you. One of the first truths I learned from God, as a child, was, "God is love" (I John 4:8). His love is not circumstantial. God loved us long before we learned to love Him. The apostle, Paul, writing of God's love said, "But God commendeth His love toward us, in that, while we were yet sinners, Christ died for us" (Romans 5:8).

There are times, in all of our lives, when our hearts ache. It is often reflected in our countenance. Our smile is faint. Yet, in those times we can take confidence in the words of the poet, Harold Lillenas, who wrote, "Your roses may have thorns, but don't forget. Your thorns may have some roses too. The Lord of great compassion loves you yet, and He will never fail to see you through."

As children, there were times when we thought our parents did not love us. We were not permitted to have our own way. When we were disobedient we were punished. It was difficult to smile under those circumstances, we would rather cry, and we often did. We know now that those wise parents loved us and they were striving to help prepare us for our future. "For whom the Lord loveth He chasteneth and scourgeth every son whom He receiveth" (Hebrews 12:6). God, too, is concerned that all of His children grow into fit subjects of His kingdom.

If we would encourage others, we must help them to see the truth in the words, "Smile, God loves you." When the days are dark and despair crosses our pathway, "Smile, God loves you."

O God, we are grateful that you love us. Help us each day to be more loveable. In the name of Christ, AMEN.

Seeing The Beautiful

THE HARVEST ripens! The fruits of another summer's labor are seen all about us. The beauty of the harvest and the changing seasons makes one feel all the more that truly it is the beauty of God's presence.

One cannot be blind, however, to those who would pollute the streams, the air and landscape. Or those who would, through greed or lack of concern for others, destroy instead of perpetuate. But in spite of all of this, there is the beauty of His presence all about us. We need only look for it.

Someone has said that beauty seen is partly in him who sees it. Life is like this. Beauty can degrade some and inspire others. That which is beautiful is now always good, but that which is good is always beautiful. True beauty is more than skin deep.

I remember a teacher who came to our school when I was a lad. At first glance she was far from beautiful. However, it wasn't long until, by her spirit and personality, she had won us all. I look back upon her as one whose life was truly filled with beauty. My dear old Quaker grandmother used to say, "Pretty is as pretty does."

There are some words written by the prophet Isaiah that used to bother me. Then I learned to understand what the prophet meant when he wrote, "When we shall see him, there is no beauty that we should desire him" (Isaiah 53:2). He was foretelling how many would feel about Jesus of Nazareth. But when they would come to know Him and why He came, they would see Him in a new light.

The beauty of the Master was manifested through who He was and what He did. That beauty He instilled in all who believed in Him. This He still does today.

There is a French proverb that says, "Beauty unaccompanied by virtue is as a flower without perfume." The test of lasting beauty is in the depth of character. It is not something that is applied without, but rather created within. It was Socrates, the Greek philosopher, who prayed, "I pray thee, oh God, that I may be beautiful within."

Albert Orsborn, pastor and writer, gave us the little prayer song. A part of it says, "Let the beauty of Jesus be seen in me, All His wonderful passion and purity."

When we possess this kind of grace we will, likewise, better be able to see the beauty of life around us. In turn our lives will take on a grace that others may see in us.

O God of beauty and of love, may we have the beauty of character that Thy Son our Lord had. That others may see Him in us. AMEN.

Slow Down

RECENTLY, as I neared the village limits of a small town I noted an attractive sign on which were the words, "Slow down and live." Of course, the words had to do with the speed of the cars that approached the city limits. I could also see that those words might have something to do with our physical and mental speed.

During the past two years there has come to my desk, from at least four persons, the prayer poem, "Slow Me Down, Lord." The author, to me, is still unknown but it has much food for thought and a definite warning to all in this age of speed.

It is not work that kills but the worry and the strain that goes with it. The danger is in the hurry and the urge to keep up, for fear of being left behind in the achievements of this world and its goals.

A friend of mine gave me this little quip, recently, in which there is real wisdom, "We had better be twenty minutes too late down here than twenty years too early up there."

"Slow me down, Lord, ease the pounding of my heart by the quieting of my mind," says the prayer poem. Slow down, take time to meditate upon the common every day blessings that are all about us. Take time to smile, it eases the strain the lightens the worry. Take time to read, it refreshes the mind. Take time to pray, it strengthens the soul.

There is more to life than increasing its speed. What is the reason to hurry if you are not sure where you are going or what you shall do when you arrive?

The creation of the world and every living creature, including man, in short span of six days, was a mighty miracle of God's hand. On the other hand, the fact that God takes a hundred years to grow a mighty oak proves that He is not hurried.

The life of Jesus is an illustration of the necessity of the unhurried life. He felt the need and found time to pray for strength of His own soul and the needs of others. He was never in such a hurry to seek out the multitude that He did not have time for the need of one individual.

If we would grow taller we must go deeper. We will do well to send the roots of our soul down that they may grasp the richness of the enduring values of life.

The writer of the Psalms often wrote, "Wait on the Lord; be of good courage and He will strengthen thine heart." Time spent in meditation upon the enduring values of life is never wasted. It is rather an investment of time that will continue to pay rich dividends.

Lord, help us to turn aside from the rushing ways of life, that we may catch the real meaning of living with trust in Thee for today and tomorrow. AMEN.

Spend Or Invest

SOMETIME back I spent three hours in our State Penitentiary. I was visiting, of course. There in a penal institution, built to house fifteen hundred inmates, were twenty-five hundred. Their ages ranged from fifteen-to ninety-years-old. Many of them will spend most of their lives in cells of solitary confinement.

Some of these men are preparing themselves to try and start a new life when they are released. In one of the buildings where these men are given opportunity to obtain an education, I saw these words, "It is not the hours you put in, but what you put into those hours that counts."

Three hundred of these men can neither read nor write. Many of those, no doubt, will do nothing more than spend their hours. Many others, though in forced confinement, will invest their time.

As I studied many of the faces that day, I recalled the words, "It is better to build youth than to mend men."

We are told that none of the disciples of Jesus were elderly men. The Master needed young men whose minds and characters were pliable. He also believed that it was better to build youth than to mend men. However, this lover of all men was concerned with mending men, as well as building youth.

Jesus encouraged the prisoners of sin not to go on spending their lives in useless living, but rather to invest what they had in fruitful service. His invitation was, "If any man will come after me, let him deny himself, and take up his cross daily, and follow me" (Luke 9:23).

Ever since childhood, the Bible story of Samson has always held my interest. This man was given such physical strength that he was an army all by himself. But he was an undisciplined young man. That which could have strengthened his character became his weakness. Too much of his life was wasted instead of invested.

Joseph, the eleventh son of Jacob and brother of jealous kinsmen, was the opposite of Samson. He also was given power even while he was a slave in Egypt. His life was disciplined and when the time came for him to get even with his brothers for selling him into slavery, he forgave them instead. Those years growing up in Egypt were invested not just spent. The world has never forgotten his contribution to decency and the disciplined life. His faith in God gave him strength to not stoop to revenge, but rather to forgive and forget.

It may be that we have emphasized the discipline of life too much and not placed enough emphasis upon the goals that have been won due to discipline. Each of us may help to make the world better if we encourage others to invest their time and talent with Him whose cause is never lost.

Keep us ever mindful, Lord, that we are here to invest our lives in making this world a better place in which to live, and a more hopeful world to leave to those who follow us. AMEN.

Seeing God

IN THE top favorite hymn, "How Great Thou Art," author Carl Boberg expresses his awesomeness of God when he writes, "I see the stars, I hear the rolling thunder; Thy power throughout the universe displayed." In this entire hymn Carl Boberg's foremost thought was, "How Great Thou Art." Millions have been inspired by these expressions of grandeur. Most all of us are moved to enter into the singing of this great hymn, for in it we see God as we have always hoped to see Him.

One Sunday morning I was at a camp where I was to speak. I stood out there in the open campground, waiting for my part in the service. I looked and there on the grounds stood a windmill. Its wheel was gaily turning in the wind and in so doing it was pumping water. Nearby was an electric power line bringing power to the camp. On one of the wires at least two dozen sparrows were perched, singing their anthem of praise. In all of this I saw God's power. The power which was available and had been harnessed by man and trusted by bird.

One day I talked with a most successful neuro-surgeon following four hours of complicated surgery on a young man. I asked this doctor how the future looked for this young patient. This very capable yet humble surgeon answered, "I operate, God heals."

We express our faith in God as we see Him. Words, many times, cannot express our feelings. The Psalm writer says, "O Lord, how great are Thy works! And Thy thoughts are very deep" (Psalm 92:5). At another time he writes, "The Lord is my light and my salvation; of whom shall I fear? The Lord is the strength of my life; of whom shall I be afraid" (Psalm 27:1).

I see God in the life of a little child. His presence is found in the touch of a mother's hand. The work of His art is seen in the early morning light and the evening sunset. The stars reflect His glory. We see Him at work in nature's harvest. The poet Babcock writes, "In the rustling grass I hear Him pass, He speaks to me everywhere."

The Lord of the Psalm writer and the poet is the God of all who will avail themselves of His goodness and power. Just as I was writing the above words, the telephone rang. As I answered it a friendly voice announced that a new radio station in our community had just come on the air this morning. Their programs were available, but I had to tune into their wave length to get them.

The most significant thing about the opportunity of seeing and feeling God's presence is found in the words of Jesus. What Jesus had endeavored to do throughout His brief ministry He was doing that night that He said to Philip, one of the disciples, ". . . he that hath seen me hath seen the Father . . ." (John 14:9) God made Himself available that all might come to know Him and feel Him near through His Son, Jesus Christ.

Lord, we know that Thou art ever present with us. Help us to so live that we can feel You near. Without You we are lost. AMEN.

Sing, Smile And Pray

"SING, SMILE and pray the clouds away," so wrote and sang Virgil and Blanche Brock many years ago. This song has been an encouragement to a host of people down through the years. The Brocks proved by their singing and their spirit that it can be done.

It requires a lot of courage to keep a song on your lips while there is a sob in your heart. The Psalm writer knew the secret. In words of confidence and praise he wrote, "He hath put a new song in my mouth; even praise unto our God: . . . (Psalm 40:3) This is why, when the days are clouded with burdens too heavy to bear alone, that by God's help we can sing the clouds away. By our singing our own burdens are not only made easier to bear, but we encourage others along the way.

The song also says, "Smile the clouds away, night will turn to day." A sincere, infectious smile can do more good than we can ever measure. It can help to "turn the night to day."

A cheerful countenance brightens the day; it scatters the gloom and drives the clouds away. It was a wise physician, Dr. Paul Haliburton, who observed that cheerfulness is health; its opposite, melancholy, is disease. It was said of a nurse of my acquaintance, "The smile she wears makes the sun shine everywhere."

Jesus encouraged His disciples by not exhibiting a defeatable countenance, but rather by saying, "Be of good cheer, I have overcome the world" (John 16:33).

This little gem of a song goes on to say, "Pray the clouds away, Pray and pray and pray; Night will turn to day — no matter what they say." Many years ago I had a radio program. This song was my theme song.

One day I received a letter from a listener in southeastern Ohio. In the letter the listener wrote, "There are times when I have been unable to sing the clouds away, or to smile them away, but there has never been a time that I have been unable to pray the clouds away."

Prayer is the confidence of the soul; the expression of belief in a Power beyond ourselves. During the last week of His life on earth, Jesus encouraged the disciples by His promise, "All things whatsoever ye shall ask in prayer, believing, ye shall receive" (Matthew 21:22). Praying with faith was and is the formula for a fruitful prayer.

Most of us have experienced those times when a song would not come to our lips, and our countenance could not display a smile. In our weakness and despair we turned in prayer to God, the source of our peace and strength. By His help we were not only able to pray the dark clouds away, but our countenance changed and a song once again came to our lips. "Sing and smile and pray—that's the only way—If we sing and smile and pray, we'll drive the clouds away."

I pray, O God, for that one who is discouraged, that they may look up and catch the smile of Thy countenance and have a song in their heart. AMEN.

Start Here

OUT IN Ohio there used to be a sign at a crossroad. On this sign were the words, "This is the center of the world. Start here and you can go anywhere, if you want to bad enough." Whether the sign is still there or not, the words will always be true.

Who determines my destiny? God holds the major part of our destiny in His hands. But, I determine whether I accept the opportunity God gives me. It is not so much what destiny does to us, but what we, by God's help, do with destiny, that counts.

Wilma Rudolph, as a child, had polio. She never walked until she was eight-years-old. Her mother never gave up. She kept encouraging Wilma and working with her. Wilma was just as determined as her mother. She learned to walk and then to run. She kept running.

A few years ago Wilma Rudolph won the Triple Olympic Gold Medal in the one hundred meter race in the World Olympics. She would not give up. She believed that if she would start where she was she could, by God's help and her determination, go anywhere.

When I was a youngster, every boy was told by his school teacher that he could grow up and become the President of the United States. Most of us, however, were willing to settle for much less. The opportunity was ours if we were determined to do so.

In the Sermon on the Mount, Jesus gave many words of wisdom. In one of the Beatitudes the Master said, "Blessed are those who hunger and thirst after righteousness, for they shall be filled." He was saying that if we really have a determined thirst and hunger for goodness we may have it. How determined are we that we may have the best in life, for ourselves and those around us?

We might translate the familiar verse above to read, "Happy are those whose greatest desire is to do what God requires, He will satisfy them fully." Or it might read, "Blessed are those who hunger and thirst to see right prevail, they shall be satisfied."

This is the center of the world, start here, where we are now. Where else? The man of wealth might say that my billfold is the center of the world. Purchasing power is necessary but cannot buy peace of mind. There are those who might say the head and the mind is the center of the world. Education is necessary, to any field of endeavor. But the truly educated realize that the best things in life must go deeper than the mind.

A wise man of long ago wrote, "As a man thinketh in his heart, so is he" (Proverbs 23:7). This same man had counseled his son, "Keep thy heart with all diligence, for out of it are the issues of life" (Proverbs 4:24). This is the center of our world. Start here and we can go anywhere. A hungry and thirsty heart God will not deny.

O God, help us to truly believe that all things are possible with you. AMEN.

Things That Last

"BUILD NOT your life on shifting sand; but rather on that which you know will stand." The above words was a bit of wisdom repeated, many times, by Uncle Orlo, my good neighbor and friend for many years. As I recalled those words, recently, I thought how true they were and are today.

Styles change. Appetites do likewise, especially as we grow older. Physical beauty fades but a beautiful life endures. Youth may deteriorate, but wisdom increases. Our eyes may grow dim but vivid visions continue to be ours.

The scent of a fragrant rose; the sincere smile of a little child; the love in a mother's prayer; the memories of one whom we have loved and lost awhile. These are some of the things that last. The song may end but the melody lingers on.

I never grow weary of the Love Chapter (I Corinthians 13). It is like quoting, again, a favorite poem or the singing of a familiar hymn. In reading it again, recently, I came to the last verse. One word stood out as it had never done before. That word was "abideth."

What are some of the things that last? The conclusion of this beloved and familiar chapter says, "And now "abideth" faith, hope, charity (love), these three; but the greatest of these is charity (love).

And now "abideth" FAITH. A glow worm faith is not enough. Most of us remember, as children during a summer evening at dusk, catching "lightening bugs." Those bugs had a way of turning their lights on and off, making it difficult to see them. This kind of faith is not dependable.

Jesus once said to a young father, who had brought his son to be healed by Jesus, "If thou canst believe, all things are possible to him that believeth" (Mark 9:23). Faith is not only essential but it is enduring and will help to make all things possible.

And now "abideth" HOPE. "Hope is like a gleaming taper's light/Adorns and cheers our way/And still, as darker grows the night/Emits a brighter ray," so wrote Oliver Goldsmith, English poet.

Hope is not a substitute for our own efforts. Hope encourages us to do our best and leave the rest to God.

And now "abideth" LOVE. The greatest of the three is love. How much richer life would be if all our decisions, deeds, and actions were motivated by love.

Love thinks not of itself. Love is continually giving and not counting the cost. Love is the one thing that will last when all else is gone. "Greater love hath no man than this, that he lay down his life for his friends" (John 15:13). So spoke Jesus to His disciples in those last hours. Yes, love is the greatest of all possessions, yet, love is not love until we give it away. This is true of all things that are enduring.

Dear Lord, we give Thee thanks for those things in life that abideth. They, like Thee, shall never fail. AMEN.

The Highest Calling

"BASKETBALL IS not the ultimate. It is of small importance to the total life we live. There is only one kind of a life that truly wins, and that is the one that places faith in the hands of the Saviour." Under Mr. Wooden's leadership the Bruins had won their tenth NCAA basketball championship.

Russell Chandler, of the *Los Angeles Times,* reports that Mr. Wooden, on his retirement from coaching, expressed his gratitude for the honors that had come to him. He added, "Material possessions, winning scores, and great reputations are meaningless in the eyes of the Lord, because He knows what we really are and that is all that matters."

The truly great men and women, who have helped to mold and build the character as well as the physical well being of our youth, never forget the highest calling. They believe and teach that one cannot separate material success, in any avenue of life, from the spiritual.

Paul, the apostle, speaks of the high calling more often than any other writer in the Bible. He was a well educated man. He was able to hold an audience by his magic words. About one-fourth of the New Testament was written by him. But Paul's highest calling was, "I press toward the mark for the prize of the high calling of God in Christ Jesus" (Philippians 3:14).

To have a goal in life of being the best in one's profession, business or vocation, is good, but to seek God's will in all of life is better. Whether it is coaching a famous basketball team; raising blue ribbon livestock; seeking to win the high school musical contest; or being the best cook in the neighborhood, we need guidelines and worthy goals.

John Wooden gives much credit for his success in life to the homespun philosophy and New Testament Christianity that he first experienced on an Indiana farm where he was born and reared. He never lost sight of the highest calling, that of first being a faithful, unashamed follower of Christ.

The words of Jesus are as true today as when the Master spoke them long ago out there on the hillside, "Seek ye first the kingdom of God and His righteousness; and all of these things shall be added unto you" (Matthew 6:33). It is sufficient to say that the will of God will never lead you where the grace of God cannot keep you. This is the highest calling.

O God, we thank Thee for those who have influenced our lives for good. As you have come to us through them, help us that you may speak to others through us. AMEN.

The Tongue

IN THE early days physicians examined the tongues of their patients to assist in diagnosing their disease. Most of us can recall in our childhood a visit to the doctor when he would say, "Open your mouth, stick out your tongue, and say Ah." In these days of modern medical science they now analyze the chemistry of one's entire body.

A good doctor friend of mine recently told me that the condition of the tongue is still good evidence of the state of one's health, physically, mentally, and spiritually.

The Bible has much to say about this most important member of our body. We are advised that the tongue can be a blessing or a curse to ourselves and to those around us. Our spiritual and mental condition, as well as our physical health, is determined by the state and action of our tongue.

"Whoso keepeth his mouth and his tongue, keepeth his soul from trouble," so said the wise man of Proverbs (21:23). It was President Calvin Cooledge, a man of few words, who once said, "No man has ever gotten in trouble by a thing he didn't say."

The epistle or book of James has been called "The Christian Book of Proverbs," because its teachings are in the form of moral precepts. At one time James writes, "If any man offend not in word, the same is a perfect man, and also able to bridle the whole body" (James 3:2). Knowing when to speak and when to be silent, is an art or a grace. To learn this art takes wisdom and patience.

I once learned a poem, a part of which says, "Boys flying kites/Pull in their white winged birds/But you cannot do it with flying words." Words spoken in haste cannot be retrieved. The harm they inflict cannot be measured.

But the tongue is not all bad. A tongue under the control of love can encourage the discouraged. Each of us has felt the inspiration of words spoken with wisdom and concern.

"Keep thy heart with all diligence, for out of it are the issues of life" (Proverbs 4:23). The above words, spoken long ago, tells us that life's actions is of the heart. A life so controlled is echoed in the words of our tongue.

A prayer loved by many of us says, "Let the words of my mouth, and the meditation of my heart, be acceptable in Thy sight, O Lord, my strength and my redeemer" (Psalm 19:14). Our tongues under the control of the great Physician, Jesus, will ever be acceptable to Him and a blessing to others.

O Lord, our strength and redeemer, may we so live that others may feel Thy presence as we linger in their presence. Through Christ, we pray. AMEN.

This Is The Day

APRIL SHOWERS bring May flowers, but what about a downpour in June? As I drove that Sunday morning in June, the rain was coming down like the clouds had been saving up for this special day.

I was just a young pastor then with the feeling that this Sunday, for which I had prepared a special sermon, should be a bright day full of sunshine.

I entered that country church, greeting the few people who had braved the storm. I stopped to greet Grandma Jackson. I groaned, "Grandma, isn't this a terrible day?" Grandma responded with, "The Lord made it so."

I walked on to the pulpit, ashamed of what I had said. I forgot my special sermon that morning. All I could think of was, "The Lord made it so."

I can honestly say that, as I looked at that little group of farmers and their families, all I could think of was, "This is the Day which the Lord hath made, we will rejoice and be glad in it."

As I spoke that morning I could hear the rain beating in happy rhythm on the windows of that little church. I could see the cattle out on the hillside, grateful for the rain that would freshen the grass in the pasture. I could almost hear the corn growing as it drank in the much needed June rain.

"This is the Day which the Lord hath made." Who, but God, knows what we really need? How often we have complained because of what we thought was a calamity, when it was a blessing in disguise.

Several years ago I read, for the first time, Jesse Stuart's book, *The Year of My Rebirth*. It is a true story of a famous young writer and lecturer who, at the very height of his life's activities was struck down with a severe heart attack.

It seemed to Jesse that it was the end, but it proved to be a "rebirth." God came very near, "Death held me prisoner till God stepped in, and took me by the hand and gave me breath," so wrote Jesse Stuart.

"This is the day which the Lord hath made, we will rejoice and be glad in it" (Psalm 118:24). Glad for heart attacks; Rejoice for the storms of life? Glad for trouble? No, we do not rejoice because of these things, but rather we rejoice in the way that God steps in to show us that, in spite of these things He will have the last word for our good.

After the storms there comes the sun and we are sure then that, "This is the day that the Lord hath made." Moses was not only speaking to the tribes of Israel but, likewise, to us, when he wrote, "The eternal God is thy refuge and underneath are the everlasting arms."

"This is the day" . . . "The Lord made it so." He will do likewise for tomorrow and our needs, for our good and His glory.

Our Father in Heaven, we thank Thee for this day. It was made for each of us. Help us to live today for what we can give to the day, as well as what we can get from it, for our good and Thy glory. AMEN.

This Is Life

THEODORE ROOSEVELT, American statesman and twenty-sixth President of the United States, once said, "The poorest way to face life is to face it with a sneer." Mr. Roosevelt knew what he was talking about, for in his early youth he had to fight poor health. He did not give up. History tells us how he overcame his weakness and went on to become one of the great statesmen of our world.

There are many people who go through life broken by bad breaks. What one of us has not felt, at times, that the world has given us some hard blows? Some have taken the fatalistic attitude and gone down in despair. Many others have faced life, not with a sneer, but a smile and determination. Life can be a load or a lift. It can be frustrating or invigorating, it all depends on how we face it.

A good doctor friend of mine told me one day of a patient of his who had threatened to commit suicide. Knowing that Dr. John Hall's spirit and words were as helpful as his treatment and medicine, I asked him what he said to the man.

"I made him promise me," Dr. Hall responded, "that he would leave my office, go out and walk six blocks. Each step you take, I said, thank God for two good legs; listen for the birds, and thank God for two good ears. Look for the flowers and beauty around you and be thankful for two good eyes. See how many people you can speak to with a smile on your face. The man is alive and happy today," concluded the good doctor.

Life need not be futile. We may not be able to avoid the storms that threaten us, but we can lower the anchor of faith and ride out each storm.

Someone has said that most of what Paul, the apostle, wrote of the New Testament was written in prison. At one time he wrote to the Christians at Corinth, "We are troubled on every side, yet not distressed; we are perplexed, but not in despair. Persecuted, but not forsaken; cast down but not destroyed" (II Corinthians 4:8-9). He also wrote to Timothy from prison, "I know whom I have believed and am persuaded that He is able to keep that which I have committed unto Him against that day" (II Timothy 1:12).

Some of the most inspiring hymns and poetry have been written by those with physical handicaps but with spiritual victory in their hearts.

Henry Wadsworth Longfellow, American poet, wrote a poem in answer to a discouraged friend. The poem opens with the words, "Tell me not in mournful numbers, life is but an empty dream" He went on to write that life is real and the returning of the body, at death, to dust was not spoken of the soul. He concludes with: Let us then be up and doing, with a heart for any fate; Still achieving, still pursuing, learn to labor and to wait.

It was Jesus, in His last prayer with His disciples Who prayed, "This is life eternal, that they might know Thee, the only true God, and Jesus Christ whom Thou hast sent" (John 17:3). This makes the difference between defeat and victory.

Forgive us, Lord, when we grow lax in our living and waste our lives in foolish living. Give us Thy grace to share with others what Thou hast shared with us. AMEN.

The Magic Words

THE MAGICIAN was ready to begin his special program for the children. "Before I perform any magic," said the showman, "I must have the magic word. Who kows the magic word?"

A little fellow on the front row called out, "Please." "I'm afraid you are wrong," answered the magician. Another boy in the group spoke up, "I think the magic word is hocus-pocus." "You are right," exclaimed the magician, and he began his show of magic.

Hocus-pocus may be the magic word for drawing rabbits out of hats, but I agree with the first boy. "Please" is the word that works magic in everyday living. Please and thanks, are words of appreciation, respect, and courtesy. They work like magic.

It is well to learn the meaning, power, and use of these magic words in childhood. They not only bring results to children, but big dividends throughout life.

Our national Thanksgiving Day is truly an American special day. But, showing gratitude is an international spirit. It cannot be saved up for a specific day but should be an attitude of the mind and heart continuously.

A mother of several children once said to me, "I have tried to teach my children to be courteous in their requests and grateful for what they receive."

As a nation, we Americans have been blessed with abundance. Our gratitude should be as abounding as our blessings.

I think of the time when the ten lepers who were waiting by the roadside in their misery. They had heard that Jesus, the great Healer, was passing through their village that day. As they saw this Master of men, they cried out, pleading with Him to have mercy on them.

Luke's Gospel tells us that Jesus heeded their plea and healed them. These ten men went on their way to show themselves to the priests. One of the lepers, when he saw that he was healed, turned back to Jesus, "And fell down on his face, at His feet giving Him thanks . . ." (Luke 17:16)

I have always felt that this leper who returned to give thanks, received a double blessing. He was not only healed like the other nine, but by returning to give thanks his whole life was changed.

The Psalm writer was inspired by God to write, "Call upon me in the day of trouble; I will deliver thee" (Psalm 50:15). He also wrote, "Offer unto God thanksgiving and pay thy vows unto the Most High" (Psalm 50:14).

We owe much to those stalwart Puritan fathers who, in those tragic days, prayed for deliverance. In their prosperity they, likewise, gave thanks to God for His goodness. The spirit in which they did this didn't work like magic; but the continued attitude of those who followed them has helped to make this Land a great Nation.

If we are to continue to follow in their train, we will do well to not only ask God for our needs but, likewise, thank Him for our blessings.

Dear Father in Heaven, help us to have a spirit of gratitude each day and to so express it, for Thy loving goodness to us. AMEN.

The Art Of Talking

THE ART of talking comes not through the use of many words, but by the weighing of each word. The above statement came to me as a young student from a wise professor. His words were well chosen.

The art of talking is not acquired overnight. It is somewhat like another wise man who said that as a man grows wiser he talks less and says more.

I have often thought if one could only have the enthusiasm of youth and the wisdom of age at the same time, it would be a great asset to life. It would, likewise, save a lot of heartache and embarrassment.

The writer of the Book of James gives us some well chosen words when he says, ". . . let every man be swift to hear, slow to speak and slow to wrath" (James 1:19). He is saying that the art of talking can better be achieved by first learning the art of listening.

It has often been said that some speak before they think, others speak without thinking. The best philosophy is to weigh our words before we speak.

My mother used to have a philosophy of life that she practiced sincerely. She often said, "If you can't say something good about someone, don't say anything."

Her favorite Bible verse was Psalm 19:14; "Let the words of my mouth, and the meditation of my heart, be acceptable in thy sight, O Lord, my strength and my redeemer."

James, also, writes in his letter, "Even so the tongue is a little member, and boasteth great things. Behold, how great a matter a little fire kindleth" (James 3:5). We, likewise, know that one cannot measure the good that words, well chosen and spoken at the opportune time may accomplish.

Many a person who is tempted to give up, has been encouraged to go on through the wise counsel of a friend. A well chosen word at a crucial time in a child's life has saved that child from failure.

Jesus was a Master at this. Even though He condemned the sin, He loved the sinner. Many a time He gave new hope to a potential failure by encouraging them to "go and sin no more."

Certainly this Master of men was experienced in the art of talking. His well chosen words have been pondered by the wisest of men for centuries.

His words have brought comfort to the sorrowing, rest to the weary, and healing to the sick. As He talked the common people understood Him and the learned wondered at His wisdom. We would do well to practice His spirit as well as His words.

Lord, grant that whatever we say, think or hear, that it may be acceptable in Thy sight. AMEN.

The Value Of A Friend

"EVERYONE NEEDS someone." Such were the words spoken to me by a new acquaintance one day. He had told me how that life, for him, had seemed impossible, then someone came to his aid. He went on to say, "No one knows the value of a true friend until that one comes to you in time of desperate need."

What does it mean to be a friend? Someone has said that a friend is one who knows all about you but still loves you. Most of us have friends like this, whether we deserve them or not. Many of us have found that a friend is one in whom you can confide. A friend listens to your innermost longings; shares your hopes; comforts you in your sorrows and helps bear your burdens.

Slaves and servants were words quite common more than two thousand years ago. Those who served willingly or unwillingly, someone over them, expected to be called slaves or servants. Then there came a young man into the Galilee area one day. He urged twelve other young men to become His disciples.

In the course of time Jesus gave these disciples new hope by saying to them, "Henceforth I call you not servants; for the servant knoweth not what his lord doeth: but I have called you friends; for all things I have heard of my Father I have made known to you" (John 15:15).

Friend was a word fasioned from a spirit of love and trust. Jesus knew all about His disciples. He knew their weaknesses, their fears, their sins, yet He loved them.

One of the most commendable things the enemies of Jesus ever said about Him was, that He was the Friend of sinners. This was and is quite true. He showed that He cared. He loved the sinner but not the sin. If He had not been the "Friend of sinners," what hope would we have today?

It has been said that a friend is one who comes in when the world has gone out. One cannot place an estimate upon this kind of friendship. Such is the Friendship of Jesus. His promise was and is, "I will never leave thee nor forsake thee" (Hebrews 13:5).

Jesus exemplified this kind of friendship. Mary, Martha, and Lazarus, of Bethany, experienced it; Peter, James, and John, three beloved disciples, felt it. We too, may know that kind of friendship. The kind of companionship that may be warm and understanding; forgiving and true; refreshing, enlightening and strengthening. The kind that the poet writes of when he says, "And He walks with me and He talks with me."

Austris Whitol, who penned the song, "My God and I," felt this friendship when he wrote, "My God and I will go for aye together, We'll walk and talk and just as good friends do. This earth will pass and with it common trifles, But God and I will go unendingly." This experience may be ours too. This is what He would have it be.

Our Father, we know that you want us to trust you day by day. Help us to so live that we may have a walking friendship with You each day. AMEN.

The Decision Is Ours

IN THE MIDST of January's snow storms, the seed and flower catalogues begin to arrive. I am always carried away with all of the new creations, as well as the familiar standbys. It makes me wish that our little plot of ground was large enough to have a little of each flower, vegetable, and fruit.

When April comes, I know then that I cannot find room for all that I wished for in January. I must use good judgment and make certain choices. We must have a well ordered landscape, not a conglomeration of this and that.

Life is much like the above experience. True satisfaction comes only when one sets his mind on those goals that will produce a well ordered life. He whose goal is everywhere usually arrives nowhere.

In the first gospel, Matthew tells of a young man coming to Jesus. No doubt this young man has observed the life and ministry of Jesus. He had noted the satisfaction in the lives of those whom Jesus had touched.

This young man came, asking what good thing he could do that he might have the more abundant and eternal life. Jesus held up the goals and gave him the challenge. "But when the young man heard that saying, he went away sorrowful: for he had great possessions" (Matthew 19:22). So it is that God gives us the challenge — the decision is ours.

Opportunity is easier to see than responsibility is to accept. There have been many who have fallen by the wayside, or failed to reach the goals for which they had hoped, all because they were not willing to pay the price.

Most of us have never reached our highest plateau of living and service. We could have done better if we had not been satisfied with "good enough."

A young college student approached a farmer who was resting on his front porch. "Sir," spoke the student enthusiastically, "I have a book here that will tell you how to raise more and better crops." The farmer smiled and replied, "Son, I already know more than I have put into practice now."

To most of us it is not the lack of knowledge on how to live better. It is rather the lack of the will and courage to do it.

When God challenged Abraham to leave his country and go out "into a land that I will show thee" (Genesis 12:1). Abraham accepted the challenge. He went out not knowing where he would be led. His life was blessed and all those who followed him. So it is with all of us who accept the challenge of the Master. The final decision is ours.

Our Father, we thank Thee for the many opportunities of life. Help us, that we may have the wisdom to make the right choices. AMEN.

The Passing
And The Abiding

AS I SIT at my desk I look out upon a scene of beauty, but a cold one. Only a few weeks ago our lawn, with its blossoms of summer and fall was a thing of beauty. This morning it is no less beautiful. A new fallen snow is clinging to the branches of our evergreens. It is the changing of the seasons.

As sure as the seasons come and go, so surely change comes to each of us, for we live in a world of change.

An ancient writer saw his nation going to pieces all about him. Palestine, the nation he loved, had been conquered by Rome. But this writer's faith could not be destroyed. He pleaded with his people to trust in those things which would continue to abide, "that those things which cannot be shaken may remain" (Hebrews 12:27).

When it seems that our world around us is in danger of going to pieces and those things we have always held dear are in danger of being destroyed, take heart, there are the abiding things, "which cannot be shaken which will remain."

During the presidency of Calvin Cooledge, a friend of his was lamenting the condition of the country. President Cooledge, known for his few words, rose from his chair, walked over to the window and said with confidence, "I see that Washington's monument is still there."

It is good to know that we too can look out of our window of faith, in trying times, and see that God's creation is still with us and His promises will not fail. He not only created but is creating and will continue to do so long after mere man has turned again to dust.

It is good to hear again the words of the Psalm writer who said of his faith in God, "Before the mountains were brought forth, or ever thou hadst formed the earth and the world, even from everlasting to everlasting, thou art God" (Psalm 90:2).

It is encouraging, likewise, to read of the faith of the man who faced a changing world, saying, "Jesus Christ, the same yesterday, today and forever" (Hebrews 13:8).

Henry F. Lyte, English pastor and poet, knew that physically he was fighting a losing battle. As he came to the eventide of his faith, he did not waver. In that beloved hymn, "Abide With Me," he writes, "Change and decay in all around I see; O Thou who changest not, abide with me." We too can take heart, many things are passing but we can trust Him who changest not.

We are grateful, our Heavenly Father, we can trust in Thee who art the same yesterday, today and forever. AMEN.

The Good Seed

RECENTLY, I was showing surprise at the amount of money a farmer friend of mine had invested in some seed for his farm. He looked at me, smiled, then said, "Good seed costs money, but it is the most rewarding in the long run." He was right.

As you drive through the countryside you can see the result of the foresight of those who are building, not alone for the present, but the future. They are sowing good seed. You will not only see fruitful and well kept farms, but in the distance adequate schools and church spires pointing heavenward.

Life's future depends upon the wisdom of our investment and the sowing of the good seed. The apostle, Paul once wrote, "I have planted, Apolles watered; but God gave the increase" (I Corinthians 3:6).

Disheartened, I stood one night at the ruins of a village church that had burned to the ground that very afternoon. The remains of the building was still smoldering. As a young pastor, I had just come to that community a few weeks before. I wondered what was to be done. That afternoon I had been informed that the insurance had been dropped three months before.

I heard footsteps. I turned, and there beside me stood an elderly man whom I had never met before. He took me by the arms and said rather abruptly, "Preacher, we've got to rebuild it. There has to be a church for all of these boys and girls around here. I'll give a thousand dollars to start it.

It took some real sacrifice on the part of many of us. Today, that good seed sown long ago, is bringing in a good harvest. All because some of us planted, others watered, and God has continued to give the increase.

The above experience could be duplicated again and again by those who have met the challenge. That plot of ground could have grown up in weeds. This could very well be true of our homes, communities, and our individual lives.

My father's favorite Bible verse was, ". . . whatsoever a man soweth, that shall he also reap" (Galatians 6:7). Dad practiced this rule and impressed it, over and over, upon his children. His philosophy was that anyone could sow wild oats without trying, but it took high aim and courageous living to sow the good seed.

The farmer was right; good seed costs more, but it is the most rewarding in the long run.

Integrity, discipline, purity, courage, these and many others, may be old-fashioned virtues, but they are still good seeds to sow. They are still needed in the halls of government, in the pews and pulpits of our churches, and within the portals of our homes. They will bring a bountiful and rich harvest.

Help us, O Lord, to sow the good seed of faithful living and then leave the outcome to Thee. AMEN.

The Art Of Giving

ONE BEAUTIFUL Spring morning I stood on a hilltop looking out over a farm of a hundred and twenty acres. Beside me was a successful farmer of many years. His son, Jack, was standing close by.

The son was interested in buying the farm and had invited us to look it over. The farm was in poor condition, and anyone who loves the soil could see that it had known better days.

The father, after surveying the situation, turned to his son with this conclusion, "Jack," he said, "if you will give back to this soil that which belongs to it you can make it a good farm again."

Many of us were brought up with the ideas that life's main goal is in getting. Getting ahead. Getting an education. Getting rich and getting happiness. We eventually discover, however, that to get we must first give. This is true whether it be with the soil or the soul. The true art of giving is discovered through the experience of giving yourself.

A few years ago I stopped at my favorite station for gas. The cheerful operator of this station had made many friends. He always met his customers with a smile in his voice as well as on his face.

On that particular morning I was told that the oil company, for whom our friend worked, had presented him with a new car. At the time of the presentation he was told that the car was given to him because of his courtesy to a stranger as well as his friends. This young man not only sold gas and oil but gave himself, cheerfully, in so doing. He not only serviced your car, but he seemed to have a way of adding extra miles to your entire day.

Much of Jesus' teaching had to do with man and his possessions. He explained to His hearers that man's life consisted, not alone in the things which he possessed. Many came to Him rich in the fruits of the soil, but poor in the increase of the soul. This Master of successful living taught that if we give it shall be given us. His philosophy for living was that the gift without the river was bare.

On one occasion He told the difference between the hireling and the shepherd. The hireling loves his job for what he gets. The shepherd loves his sheep as well as his work. He gives not only his time, but himself. The hireling takes from the soil and robs his soul. The shepherd feeds the soil and replenishes the soul. Long and tiresome is the day of one who looks forward only to the sunset and the paycheck. No day, however, is long enough for the one who gives himself in love to his work.

"Give and it shall be given unto you," were not only words spoken by Jesus; He also practiced them in His daily living. He practicied the rule, not for what He received, but for the joy He could bring to others.

There are many whose lives are an example of this rule for fruitful living. These have learned the true art of giving.

Lord, help me this day, as I give of myself that I shall forget what might come back to me and remember that it is more blessed to give than to receive. AMEN.

The Checkered Flag

PALM SUNDAY, 1965, will long be remembered by many of us as a dark day of tragedy in Indiana. The tornadoes that struck Elkhart County between 6:30 and 7 p.m., left fifty dead and many others in hospitals. Hundreds were left homeless. Many of our homes and families felt the effect of this indescribable disaster.

Surveying the ruins of the homes of several of the families of our area brought to light some calamitous experiences.

I stopped at one place where one of our families of our church had once lived. As I looked about I noticed that the only thing, amongst the rubble that was left standing, was the bathroom vent pipe. In the top end of the pipe an undefeatable son of this family had stuck a checkered flag. To me, the flag denoted a winner.

This was the spirit of not only this Christian family but many others in that area. They had been struck down but not defeated. They had put up the checkered flag.

A great general once said that we may lose a battle now and then, but by determined effort we will win the war.

As I survey the experiences of life that seem, at times, to be utter defeat, I find myself thinking of what Paul the apostle once said. In writing to the Corinthian Christians he gave words of encouragement. He wrote, "We are troubled on every side, yet not distressed; we are perplexed, but not forsaken; cast down but not destroyed" (II Corinthians 4:8-9).

Many calamities have struck our nation, with terrible destructive force, since its beginning. Our people, on each occasion, have proven themselves to be equal to every disaster. This is one of the courageous powers that God has given man, that courage to start over again.

The spider's web was destroyed time after time but I noted that after each misfortune this undefeatable creation of God's hand set out to rebuild. Such examples give each of us greater moral courage.

Recently, I met a young man who had lost both hands in a corn picker accident. The spirit with which he set about to adjust himself to the use of manmade hands was an inspiration to all who knew him. This young farmer's attitude was that "it wasn't what you have lost but what you have left that counts."

God, Himself, has never known defeat. The enemies of Jesus thought they were rid of Him when they nailed Him to a wooden cross. They had not reckoned with the proven truth that God always has the last word.

When, with courage and faith in Him, we hang up the flag that denotes a winner, we do so not in vain. The reward of such courage is valuable.

O God, give us the courage to never lower the flag of faith, but to lift it high and trust Thee for the outcome. In Jesus' Name we pray. AMEN.

The Cost Of Living

THE COST of living is one of the real problems of our day. It has been the problem of every generation. The young couple getting started, with a family coming on, faces life with a great deal of energy but also frustration. The parents with children in college, as well as the grandparents facing inactive years, both realize that it takes much planning and thrift to meet the daily needs.

Someone facing this everyday problem has said that one of the difficulties of the modern family is that there is too much month left over at the end of the money.

To solve the problem of the cost of living means the making of decisions and the practicing of disciplines. Life is made up with making choices. Most battles are won or lost the day before, by wise or foolish decisions.

Luke, the Gospel writer, tells us that Jesus turned to His disciples one day and gave them a challenge. He said, ". . . If any man will come after me, let him deny himself, and take up his cross daily, and follow me" (Luke 9:23). This was the cost of real living. It meant the making of a decision, and the practice of discipline. It was not easy.

Discipline is a confining word. It suggests crosses, hard work and sacrifice. Discipline also suggests success, victory, and the feeling of having accomplished those things that are really worthwhile.

Recently, I talked with a mother who had two sons in the ministry and a daughter who is a missionary. This woman had lost her companion early in their married life.

It was not easy to keep the home together and educate her three children. By teaching in the public school and farming she had been able to help her chldren to prepare themselves for life.

A neighbor commending her on what she had been able to do, said, "I'd give anything for a family like your's." The mother's quiet reply was, "I did."

This leads us to say that the cost of living a life like this is the cost of caring. Jesus would say, if you do not care for others you cannot be my disciple. This Master of men proved that He cared for others. He gave much more to others than He ever received from them. The cost of caring has made many a load lighter when, otherwise, it would have been drudgery.

It was Paul, the apostle, who once said, "We were ready to share with you, not only the gospel, but also ourselves."

A life invested in worthwhile living brings rich dividends. At the close of each day there is a feeling that the dedication of this kind of life is worth all that it has cost and more.

Lord, You know how often we have felt that we have failed. We pray that You would take what we have and are, and make us what You would have us to be. Through Christ we pray. AMEN.

The Simple Things

SEVERAL YEARS ago I was the guest speaker for a preaching mission in one of our Indiana churches. At the end of the week a lady of the church came to me to express her appreciation of the services. She concluded by saying, "I certainly have enjoyed your preaching, you are so simple minded."

I think that I understood what the young lady meant. At least, I accepted the words as a compliment and not as an insult.

Emerson, American philosopher and poet, once said, "Nothing is more simple than greatness; indeed, to be simple is to be great."

Eloquence of language may not be the power of all of us; but simplicity may be. A teacher who left an impression upon all who knew her, once said, "I have always tried to keep the cookies down on the lower shelf so that even the children could reach them."

Those whose lives have influenced us most have practiced simplicity. They have lived, spoken, and written down where we live. When they have used terms understood by the unlearned, the wise appreciated them likewise.

Jesus, himself, was a noble example of this. He talked to the people with whom He came in contact, about the things with which they were the most familiar.

His teachings are still pondered over by the most learned, yet understood by the common people. He taught them as one having authority, yet as one having cmpassion.

As He stood by the seashore, with the multitude gathered about Him, He spoke of the sower and the seed. Those acquainted with sowing and harvest, understood better His parables of the Kingdom of God.

On the hillside Jesus gave to them the Beatitudes. These were the "blesseds" with promise. Along the busy highway He paused to take a little child in His arms. Here He compared a member of the Kingdom of Heaven with a little child.

To live and speak with simplicity was one of the many attributes of Jesus. It was said that, "the common people heard him gladly." They heard Him because they understood Him, at least, they understood that He was concerned about them and their future welfare.

It is not always the simplest things in life that make the most lasting impression. We do not forget, however, those persons who talk our language. This the Master did. We could do no better than to try, by His help, to exemplify His way.

Our Father, keep us humble but wise that others may see the better way of life, because we have walked humbly in that way. AMEN.

Togetherness

A NEIGHBOR of mine has lived many years and has seen many changes. He said to me a few days ago, "The world seems smaller than it used to be. We have better communication and faster mode of traveling." He continued, "But I doubt, that in this busy, hurried day, that there is as much 'togetherness' as we had when I was a boy."

This bit of wise philosophy by my good neighbor set me to thinking. Togetherness is a most meaningful word. It is something that we need more of today. Families break apart where it does not exist. Nations are defeated where it has failed. Churches grow and a right spirit prevails where it is found.

I stood one day in the room where the founders of our Country signed the Declaration of Independence. As I studied the picture of those men before me, I recalled that one of those men had said, "Unless we all hang together, we shall all hang separate." In unity there is strength. In unity there is harmony.

In times of great emergency the citizens of our country have always forgotten their differences and pulled together. Think what could come to pass if we would continue to do so.

In my early boyhood days we used to cut out winter's wood with a cross-cut saw. It was a saw for two men, or a man and a boy. My father spent a great deal of time trying to teach us boys that we had to work together to run the saw to the best advantage. The right and wrong kind of togetherness was illustrated many times as my brother and I worked on either end of the saw. We had to learn to push and pull together. Even in this age we still need to learn that lesson.

The wrong kind of togetherness was illustrated at the unjust trail of Jesus, when with one accord the mob cried out, "Crucify Him." This was the kind of togetherness that was incited by evil men interested only in their own selfish desires. Many, today, want a world brotherhood without giving up their prejudices and unbrotherly actions.

On the other hand, the right kind of togetherness is illustrated by those who gathered in the Upper Room, after the ascension of Jesus. While they continued with one accord in prayer something came to pass. On the day of Pentecost they were filled with the Holy Spirit. They then went out to be witnesses of what always comes to pass when there is fellowship of kindred minds.

All worthwhile movements have been accomplished through the "oneness of spirit." If our world is to be saved for the future it will be only as we share together one with another, under God.

Father in heaven, when there is so much disunity in our world, help us to see the good that can come from togetherness. Give us the spirit of love which helps us to better understand one another. AMEN.

The Voice Of God

TWO BOY SCOUTS on a camp-out with their scout master, were asked to make a brief observation tour. When they returned, each of them was asked to report on what they had observed.

The first boy to report said, "There was nothing unusual, just the same old things. The countryside has not changed much." The other boy eagerly reported that the clouds were white as mountains of snow and their whiteness made the sky all the more blue. "I watched," he continued, " as a mother bird fed her young and I listened to the music of the river as it trickled over the rocks." Life's experiences are dull or rewarding, it all depends on our expectancy.

John Burroughs, the naturalist, observed, "The great Creator has a message for us each day, in the world about us, if we will only take time to observe and listen."

The poetess, Maltbie Babcock, wrote, "This is my Father's world, In the rustling grass, I hear Him pass; He speaks to me everywhere." It is as the Psalm writer says, "The heavens declare the glory of God and the firmament showeth His handiwork" (Psalm 19:1).

Moses, the early leader of Israel, was keeping his father-in-law's flocks in the mountain of Horeb. He noted something unusual. It was a bush that continued to burn yet not being consumed. Moses turned aside to see this amazing sight. From the burning bush came a voice that said, ". . . put off thy shoes from off thy feet, for the place whereon thou standest is holy ground" (Exodus 3:5). From that burning bush experience Moses was given proof of God's presence and the task that was to be his in the coming years.

God spoke not only to Moses, but to Samuel, the prophet, still a young lad; Saul, the persecutor, who later became Paul the apostle; and to many others down through the ages. There is a burning bush and a voice for each of us. God speaks in marvelous ways His wonders to perform. Our present and future welfare depends on how we observe and listen in our pilgrimage through life.

Joan of Arc, a French heroine, proclaimed that the voice of God had spoken to her. The King, in amazement, asked her why it was that this voice of God had not spoken to him. Joan of Arc replied, "Might it be, your Majesty, that you have not been listening?"

In the world about us, in the printed word, or avenues of communications, God is trying to speak to us. Might it be that we are not always listening? Wisdom to solve each day's problems; strength to live victoriously and to help others to do likewise. all of these are ours if we listen to the still small voice of God.

O God, teach us the wisdom of being still and knowing that Thou art God, that we may better know Thy will for us. AMEN.

True Friends

NAPOLEON BONAPARTE, French Emperor and military leader, met his defeat at Waterloo. He once said, "I made courtiers; but I never pretended to make friends." He fretted away his last years on a rocky island — alone. No one is so alone as one who has no friends.

It was a man of wisdom who once observed that a faithful friend is a strong defense; and he that hath found him hath found a treasure. I cannot begin to estimate the value of my many friends. I have had many more than I have ever deserved.

Homer Rodeheaver, song leader for the evangelist Billy Sunday for twenty years, once quoted in my presence, the following words: "It is a joy in life to find/at every turning of the road;/the strong arms of a friend so kind;/To help me onward with my load./And since I have no gold to give/and love alone must made amends,/My daily prayer is while I live/God make me worthy of my friends." Friendship is a good investment. The dividends are never reduced.

True friendship is not seasonal. The wise author of Proverbs once wrote, "A friend loveth at all times, and a brother is born for adversity" (Proverbs 17:17). A sincere friend does not depend upon certain conditions. A true friend is one who knows all about you and still loves you. You cannot buy them, or steal them; you have to make them.

Genuine friendship knows no limitations. In those final days of Jesus, before His trial and crucixion, the Master tried to instill confidence in the minds of His disciples. He assured them that, "Greater love hath no man that this, that a man lay down his life for his friends. Ye are my friends, if ye do whatsoever I command you" (John 15:13-14). The test of ones friendship is found in the extent of ones love.

Friendship, then, is a sincere, mutual understanding. It is a companionship. It does not wait to receive, but rather to share. It knows no limitation; it is mutual in its concerns.

It was said of Enoch, of Old Testament days, "And Enoch walked with God; and he was not for God took him" (Genesis 5:24). This good man must have known what it meant to have had a confidential friendship with God. So much so that they walked together; the walk that did not end, but continued into the eternal world.

Austris Wihtol, poet and song writer, expressed his feelings of friendship by saying, "My God and I, go in the fields together. We walk and talk as good friends should and do." This kind of friendship each of us may experience, and many of us do.

"Can we find a friend so faithful, who will all our sorrows share?" Joseph Scriven, author of "What a Friend We Have in Jesus," answers his own question by saying, "Take it to the Lord in prayer." In time of deep sorrow this man found a Friend that did not fail.

A friendship tested in time of adversity, mellowed with mutual understanding and enriched by the warmth of companionship. This is the longing of us all. This is met in Jesus, greatest Friend of all.

O Christ of God, we are grateful for the feeling of knowing that you are our dearest Friend. Help us to do nothing that would endanger that friendship with Thee or those near and dear to us. AMEN.

The Goal Of Life

"KEEP A tight line and your eye on the goal," were the familiar words of my father long ago. They did not mean as much to this boy, when he was thirteen, as they did years later.

It was Springtime and we were starting the plow. One of the horses of my team was blind and the other was unpredictable. Starting a "haw" land in the middle of the field was my father's procedure. He would step off the land and set a stake at the farther end of the field. "Now," he would say, "keep a tight line and your eye on the goal."

As I recall now, this was the advice of not only my father, but it was the philosophy of most of my teachers, as I grew from youth to manhood. Growing up is not easy, either on the child or the parent; on the youth or the adult.

Uncle Orlo, my good neighbor, once said, "Growing pains are not easy to cope with. In our youth we want to move with speed. We are ready for venture, but speed is not nearly as important as direction." I have often thought of Uncle Orlo's advice. His words of wisdom were much like my father's, "keep a tight line and your eye on the goal."

Sitting at the dinner table recently, we were recalling some of the mistakes we had made in the past and some of the hopes for the present. Thelma, my faithful companion for fifty years, said "If we could only have as much enthusiasm at our age as we had when we were young, along with the wisdom of maturity, think what we could do." This is one of the reasons that we should do all within our power to give encouragement and direction to youth in their enthusiasm.

Paul, the apostle and man of wisdom, loved Timothy as though he were his son in the flesh. Paul paid tribute to Timothy's family background, the faith of his grandmother Lois, and the influence of his mother Eunice. No one can estimate the influence Paul must have had on the life of young Timothy.

"Stir up the gift of God," Paul once wrote to Timothy. At another time he advised, "But refuse profane and old wives' fables and exercise thyself rather unto godliness" (I Timothy 4:7). "Let no man despise thy youth," he later writes. Then, seeing life as not only earthly but eternal, he implores Timothy to, "Fight the good fight of faith, lay hold on eternal life, where unto thou art called . . ." (I Timothy 6:12)

Real living takes time. We are tomorrow what we are becoming today. It also takes discipline. To a young man whose urge to follow Jesus was defeated by the pull of things less important, the Master said, "No man, having put his hand to the plow, and looking back, is fit for the kingdom of God" (Luke 9:62).

It is true, many are turning away from God and the Church. But, we are also witnessing a movement of youth and adults who have discovered the real importance of "keeping a tight line and their eye on the goal." Their faith in God and His promise is our hope for tomorrow's world.

Our Father, there are so many things that tempt us to turn aside from those goals that we know are worth striving for. May the light of Thy countenance ever guide us in the right way. AMEN.

The Golden Rule

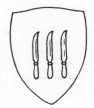

RECENTLY I received a most interesting communication from my good friend, Wheeler McMillen, former editor of *Farm Journal*. It was on the occasion of his eightieth birthday.

This man of wide experience and profound wisdom wrote, "If I live to be old, and ever acquire a franchise for pontificating, this will be the message: Human experience has yielded no higher wisdom than that expressed in the Golden Rule."

I knew that my good friend was referring to the words of Jesus. The occasion was the Sermon on the Mount when He said, "Therefore all things whatsoever ye would that men should do to you, do ye even so to them: for this is the law and the prophets" (Matthew 7:12). This is the Golden Rule.

There are those who have taken as their creed the negative translation of the above Rule. Their affirmation is: Do not do to others anything that you would not want them to do to you. This is good, but not enough.

In a community where I once lived, a certain man died. Those who had known him said that he had never harmed anyone. He had never belonged to anything, no P.T.A., no Chamber of Commerce, no union, no church. He lived sixty years in the community without throwing his influence for or against any organization. He kept the law. He kept out of jail. Someone observed that here was a man who lived by the negative translation of the Golden Rule.

It be a good citizen, in any community, one must do more than abstain from doing anything. The teaching of Jesus was always positive. This is why the Golden Rule has never been improved upon. Jesus not only taught this, but it was the guiding principle of His life.

Millions of people have been affected by those who have practiced doing unto others as they would want others to do to them.

This Golden Rule teaches us that if we want a good neighbor, we must be a good neighbor. If we want to be loved, we must show love towards others. We must forgive if we want to be forgiven. He who sincerely lives by the Golden Rule thinks not of the reward he shall receive by doing so. He practices the standard because of the compassion he has for others.

How much better our world is today because of those who have been an example of this noble teaching of Jesus. How much better it would be if all of us lived by it.

Help me, Lord, that this I shall be, a true example of the Golden rule in my words and deeds. That, in so doing, I may influence others to do likewise. AMEN.

Today

WILL ROGERS, the humorist and philosopher, once advised, "Don't let yesterday use up too much of today." Too often we spoil today's joys and tomorrow's hopes by letting them consume "too much of today."

Someone placed true value on today when they said that "I have no yesterdays, time took them away; tomorrow may not be, but I have today."

The winter has been a hard one, with snow, icy roads, and freezing winds. But, that was yesterday. Today the sun shines warm and bright. The fields have changed their coats of white and brown to green. The flowers bloom, the harvest comes. True, the winter winds will come again some day, but we have today.

Whatever accomplishments may have been mine yesterday, they will not suffice for today. I must give myself to the tasks of this day. Even though I may have failed yesterday; overcome by some temptation; discouraged by some failure; I have been given another day.

Giving us another day to try again. This is God's way. I never grow tired of the words, "This is the day which the Lord hath made. We will rejoice and be glad in it" (Psalm 118:24). Be glad for today and all that it may bring to us.

Wait not for a better day. This is the word that comes to us from the wise man of long ago, "Boast not thyself of tomorrow, for thou knowest not what a day may bring forth" (Proverbs 27:1).

When Jesus taught His disciples to pray, He taught them to say, "Give us this day our daily bread." He did not suggest that they pray for bread for tomorrow or the next week. If God can supply our needs for today, certainly when tomorrow comes, He can do the same. If we use what God has given us for today, we will be prepared for tomorrow.

I will give myself, then, to the tasks and opportunities of today. From the rising to the setting of the sun, I will rejoice that God has given me another day. I will be a little kinder to those who cross my pathway. I will be a little blinder to those mistakes others may make. I will encourage the discouraged today. At the evening time I will thank God, who in His mercy, has given me today.

The day in which we live is far spent. God's mercy abides, but His judgment finally comes. Someone waits for me, for you to come, in the Master's name, to help lighten their burden today.

Lord, for tomorrow and its needs, I do not pray; help me to labor earnestly, and duly pray; let me be kind in deed, Father, today. AMEN.

The Majority Report

FACT FINDING boards, investigating committees, majority and minority reports. These are present day terms of speech. They are, likewise, as old as Moses. It was Moses, the illustrious leader of the Israelites, who appointed the first investigating and fact finding committee.

The account of the twelve spies, sent out by Moses, to investigate the Promised Land of Canaan, has always been interesting to me. At the end of forty days they returned. In their report they were in one accord on one thing about the Land, "surely it floweth with milk and honey; and this is the fruit of it" (Numbers 13:27). They showed the people the fruit of this rich country. "Nevertheless, the people be strong that dwell in the land" (Numbers 13:28).

You may remember that there was also a minority report. There was in the group a strong, stalwart young Israelite by the name of Caleb. His response was, "Let us go up at once, and possess it; for we are well able to overcome it" (Numbers 13:30). Where the majority saw the difficulties; the minority, like Caleb and Joshua, saw the opportunities.

Too often, today, the majority report is quite audible, "Sure, world brotherhood would be fine, but there are too many obstacles. As long as we have greed and hate we can't have world brotherhood; " . . . Sure, a peaceful world is the ultimate goal, but as long as human beings are as they are, there will never be peace; ". . . Sure, the Christian life is worthwhile, but there are too many temptations, we can't overcome them." Each of these are saying, "There are too many giants in the land."

However, there are many like Caleb of old who, with courage, are saying, "We are well able to overcome them." It is to this minority that we shall never be indebted.

One of the giants, whose phantom presence defeats more people than any other is FEAR. It was all right for the ten men who returned to see themselves as "grass hoppers," but they failed to see God in the project.

God is greater than all our problems. He knows no defeat. His is the last word. A courageous man, with all of his enthusiasm, once prayed, "Thank you, Lord, things are in a pretty mess, we have a big job, but there is nothing but what you and I cannot handle."

There are many problems that some say cannot be solved. They cannot be, as long as we see only the giants involved. But if we take the obstacles that are facing us; pray for God's strength and wisdom and then go forward with courage, the victories that are needed will come.

With God's help we can substitute faith for fear. World brotherhood, peace in our time, these and other needs, will be found only in the pathway of God. Like Caleb, let us say, "We are able."

Lord, we are able, Our spirits are Thine, Remold them, make us like Thee Divine. Thy guiding radiance, Above us shall be, A beacon to God, To love and loyalty. AMEN.

The Countdown

MAY 5, 1961 is a date that will be long remembered, especially in the life of Commander Alan B. Shepherd. It was the date of his flight into Space. What were his thoughts just before the zero hour, during the Countdown? He said that he felt all preparations had been made, he trusted that all would go well, and that during those minutes he was praying.

Did you ever wonder what the athletic coach says to his team at the zero hour just before the start of a crucial game? What does the surgeon think about just before that serious operation? What about the thoughts of the patient?

The countdown comes to every individual many times in life. In each emergency one must know what to do, and in what spirit to face that zero hour.

Paul, the apostle, was writing of his concern for the Christians he had left at Ephesus. "Finally," he writes, "be strong in the Lord, and in the power of His might" (Ephesians 6:10). He goes on to urge them to be alert, "watching with all perseverance."

If one is to be alert he must have a clear head and a steady hand. Someone has suggested that our United States has lost conviction and impetus because we have confused the free, with the free and easy.

Many have learned that to have freedom and influence, in every sense of the word, is not something that comes through ease of living but rather through sacrifice and dedication. Being alert is being ready at all times and all places in all emergencies.

My father used to enjoy telling the story of the days of the horse-drawn fire engines. He said that they retired an old fire horse from duty and a junk dealer bought him. However, each time the fire bell rang, if the old horse was near enough to hear it, he headed for the fire, junk wagon and all. What a parable of the life of an alert Christian. There is no such thing as retiring him and letting him get near the call of duty.

Also, in the countdown in this zero hour, we will be courageous. Frank Laubach, missionary to the illiterate of the world, has a slogan that says, "Lift the world or lose it." Deeds of mercy, not just words is the price we must pay if we would save the world from self-destruction. J. Edgar Hoover once said, "Unless we reform our morals we shall reap the harvest of folly." We are a rich nation but we are in serious danger of sqandering ourselves into moral bankruptcy.

Jesus, in His zero hour in the Garden of Gethsemane, returned from praying to find his most faithful disciples asleep. He urged them to "watch and pray, that ye enter not into temptation" (Matthew 26:41).

We are, without a doubt, living in a zero hour. It is the countdown of civilization. Only through being alert in the face of duty and opportunity and with faith in God's power can we save our world.

God of grace and God of glory, Grant us wisdom, Grant us courage, For the facing of this hour. In Christ's Name. AMEN.

Too Much Sunshine

HOW WOULD you like to live in a place where the sun shines continually every day? A friend of mine, who has lived in South America for some time, told me of that place in northern Chile. There is too much sunshine. It never rains; therefore, nothing will grow there.

A farmer friend of mine, who has made a success in his chosen field, says that it takes all kinds of weather to make good farming. He goes on to say, "It is the timing of this weather that pleases or displeases us." As in the successful production of the soil, so it is in the growth of the soul. All sunshine does not produce strong character. The winds of adversity do not weaken, but rather strengthens our character.

Someone has suggested that John Bunyan might not have written *Pilgrim's Progress* had he not have had the experience of being in prison. Paul the apostle, might not have been the man he was had it not been for his "thorn in the flesh." His hope was for sunshine every day, but God permitted the thorns to test him. Paul's final decision was that he had learned that God's grace was sufficient for every trial.

No words were ever more true than, "smooth seas do not make a good sailor." Oftentimes too much prosperity causes one to trust to their own self-sufficiency. It is when the storms come and it seems that our boat is about to sink, that we realize that we need the Captain of our soul who cannot be defeated.

The 1965 tornadoes that struck our part of northern Indiana on Palm Sunday brought destruction that will leave its scars for years to come. I talked with a man in our hospital who had lost everything he had; house, personal belongings, and worst of all, his companion of forty-eight years.

Everything? Not quite, so he said. As I held his hand that day, I felt the grasp of determined faith. With tears in his eyes he said, "I do not blame God for this calamity that has come upon me. I am only thankful that in times like these I have one like

140

Him that will stand by me." The question that faces us today is not, will we escape the adversities of life? Rather, how will we face those storms that are sure to come our way?

In the Old Testament we read of a prosperous farmer by the name of Job. The sunshine of life had never shone brighter upon any man than it had for Job. He had rich lands, flocks, houses, and family. Then destruction came. All was taken from him. There was a great time of testing for Job but the story ends by telling us that his faith prevailed and we read where, "The Lord blessed the latter end of Job's life more than his beginning" (Job 42:12).

We do well to be grateful for the sunshine of life, but we will also do well to accept the storms. In all of this, God works together with us to bring good out of what might be chaos.

Dear Lord, we believe that You know what is best for us. We know that You will never let anything defeat us if we will but trust You. Help us to have the courage to trust Thee, Lord. AMEN.

The World Of Change

THE LEAVES of the trees of the Vermont mountainside were aflame with autumn colors as we drove the scenic, winding roads of that New England countryside.

The beauty of it all was inspiring and exciting. But, it also suggested change. Winter's snow had already come to some of the highest peaks. Fodder shocks, with yellow pumpkins scattered here and there, added color to the small plots nestled in the valleys.

All of this reminds one that the changing seasons come not only to nature, but to the physical, scientific, and even to religious experiences. It was Shakespeare who said that in this world of change naught which comes stays, and naught which goes is lost.

Change, in its entirety, has not always been easy for many of us to accept. There are, however, many changes which most of us welcome, especially when they contribute to the advancement and good of mankind.

Those who have advocated change have often been called rebels or radicals. Not all of the changes that some of the so-called rebels or radicals have advocated have been good, nor have they all been bad.

Some even called Jesus a rebel and a radical. The changes that He taught and exemplified were thought by many, of His day, as impossible and even blasphemy.

Once He said, "Ye have heard that it hath been said, an eye for an eye and a tooth for a tooth. But, I say unto you, that ye resist not evil; but whosoever shall smite thee on one cheek, turn to him the other also" (Matthew 5:38-39). Thus, the Master taught the change from hate and unforgiveness to love, forgetting and forgiving.

There are certain basic standards of faith that must never change. But, fulfilling those standards, such as going the second mile, going beyond that which we have been asked to do; these were the changes that Jesus championed. This Master of life came to change words to deeds. Creeds are fine only when they are put into practice.

The experience of the past can be good seed for the future. We need the wisdom of the past. We, likewise, should not repress the hopes of youth and the future. We may be disappointed in the change that some of the youth of our day are advocating. There are, however, responsible dedicated youth who have something to say to our day.

Regardless of age we all need the wisdom of God in this day of change. We need to remember the changless truth that God is and will always be. He is the same yesterday, today, and forever.

O God, change and decay in all around I see; O Thou who changest not, abide with me. In Jesus' Name we pray. AMEN.

The Lord Made It So

IT WAS raining hard as I came to my little country church, that Sunday morning, many years ago. As I entered the church and walked toward the front, I paused to greet Aunt Jane Martin. In the course of my greeting I said, "Aunt Jane, isn't this a terrible morning?"

Looking up with a smile, Aunt Jane responded, "The Lord made it so." I shall never forget her words and their meaning. What God has made is always good if we will but accept it.

That morning I changed my text and sermon. Speaking to myself as well as to the others, I quoted the following words, "This is the day which the Lord hath made; we will rejoice and be glad in it" (Psalm 118:24).

As I thought of Aunt Jane's words and the words of the Psalm writer, I concluded that they were very much in agreement. I had not made the day, God had made it. The past summer had been hopelessly dry after a wet, cool spring. The fall rains had now come and the wheat would get a good start before winter would set in, we were forsaken not. The Lord made it so, we will rejoice in it.

Can we rejoice in the face of disaster? Do we have anything for which to be thankful? The early Pilgrim fathers did. Sickness and death had cruelly depleted their numbers. They were disheartened but God had given them a good crop of corn. They were fearful of what the Indians might do to their remaining numbers, but they discovered that there were friendly Indians who came to their aid. These determined, dedicated Pilgrims, with a faith in God, planted firm foundations and the little settlement grew to become a great nation.

Yes, we have become a great nation. But we shall remain great only as we remember from whence we have come, by Whom we have been blessed, and for what future purpose we have been prepared. "This is the day which the Lord hath made."

It is not a day to squander our blessings, but rather to invest them for the betterment of those who will follow after us. No nation can remain materially strong which does not strive to become morally alert.

No words are more familiar or in keeping at this season of the year than, "Blessed is the nation whose God is the Lord; and the people whom He hath chosen for His inheritance" (Psalm 33:12).

Every nation of the past that squandered its opportunities, lowered its ideals and dissipated its morals, went down to defeat. Happy is the nation who continues to place their trust in the mercy and justice of God.

As a people and a nation, we have much for which to be thankful. As we pause to express our thanks to God for His goodenss, we will do well to rededicate ourselves to the tasks and hopes that lie before us.

Lord, we are grateful for Thy mercies that has helped to make of us a great nation. Help us that we might be good citizens of Thy Kingdom that we might be better Americans. AMEN.

The Urgency Of Mending

ONE OF the early childhood recollections I have of my father was seeing him, on a rainy day, working over his shoe last. Keeping the shoes of a family of eight children, especially five boys, in repair was quite an undertaking.

Leather, or the money to buy it, was not always plentiful. Many a worn or ill-fitting horse collar was cut in pieces by my father to make half soles to keep our shoes in repair. O. M. Jennings' name could honestly have been O. "Mender" Jennings, for he took his mending seriously, whether it was shoes, tools, line fences, or morals.

We should and do spend much of our time mending or repairing. This is true not only in the material, but the physical, mental, and spiritual. Mending is not time wasted. A man of wisdom once observed that we should never become so busy sawing wood that we fail to take time to sharpen the saw.

Paul, the apostle, loved Timothy as though he were his own son. He had high hopes for Timothy and was continually encouraging and directing him. Paul wanted Timothy to be ever alert that he might be prepared for the opportunities ahead of him.

In the course of one of Paul's letters to Timothy, he counseled him to "Study to show thyself approved unto God, a workman that needeth not to be ashamed, rightly dividing the word of God" (II Timothy 2:15).

It was Phillips Brooks, famous pastor of another era, that said to his congregation, one Sunday morning, "Just as those humble fishermen of long ago felt it necessary to keep their nets in repair, so do each of us need to spend time mending our spiritual nets."

Among the many folk who encouraged me, as a young pastor, was a quiet, motherly, kind woman. When she prayed she always used a phrase that became quite familiar. She would say, "Lord, help us to take our places and stand in the gaps and help make up the hedges that reach from earth to heaven."

This good woman's prayer was Biblical. Israel's moral fences were badly in need of repair. The word of God came to Ezekiel saying, "I sought for a man among you that should make up the hedges and stand in the gap before me for the land, that I should not destroy it: but I found none" (Ezekiel 22:30).

We can stand in the gaps and assist in making up the hedges by helping to heal the hurts, straighten out misunderstandings and mending the hedges of peace between individuals, races, and nations. We can do this by interceding between man and God and person to person.

When we are diligent concerning the mending of our own spiritual inadequacies, we will be better able to assist others in their needs.

Father in Heaven, help us that we may feel the urgency of keeping our mending done that we may be able to help others with theirs. AMEN.

The Extra Lift

WE HAVE two clocks in our home. Both of them seem like members of the family. One of them stands on the floor. It has been standing there since the first year we were married. The other was purchased by my father the first year he and my mother were married.

Both of these clocks are called eight day clocks. I have discovered, however, that they seem to grow weary before the week is past. I have found that the Saturday night winding keeps them going but the Wednesday night winding, also, gives them an extra lift and they sound happier as they tick away the time. They strike the hour with more vigor.

I have discovered that most of the people I have learned to know, including myself, are quite like our clocks. Some get just enough exercise, vitamins, and religion just to keep them going. The extra lift is what most of us need.

Uncle Orlo used to say that some folk had just enough religion to make them miserable, but not enough to make them happy.

It takes very little of the necessities of life for one to exist. However, our lives to be lived to the fullest, needs more than a mere existence.

In the Sermon on the Mount, Jesus, speaking to those gathered around Him said, "Blessed are they which do hunger and thirst after righteousness: for they shall be filled" (Matthew 5:6). That is to say that they shall have that extra lift.

The Master also said, "I am come that they might have life and that they might have it more abundantly" (John 10:10). Sabbath worship was important but this Master of life was trying to help the people of His day to see that abundant living came from going out and putting into practice what they learned on the Sabbath. It was, and is, going the second mile that gives one the extra lift.

Private devotions and prayer once a day gives one a lift but Paul, the apostle, once wrote, "Pray without ceasing." This gives one the extra lift.

Abundant living, peace of mind, confidence in the future, and many more like unto these is the longing of this age. With frustrations, fears, hates, and mistrust of one another on all sides of us, we find that we must have something to which we can cling.

It may sound old-fashioned, but the new ideas of leaving God out and trying our own way has already failed. Why not confess that we have failed, and will continue to do so, until we turn back to the God of our fathers.

If keeping a full spring in the clock is important, how much more so a full spring in the spirit. Don't forget to give your spiritual clock the extra lift. It will pay good dividends.

Help us, Lord, when our spirits are low to remember that you are willing and able to give us that extra lift for the day. AMEN.

True Greatness

HOW DOES one attain the status of greatness? What are the marks of greatness? Rich in material possessions? Well educated? A leader among men? Is true greatness found in becoming famous in the world of entertainment, science, or politics? Some of these things may be found in one who has attained greatness, but this is not the true image of greatness.

A truly great man is not one who can only command service, but he who can render it. Luke, the Gospel writer, tells us that, on one occasion, there was an argument, among the disciples of Jesus, as to which one of them should be thought of as the greatest. Jesus gave them the true definition of greatness. ". . . he that is greatest among you, let him be the younger; and he that is chief, as one who doth serve . . ." (Luke 22:26)

Phillips Brooks, who attained greatness as a minister of another generation, influenced many people by his words of wisdom. He once observed, "No man has come to true greatness who has not felt that his life belongs to others, and that what God gives him he gives him for mankind." Jesus taught, by precept and example, that greatness is found in one whose life is spent in serving others. It is found in one who does not think how much this may profit me but what it may do for someone less fortunate.

Florence Nightengale is remembered for her leadership and endowment in the field of hospitals and nursing. She is remembered best for her untiring ministering as a nurse to the soldiers of the Crimean War. She was asked for the secret of her unending, fruitful life. She answered, "I work very hard and let the Lord Jesus have all there is in me." She was great in her spirit of capable, humble service to others.

True greatness is often found in deepest humility. It is not how much we have, but how much we give. Not, alone, what we do, but what we are. Aunt Pearl was always a loveable, sincere, concerned person. She was always interested in what she could do for others. We visited with this good woman in Florida recently. She has now reached the coveted age of ninety-two. She is unable to get around and do for others in the way she once did. But she is still serving. She spends much of her time writing letters to those of all ages, whom she feels needs a word of encouragement. She doesn't have much of this world's goods, but she is rich in heavenly endowments.

There are many of us who will never be known to grace the pages of "the greats." We may never command the attention of the world of great leadership. We can, however, remember that the greatest Master of all was willing to be the servant of all. If we follow in His train, we can then leave the outcome to eternity.

O Thou who became great by being humble, help us to pattern our lives after Thee. AMEN.

Treasures

IT WAS said of a once famous actress, "Her jewels were her life." This actress, in her own words said, "For ten years my jewels were such a comfort to me. I bought them carefully as a proof that I would never be poor again. Then one night I was robbed. Five hundred thousand dollars worth of jewels were gone forever."

That which would be a treasure to one might be a burden to another. It all depends on ones sense of values. The estimate of a treasure should not be based, alone, on its market value, or the pleasure for the present it gives the possessor. Its appraisal should also be based on the eternal peace of mind this possession brings one.

So much of the material is so uncertain. As someone has said, it is like a handful of sand that slips through your fingers and is gone. A prophet in the Old Testament gives good advice when he says, "Wherefore, do you spend money for that which is not bread? And your labor for that which satisfieth not? Hearken diligently unto me and eat that which is good and let your soul delight itself in fatness" (Isaiah 55:2).

What is the best investment to assure security? Jesus cautioned His listeners by saying, "Lay not up for yourselves treasures on earth where moth and rust doth corrupt and thieves break through and steal, but rather lay up treasures in heaven where moth and rust cannot destroy and thieves cannot break through nor steal" (Matthew 6:19-20).

Some of the treasures of life are priceless, yet can be had by each of us for the asking. There is the beauty of the sunset, the starlit night, the song of the bird, and the touch of the hand of love upon us. These are the kind of treasures that bring heaven down to earth. These may be ours and heaven too. These are the kind of treasures that no one can take from us.

One of the treasures in which we may invest for a good return is the treasure of service. The dividends from investing our lives for the sake of others are eternal.

The treasures of memory is priceless. A wise man once said that a thief may steal one's earthly possessions but only man, himself, can dissipate his memories. Man cannot live upon his memories but those memories can add much to his state of mind.

This leads us to say that one of the most valuable treasures is peace of mind. When Jesus was about to leave His disciples, He consoled them by saying, "Peace I leave with you, my peace I give unto you: not as the world giveth, give I unto you. Let not your heart be troubled, neither let it be afraid" (John 14:27).

Our investment in this kind of treasure, through Christ, assures us not only peace of mind here, but eternal security.

O Thou, in who's storehouse are the treasures that endure; help us to lay up the riches that are eternal. AMEN.

The Fading Art

WALKING IS, according to many heart specialists, the perfect exercise. But, walking is fast becoming a fading art in America. Uncle Orlo, my good neighbor of several years ago, once said in my hearing, "We are spending millions on buses to transport the younger generation to school, and more money on gymnasiums to give them exercise after we get them there."

That statement by Uncle Orlo may have been a little too strong. It did make me think how I used to walk the mile from our farm home to school, then run home for lunch at noon. No doubt all of this did me as much good as what I learned while in school.

The walking plow, which I would not recommend we return to, did give us opportunity for reflection and meditation, as well as the perfect exercise of walking.

Walking, however, has become an un-American activity. In our day we do not have time to walk. In our hurry we have been the losers, mentally, physically, and spiritually.

Recently, I turned to the concordance of my Bible. It was surprising how many times the word walking appears in the good Book. God walked in the cool of the evening in the Garden of Eden. Enoch walked with God. Jesus, Himself, spent three years as a walking Teacher.

The hymn writers have made much of the theme of walking. One wrote, "I walked today where Jesus walked." Another testified, "And He walks with me and He talks with me." Still another urges us to, "Walk in the light and thou shall find, Thy heart made truly His." Finally, one writer asks, "Shall I be carried to the skies on flowery beds of ease?"

I hasten to say that many are unable to walk, physically speaking. Anyway, this fading art is a parable of our day. Our spiritual limbs are our opportunities. Walking is faith in action.

What is happening to the Christian religion today? Is the practice of it really a fading art? There is nothing wrong with Christianity. The wrong is in we who represent it. A religion lives only as those who believe in it live.

In Jesus day He found much of the practice of religion only a form, not a spirit of action. The Church for which Jesus gave His life needs, as never before, believers who are willing once again to walk the paths where Jesus walked.

The need for a religion that touches every part of ones daily living, is as urgent in our world as ever. In fact, it is the only way that our world can be saved from those elements that would destroy all that is good. Jesus, once again, bids us take up our cross daily and walk with Him.

Give us courage, Lord, to walk, with faith, the paths that you choose for us. AMEN.

This Day Is Mine

BENEATH the glass top on my desk is a little poem of challenge. It was sent to me by my good friend George C. Biggar, who was for many years program director of WLS Radio, Chicago. This poem was written by his brother, H. Howard Bigger, whose home was in South Dakota.

The poem begins with, "This day is mine . . . I only hope that I can fill each precious golden hour/With deeds that help to cheer some lonely heart/I trust that somehow I may have the power/To comfort souls that may be sad/To make some fellow toiler glad/To help to bear another traveler's load/Along life's well-worn road/This day is mine."

How many times I have looked at those words and asked myself, "Am I making the most of this day that is mine? Am I wasting it or investing it? Is someone happier because I am using this day to share with them the blessings that have come to me?

I have often said that it is not how long but how well we live that counts. It is not the length of our day but the investment of it that enriches our lives and influences those around us.

This day is mine. It is a gift from God, therefore I am only a steward of it. I must give an account of how I use it. What tomorrow shall bring depends on what I do with today.

The Epistle of James, the brother of Jesus, is filled with the philosophy of living. In the fourth chapter James is speaking of the uncertainty of life. He tells us that we have no assurance of what tomorrow shall bring us. Then he says, "Whereas ye know not what shall be tomorrow. For what is your life? It is even a vapor that appeareth for a little while, and then vanisheth away. For that ye ought to say, If the Lord will, we shall live and do this or that" (James 4:14-15).

In spite of the uncertainty of tomorrow we are not to become over anxious or worry about it, for we have today. Is not this what Jesus was talking about when he implored His listeners not to be overly concerned about the material things of today and tomorrow?

One of the happiest persons I have ever known was so busy thinking of others that she seemed to forget her own problems and needs. In so doing, her own difficulties were minimized and her needs always supplied.

E. Ruben Wilberforce, minister and poet, gave himself to the neglected children and youth of his day. In his poem, "Just for Today," he has a line that says, "Lord, for tomorrow and its needs, I do not pray, Let me be kind in word and deed, Father, today." We would do well to make this our prayer and remember that, "this day is mine."

Lord, help us to live this day as though we might die tonight, and work this day as though we might live forever. AMEN.

The Greatest Of All

WHAT IS the greatest power in the world? There are many great powers. There are so many that we would not have room to list them all here. There are the powers of nature like the sun, wind, and water; the powers of the mind and strength of the body. The influence of the pen, and eloquence of the tongue. But the greatest of all is the power of love.

Love is the lubricant that keeps the machinery of life running smoothly. Love is the element of life that makes two hearts beat as one. The presence of love in the home makes it a heaven on earth, its absence can make it a hell on earth.

Sincere love helps to minimize the faults of others, wile it magnifies one another's virtues. Longfellow, the beloved American poet, once wrote, "Love gives itself; it is not bought."

The Bible is filled with many words of wisdom and inspiration. The greatest revelation is that of the power of love. The most familiar is the Love Chapter. Paul, the apostle, writing to the Christians at Corinth, says that love does not think of self; has no envy of others; rejoices in the truth rather than thinking evil. Love never fails in the times when it is needed. "And now abideth faith, hope and charity (love), these three; but the greatest of these is charity (love)" (I Corinthians 13:13).

Our gifts that we share are good, but they mean more and go farther when they are wrapped in love. The kind of love that does not measure the worthiness of the recipient of our gifts. It was Victor Hugo, French poet, who once observed that, "The greatest happiness of life is the conviction that we are loved, loved for ourselves or rather loved in spite of ourselves."

Paul, writing of this kind of love, says, "But God commendeth His love toward us, in that, while we were yet sinners, Christ died for us" (Romans 5:8). God loved us in spite of ourselves. He loved us not for what we were, alone, but what we could become with the help of His love.

Paul, who had experienced the forgiving love of God, entreats the Christians at Rome to, "Owe no man anything, but to love one another: for he that loveth another hath fulfilled the law" (Romans 13:8). We can never pay our debt of love for the way God has loved, and loves us. We can, however, continue our expression of love to one another. The love that gives itself away. The love that serves for the sake of giving, not for the sake of the returns. This, then is the greatest power. The power that makes life worth living and eternity, with peace, certain.

O Thou who art Love, help us that we may love one another as ourselves and Thee above all. AMEN.

True Acquaintanship

I HAD a letter, recently, in which the writer stated, "Even though we have never met, I feel that I am acquainted with you by reading your columns through the years." It is good to get a letter like that once in a while.

I think that it was Thomas Carlyle, English philosopher, who once wrote, "Acquaintanship is the experience of becoming friends in mind, heart, and purpose." In becoming acquainted we learn to understand one another's longings. It is like unto the hymn that says, "Our fears, our hopes, our aims are one."

At the end of three years with Jesus, His disciples had yet to really understand their Master's motives or His longings. On the night, just before He went to Gethsemane, He prayed in the presence of His disciples, "And this is life eternal that they might know Thee the only true God, and Jesus Christ whom Thou hast sent" (John 17:3).

In an anonymous letter, sometime back, the writer said, "I doubt if you have ever led anyone to Christ . . . " I am not attempting, here, to answer criticism nor boast of victories. I can only say that the highest and warmest moments of my life have been when I have seen those, with whom I had spoken and prayed, come to know Jesus as their Saviour and become acquainted with Him.

The idea for the general theme for this column "Thoughts For Better Living," came to me many years ago. My foremost "thought" through all of these years, has been that I might say something that would make it easier for someone to do right and harder for them to do wrong. It has always been my prayer that I might help to lift a burden that was too heavy to bear alone, by helping that one to become acquainted with the great Burden Bearer, Jesus of Nazareth. Whether, in a small way, I have succeeded time and eternity will tell.

On July 25, 1925 my childhood sweetheart and I were married. They have been good years. God has blessed us in spite of the many blunders we have made. but, the latter years have even been better than the former. Maybe it is because we have become better acquainted and learned to know better each other's strength and weakness and that unfailing love.

So it has been, for me, in the Christian Way. As a lad of fifteen I first came to Christ. I have made many mistakes and have had to come to Him many times to ask forgiveness. Of this I am sure, the latter days have been, by far, the best. I am certain that it is because I have become better acquainted with God through Christ and have learned that His way is always best.

There is a bit of encouragement and inspiration in the words, "And Enoch walked with God" (Genesis 5:29). Enoch walked with God because he learned to go God's way. Their acquaintanship was mutual. Theirs was an eternal walk. Acquaintanship with God comes from undivided fellowship and service with Jesus as Lord and Master.

Help us, O God, to so submit our lives unto you, that we might better know your will for us. AMEN.

The Benefits Of Praising

PRAISE CAN be a dangerous word or a blessing, it all depends on whether it is being given or received. One should give praise sincerely and joyfully, but receive it with humility. An attitude of praise lightens the tasks of each day and helps to bring peaceful rest each night.

A young man, in his early forties, was seriously ill. I stopped at his bedside, in the hospital, each day. His wife and faithful companion was with him almost continually. We prayed daily for his recovery through God's will.

One day this young husband looked up into the face of his wife and said with courage, "Donna, we should praise God more and plead with Him less." In those last days, of that brave man's life, he taught each of us a lesson.

One of the shortest, yet meaningful Psalms, says, "O praise the Lord, all ye nations; praise Him all ye people. For His merciful kindness is great toward us; and the truth of the Lord endureth forever. Praise ye the Lord" (Psalm 117).

A translation of this Psalm might read, "Think about all that you can praise God for and be glad about it." Praising, with gladness, brings a greater joy to ourselves as well as others. Someone has observed that if you can't praise God for what you have received, praise Him for what you have escaped.

The Acts of the Apostles tells of Paul and Silas, those two early Christian missionaries, being placed in prison. Not only were they placed in prison, but with their feet in stocks. "And at midnight Paul and Silas prayed and sang praises unto God; and the prisoners heard them" (Acts 16:25). These courageous men were praising God in the presence of an unhappy situation.

Praising God at midnight, when all is darkness and discouraging, takes courage and grace. In so doing, others are encouraged and take heart.

Some of the folk who have encouraged me most through the years have been those who have lived and served with a spirit of praise in their lives, even though they seemed to have little for which to be thankful.

Jennifer Lynn Clish, five-years-old, died in her mother's arms in a hospital emergency room one night recently. Only hours before, Jennifer seemed to be in normal health. As I counseled with the mother and father the following morning, the brave mother spoke with tears in her eyes yet courage in her voice, "We can't understand it now, but I believe that God will get good from this for us in the future." This mother and father were praising God from the ashes of despair. This is the kind of praise that comes from complete dedication to God. There are many others like them.

Father in Heaven, help us to have the spirit of praise in our hearts even in the presence of sorrow. AMEN.

Using What We Have

"IT IS NOT how much or how little we have, but rather what we do with what we have, that counts." Those words, spoken by a minister of my youth, helped me to decide on my life's work.

Most of us face the challenge of life with a feeling of inadequacy. We hesitate to accept certain responsibilities because of the feeling of our limitations, instead of our abilities. It is good, to a certain extent that we do so. But, in so doing, we forget the unseen power that makes the difference between failure and achievement.

Moses, the great leader and law giver of the tribe of Israel, felt his inadequacy when God called him to this place of responsibility. Moses, feeling that he was not capable, pled with God to be excused. One question God asked Moses was, " . . . what is that in thine hand?" (Exodus 4:2). The demonstration of God's power on this occasion was all that was needed to prove to Moses that God would stand by him.

It is surprising what God can do with a little talent and one who is willing to use it.

I once called upon a young father to teach a Sunday School class of boys. His excuse was that he was not well enough educated to be a teacher. I responded by saying, "Jack, you have faith in God and you have shown that you love boys. That's enough to start with." This young father was willing to start. He became one of the best teachers that class ever had. It is not always our ability but our pliability that makes the difference.

Dorcas, of New Testament days, was a shining example of doing what one can with what one has, with love. They said of her, ". . . this woman was full of good works, and almsdeeds which she did" (Acts 9:36). She went about doing good. It was not alone the garments she made for the poor, but the spirit in which she served that endeared her to all who knew her. The work we do with our hands is made more valuable when our hands are dedicated in love.

Dr. Albert Schweitzer, medical missionary, is known for his many humanitarian accomplishments, as well as his interpretation of Bach on the organ. He was unique in his accomplishments and dedication.

On one of his rare visits to London from his work in Africa, Dr. Schweitzer was addressing a class of medical students. At the conclusion of his address, he held up his hands and said, "Gentlemen, only as these are dedicated to God, can I continue to do the work to which God has called me." Then he said, "My young friends, look at your hands. Dedicate them as well as your heart to your calling and to God." Using what we have now, in the Master's name. This is all that we can do. It will be enough.

Dear Lord, we lay our talents, great or small, at Thy feet. Use them and us in whatever way Thou art able to do. We will praise Thee. AMEN.

Unanswered Prayer?

"WHY DO many of our prayers go unanswered?" inquired a young mother recently. This mother of growing children wrote that she believed in prayer and knew that many times prayer had changed things for her. "Still," she said, "there are times when my prayers do not seem to be answered."

Is it true that some of our prayers do go unanswered? It may seem that way at times, yet I believe that God hears and answers every prayer of sincere faith. The answer may be "yes" or "no" or "not yet," but He answers.

Even the Bible contains records of prayers that seemed unavailing. One occasion was of Jesus praying to His Heavenly Father in Gethsemane. Here He prayed, "O my Father, if it be possible, let this cup pass from Me: nevertheless, not as I will, but as Thou wilt" (Matthew 26:39). Three times that memorable night He prayed this prayer, but for the salvation of the world He had to drink the bitter cup.

Paul, the apostle, tells how there was laid upon him "a thorn in the flesh." He implored the Lord three times that it might depart from him. The answer to his prayer was, "My grace is sufficient for thee: for my strength is made perfect in weakness" (II Corinthians 12:9). When it seems that the response to our prayers is negative, the answer is that God knows a better way. There are two ways to lighten a burden: one is to remove it and the other is to give strength to bear it. Often the latter makes us the stronger person.

Most of us parents are unable, for our children's present and future good, to always say "yes" to their every wish. We would rather say "yes" but we realize that "no" or "not yet" is the best for them.

Prayers that seem to be unanswered, because we do not receive what we ask for, are really answered for our own good. Often, in my own life, God has closed one door of my choosing that He might open another for a greater opportunity.

Helen Keller, American writer and lecturer, at the age of nineteen months had a severe illness that deprived her of both her sight and her hearing. Through the patient, capable hands of Anne Sullivan, Helen Keller overcame her handicaps. Later in her life she voiced her faith and courage by saying, "I thank God for my handicaps, they have helped me to find my work and God."

We often become discouraged with some experience in life, because the outcome was not as we had hoped and prayed. At such times it is well for us to remember that God is still working for our good. His strength is made perfect in our weakness. He hears our prayers. He knows what the answer should be. He will see us through.

Dear Lord, help that on who feels that their prayers go unanswered. Help each of us to trust Thee in the most difficult time, that we may feel Thy presence at all times. AMEN.

Use It Or Lose It

"THE TIME of life is short. To live it basely twere too long." Thus wrote William Shakespeare, English poet, many years ago. This truth still has meaning for us today.

Too often man spends his life reasoning on the past, complaining of the present and trembling for the future. It is good for us to remember that we have only one body. We should use it sensibly. We have only one life, we should invest it wisely.

Jesus, talking with His disciples one day said, "For unto everyone who hath, shall be given, and he shall have abundance; but from him that hath not shall be taken away even that which he hath" (Matthew 25:29).

The above is not a formula on how to make a fortune in life, but rather how to keep from making life a misfortune.

In the familiar parable of the talents, Jesus gives, not only to the disciples but to each of us today, a real truth. Each of us have been given certain talents. If we use them they will increase in value. If we fail to use them we will lose them. We know how true this is in the physical and material. Our physical being, our talents, and abilities are improved by exercise. They grow rusty or are wasted through laziness or fear.

It is said that a winner of major golf tournaments retired to his ranch. Later, he was no competition, all because he had given up his daily practices.

It was Philip Brooks, famous minister of long ago, who said, "Do not pray for easy lives. Pray to be strong men. Do not pray for tasks equal to your powers, but pray for powers equal to your tasks."

Use it or lose it is true in the realm of the spiritual also. The parabe of the talents is really a lesson on spiritual increase or moral drought. The Bible contains many stories of those who grew spiritually because they exercised their faith.

Paul, the apostle, speaks about faith without works being dead. He also urges exercising unto Godliness.

It was said of a widow who was left with five children to rear and a small farm to manage, "She was a power in prayer." They said this of her because she practiced prayer, in word, faith, and deed each day. Is it any wonder that every one of her children invested their lives in the service of others.

I was asked to conduct the funeral of a physician who had given many years of his life in his community. He was a great doctor. Someone said of him, "He was a great doctor for he not only knew how to use his hands, but also his heart."

Most of us have found that in any field of endeavor, the only way to get the most out of life is to invest all we have into it. Use it or lose it.

O God, we remember that little is much if Thou art in it. We pray that Thou wouldst be in all we are and have that we might not lose it but use it for Thy glory. AMEN.

Urgency Of Sharing

I SHALL NOT pass through this world but once. Any good, therefore, that I can show to any human being, let me do it now. Let me not defer nor neglect it, for I shall not pass this way again.

No one seems to know, for certain, who gave us the above words, when or why. We do not know that those words have taken a firm hold on the minds of many, many people down through the years. The thought in them has helped many of us to be a little kinder, to show more charity and to share one another's burdens. They remind us that life is not to be lived for ourselves alone. It is urgent, for we shall not pass this way again.

No words of admonition were ever more true than those given by Paul, the apostle, when he wrote to the Galations saying, "Bear ye one another's burdens and so fulfill the law of Christ" (Galatians 6:2).

There is an old song, written by Mrs. Frank Breck, that we used to sing in our Sunday School days. A part of it says, "Look all around you, find someone in need, Help somebody today! Tho' it be little a neighborly deed, Help somebody today."

Sharing our hopes with others gives encouragement to keep hope alive when there seems to be so little hope. When hope is gone, all is gone. Keep it alive and all worthwhile things are possible.

Someone has interpreted Paul's words to read, "We should help carry one another's burdens, and in this way you will obey the law of Christ." Visit the sick. Feed the hungry. Have concern for those in prison. There are so many kinds of prisons. Fulfill the law of Christ.

What is the law of Christ? It is the law of love. The Master gave example when He said, "Whatsoever ye would that men should do to you, do ye even so to them" (Matthew 7:12).

What is our goal in life? Getting rid of burdens and crosses? Oten times the things that hold you down are the things that hold you up. Some of our burdens and our crosses help to keep us humble and looking up. Many have learned to carry their crosses with a smile. In so doing they help others to bear theirs.

Above all, helping others to know that we have Jesus who helps to lighten our burdens, but does not take them all away. Paul learned this when he prayed for the "thorn in the flesh" to be removed. It was then that Christ spoke to him saying, ". . . . My grace is sufficient for thee: for my strength is made perfect in weakness . . . " (II Corinthians 12:9)

God many times works through us when we go in His name to help bear one another's burdens. The need of sharing is urgent, for we shall not pass this way again.

Lord God, keep us ever mindful that we have only one life to live. Help us, to go in Thy name to share it with others. AMEN.

Vigilance

SEVERAL YEARS ago, while eating in a restaurant in Mitchell, South Dakota, I noticed an interesting sign on the wall above the cash register. On that little plaque I read, "If you don't tend to your business, the sheriff will."

Tending to our business surely means being vigilant or careful about or responsibilities and opportunities. This holds true in every avenue of life.

Thomas Jefferson, third president of the United States, once said, "Eternal vigilance is the price of liberty." We know that this has been true as far as our beloved nation is concerned. This, likewise, is the price of personal, physical, and spiritual liberty.

Jesus taught the importance of being vigilant. In one of His parables on the Kingdom of Heaven, He likens the Kingdom to a man who sowed good seed in his field. "While men slept," Jesus said, "his enemy came and sowed tares among the wheat, and went his way."

Jesus did not condemn the men for sleeping. On the other hand, He was trying to impress upon His hearers that it is while we sleep that the enemy makes his attack.

The opposite of vigilance is apathy. Nothing is more dangerous for the future welfare of our generation than the attitude of indifference.

My father had no great love for weeds. I was sure that I was allergic to them. That was in the days when they knew little about allergy. Anyway, on the farm of my childhood, in the fields where the best corn grew, there likewise were the most prolific weeds.

In that day the hoe was the weeds' worst enemy. My father taught us that we were in the business of growing corn, not weeds. "Get after the weeds early and stay with them to give the corn a chance," urged my father.

I enjoyed the lemonade during the rest periods more than using the hoe. However, as I think of those backbreaking days I also remember the little fishing trips after the corn was laid by. What a parable this has been in my life.

The satisfaction of a life well lived can only come to those who, with all diligence, have been careful with their lot in life.

Paul, the apostle, knew that vigilance was important to a fruitful life. Writing to Timothy, whom he called his son in the spirit, he said, "Stir up the gift of God, which is in thee . . . " (II Timothy 1:6)

Each of us has been endowed with certain God given talents. First we must discover them. Secondly, we should evaluate them. Thirdly, we must use them. Only by investing them with vigilance will we profit by these gifts.

The business of living is a daily affair. It is a trust from God. Give it our best and the best comes back to us.

Help us, O God, that we may keep alive the inspiration that comes from Thee, that we may ever be mindful of the life before us. AMEN.

Vacant Lots

BETWEEN my house and the office there are several vacant lots. I am reminded, as I pass them, that most vacant lots are invitations for those who pass by to discard trash upon them. No one is too concerned about a vacant lot.

Life is much like that. A vacant, unconcerned mind is an invitation for someone to drop trash in it. I wonder if this is somewhat like the writer of Proverbs had in mind when he wrote, "Keep thy heart with all diligence; for out of it are the issues of life" (Proverbs 4:23).

As a boy at home on the farm, one of the first chores in the spring was getting the breaking plow going. The plow did not do its work well until we were able to scour the plow share. The idleness of the winter had to be cleaned until the plow shone like a mirror.

The mind is somewhat like the old plow. Neglect is the rust of the soul that corrodes through all our best resolves. The man who procrastinates struggles with ruin. This is as true of the soul as it is of the soil.

Neglect is a type of erosion. Like the neglected vacant lot, it is found also in human living. There are those who neglect to take care of the only body they will ever have. There are those who neglect the opportunities of nurturing Christian character, as well as those who fail to see the danger in tampering with our nation's freedoms. The result of our neglect is always devastating.

I have often studied the life of Peter, one of the disciples of Jesus. Big, blundering, yet warm hearted Peter, in many ways was much like many of us. He would have been considered hopeless by many. Not so with Jesus.

It must have been a challenge to the Master to see what He could do with this big fisherman. When Peter finally let go and let God take control, he became the great fisherman of men that Jesus knew he could be.

We have all known men like Peter. One of those, whom I learned to know, was much like that wave of the sea. Even his family had given up hope of ever seeing him change his way of living. Through prayer and sincere concern, God reached him. I was grateful for having had a small part in seeing a life of neglect changed to one of concern.

Someone once said that Peter was a diamond in the rough, but with great possibilities. We are all human and if neglected to go our own way will end up in despair. However, there is a little of the diamond in all of us, possibilities that God sees. Willing to be rescued, we too can "blossom like the rose" and become the kind of person we had always hoped we might be.

God of mercy and love, cleanse us from our impurities of heart that we might be better used of Thee. AMEN.

Wayside Pulpits

TWO TWELVE-year-old boys were sent by their scout leader on a tour of field, woods and stream. They were to gone one hour. Upon their return they were to report what they had seen.

Before the hour was up one boy returned saying that he had noticed nothing out of the ordinary along the way. "Just the same old, usual things," he reported.

The second boy came back at the end of the hour with an enthusiastic account. To his report he exclaimed, "The white cloud formations were never more beautiful, and they made the sky seem bluer than ever." He reported that he had watched a mother bird as she fed her babies. He said that the fish in the brook "glistened like silver in the sun as the water, seeking its way over the rocks was like music in his ears."

The first boy lived within himself and missed the adventure about him. The second made life an adventure and the scenes around him became wayside pulpits.

Recently I stopped at a nursery to choose some shrubbery. The nurseryman, as he walked amongst his trees, spoke with feeling in his voice as he said, "Trees are my friends, not just my business. They are God's creation."

God is trying to say something from these wayside pulpits. If we listen we will be richer, if we do not we will be the loser.

The writer of the Psalms must have been a lover of nature. God seemed to have spoken to him often as he roamed the hills and walked by the rivers. At one time he said, "The earth is full of the goodness of the Lord" (Psalm 33:5).

Jesus worshiped faithfully in the temple but He also felt His Heavenly Father near in the great out of doors. He even saw sermons in the lilies of the field. As He pointed them out to His followers He said, "Consider the lilies of the field, how they grow; they toil not neither do they spin; and yet I say unto you, that even Solomon in all his glory was not arrayed like one of these" (Matthew 6:28-29). From the lilies Jesus gave the lesson of not becoming over anxious about the things of life.

Moses found a wayside pulpit at the burning bush. He must have thought to himself, "This is a strange sight. I've walked through these mountains many times but have never seen anything like this." Turning aside to see, he paused to listen and God spoke to him.

A day never passes, a trip is seldom made but what some inspiration comes to me from along the way. An odd circumstance from nature or a word from someone, these make up my wayside pulpits.

There is a burning bush or a wayside pulpit for each one of us, if we keep our eyes open, our minds alert, and our hearts in tune with God and His world about us.

O God, help us not to forget that this is your world, may we be mindful of Thy voice speaking to us in all Thy creation around us. AMEN.

Who Cares?

SEVERAL YEARS ago a young man, just entering high school, came to my study. He had a friendly personality, a fine famiy background and every promise of a success-ful future. Like many others of his age he had been overcome by temptation and found himself not only in trouble in the community, but with the law.

As I talked with him he turned to me, with tears in his eyes, and said, "Who cares what happens to me, anyway?" I answered, "Jack, your parents care, your friends care, I care, and above all God cares what happens to you."

I along, with his teachers and parents, counseled with him through those uncertain years. A few days ago I received a letter from him. He had made good. He had proven that if one discouraged, in trouble, and about ready to give up, can only be made to realize that someone cares, life can take on new meaning.

Dr. Merton Rice was pastor of Metropolitan Methodist Church, Detroit, for over thirty years. Near the end of his ministry he suffered a heart condition which confined him to his home and for many weeks. When he passed away there was found on his study desk the words, "What a Heavenly Father we have; He even attends the funeral of the sparrows."

Dr. Rice never had the opportunity of preaching that sermon. If he could have, no doubt his subject would have been, "God cares." His text, without a doubt, would have been taken from St. Luke's Gospel, the twelfth chapter which reads, "Are not five sparrows sold for two farthings, and not one of them is forgotten before God? But even the very hairs of your head are numbered. Fear not therefore; ye are of more value than many sparrows" (Luke 12:6-7).

The fact that Jesus took time to inform His hearers that, not one sparrow is forgotten by God, certainly makes us feel like saying, "What a wonderful Heavenly Father we have; He even attends the funeral of the sparrows."

It oftens seems, these days, that we have lost much of the personal concern for others. Much of the relief is left to agencies, and these are good. But, at times, when we realize that we need more than material assistance, it is good just to know that somebody cares what happens to us.

I am most grateful for those who have let me know down through the years that they cared for me and was concerned about me. All about us there are those who are asking, "Who cares what happens to me?" We can bring to them renewed faith in humanity and God, as well as courage for themselves. We can help them to see, by our concern, that we care, and above all, God cares.

Our Father, who notes the sparrow's fall, help us not to forget that You care what happens to us. Thank you for caring. Through Christ we pray. AMEN.

Waiting On God

THERE ARE times in the lives of each of us when we feel driven to a quiet place of meditation. I call it prayer. Mohandas K. Gandhi, dedicated leader of India, and a martyr to his ideals, spoke of it as "waiting for God to speak to me."

Even Jesus felt the need of a quiet place. He wanted to talk to His Heavenly Father, but He also wanted His Heavenly Father to talk to Him. Even those who knew Jesus best never knew how much time He spent in fellowship with God.

Fellowship may be talking with one another, but it is more than that. When we are in the presence of one whom we love, fellowship can be quiet and meaningful.

Someone, long ago, said that prayer was pulling the bell rope of heaven, then waiting for the answer. It was Jean Inglow, author, who said, "I have lived to thank God that all of my prayers have not been answered." Most of us have prayed and pleaded with God for certain things. But, only in our waiting have we discovered that God knew what was best.

Recently, I learned to love and respect a young man whose faith did not waiver, even though he was desperately ill. One day he said that he felt we should beseech God less and prasie Him more. This young man had learned the secret of quiet confidence and waiting on God.

Great words of wisdom come from a wise prophet by the name of Isaiah. I have often received a great deal of comfort and encouragement from the words, "They that wait upon the Lord shall renew their strength; they shall mount up with wings as eagles; they shall run and not be weary; and they shall walk and not faint" (Isaiah 40:31).

In these trying days when man's confidence is being tried, I am not anxious about God and His plans. I am concerned that we poor human beings cannot see that long before we were here God was here. Long after we are gone, God will still be on the scene.

We will do well to praise Him for what He has already done, then to lay our case before Him, wait with patience and faith for His verdict. If we do this our strength will be renewed and we shall, "walk and not faint."

I see hope for the future if we, in our day, make prayer a wholesome, natural part of our lives. If we too, "wait for God to speak to us." Then act upon our faith, that is, put feet under our prayers.

Lord, who in Thy wise providence knoweth what is best for us, help us to have the faith to pray, 'Lord we thank Thee for what you will do for us and through us this day.' AMEN.

Why Should I Pray?

GOD'S LOVE IS JESUS

"WHY SHOULD I pray? I'm healthy, strong, and capable of looking after myself." These were the words I received from a young business man recently. It made me stop and consider, again, why we pray or do not pray.

I was talking one day with a youth group at camp, on family devotional prayers. A fourteen-year-old farm boy exclaimed, "We don't have family prayers at our house and nothing has ever happened to us yet."

Do we pray because we are incapable of doing things for ourselves? Is prayer a special kind of protection against calamity?

My father, during his active years, owned several farms. Following the purchase of each farm he would immediately call the lightening rod salesman. Each barn and house had to have rods on them. This, he felt, was good protection.

Prayer may be good protection. It protects us from over-confidence and self-sufficiency. But lightening rod prayers are not enough.

James Montgomery, the poet, has said that prayer is the soul's sincere desire, un-uttered or expressed; the motion of a hidden fire that trembles in the breast.

Prayer changes things. Those words are familiar to most of us and many of us have found them to be true. Prayer may not change God's plan but it most certainly has changed man's attitude.

Kagawa, one of the great Christians of the Orient, has said that prayer is surrender. In true praying, aspiration and submission are effective ingredients. The former cannot be realized without the latter.

In the prayer Jesus taught His disciples, both aspiration and submission are illustrated. In the Garden of Gethsemane, Jesus concluded His prayer with submission and came away at peace with His Heavenly Father and Himself.

Someone asked D. L. Moody, famous evangelist of years gone by, if God answers every prayer. Mr. Moody replies, "Yes, God answers every prayer. Sometimes His answer to many of our prayers is not yet."

Jesus taught by precept and example the importance of prayer. Effective prayer as so evident in His life that His disciples asked Him to teach them how to pray.

Paul, the apostle said, "Pray without ceasing." In the epistle of James are the words, "The effectual fervent prayer of the righteous man availeth much."

Dr. Frank Labach, missionary, was invited to speak at a Senate breakfast in Washington. He has always had great faith in prayer and so expressed himself at this breakfast. After the breakfast a well known senator came to Dr. Labach and said, "My legislative duties are so great I cannot face them except I face them on my knees." These could well be the words of thousands of men and women of all walks of life. Many of us can witness to the fact that prayer does change things.

Father in Heaven, without You we will utterly fail; with Thee we cannot fail. May Thy presence be with us this day. AMEN.

"Watching"

WILLIAM SANSON, English writer, was asked what his favorite hobby was. He replied, "Watching." We might think this an odd hobby, but it is recreation as well as inspiration to many.

A large part of the history of education, science, medicine, and religion has been accomplished by watching. Think how much we miss in the world about us because we are not alert.

Helen Keller, who was blind and deaf, tells in her remarkable essay, *Three Days to See,* what she would like to see if only three days of sight were given her. She concludes by saying, "I who am blind can give one hint to those who see. Use your eyes as if tomorrow you would be stricken blind. Make the most of every sense; glory in all the facets of pleasure and beauty which the world reveals to you through the several means of contact which nature provides."

The Bible speaks of those who have eyes to see and see not, and ears to hear and hear not. How grateful are we for the sense of sight and hearing.

Watching is an interesting hobby. It is, likewise, necessary to the future well being of all who would get the most out of life.

Recently, a friend of mine said that one of the highlights of the happy memories of his boyhood days was the time spent with his father in the woods. He said that his father was always alert to nature about him. He would call the attention of my friend to the things that would have been missed, had it not been for his father's watchful eye.

Be a watcher. Watch for the beauty of God's goodness all about you. The Psalm writer has said, "The heavens declare the glory of God; and the firmament sheweth his handiwork" (Psalm 19:1).

As Apollo 8 streaked through space, over two hundred thousand miles from earth, millions of people heard one of the astronauts read from the Book of Genesis, "In the beginning God created the heavens and the earth" (Genesis 1:1).

These men, circling the moon, were watchers. As they watched they recognized the greatness of the Creator.

Be a watcher. Watch for the good in people instead of the bad. Watch for the opportunity to help people in need. Watch that we might increase in wisdom and knowledge.

We cannot afford to close our eyes to the opportunity to increase our stature intellectually or spiritually.

One of the last words of advice Jesus gave His disciples was that they "Watch and pray lest they enter into temptation." This, we too, would do well to remember, that we might better learn how to choose or refuse, thus helping to make life worth the living.

Keep us alert, O Lord, that we may see, hear and understand what you have in store for us each day, and that we might be overcome, never, by temptation. AMEN.

Walls Or Bridges?

"MANY ARE lonely because they have built walls instead of bridges." Those words, taken from a church bulletin board sometime back, have been ringing in my ears like the warning bell at a railroad crossing. Man often builds a wall around himself to protect him from undesirable circumstances. By so doing he misses opportunities of doing something for others and thus receiving a blessing in return.

Walls are a warning to those around us that we prefer to be left alone. Bridges remind others that we are available if needed. It was said of a well known and effective religious leader, that one of his notable attributes was his simple availability.

This could very well have been said of Jesus. He was never too busy but what He was available to the down and out, as well as the up and out. He did not build a wall around Himself. He built bridges. Although He was the King of Kings, He did not come to sit on a throne, but to mingle with those who needed Him. "Come unto me, He said, "all ye that labor and are heavy laden, and I will give you rest" (Matthew 11:28).

We build various kinds of walls to protect ourselves, and to a certain extent they are necessary. But some of the walls we build around us are signs of concern only for ourselves. Bridges are symbols of concern for others.

Some years ago, I had the funeral of an aged and beloved physician. What I said, no doubt, was soon forgotten. What he did was long remembered. They said of him, as has been said of many faithful, family physicians, "The night was never too dark and stormy but what he made his way to the bedside of the sick. He did not ask if they had the money to pay him. He not only gave counsel and medicine, he gave himself." This benevolent physician built not walls, but bridges. He made himself available and was long remembered for what he was.

There was Dorcas. Who was Dorcas? The Bible tells us that she was a charitable woman of Joppa, also called Tabitha, who gave much of her time to the making of garments for the needy. At the very height of her service of love, she died. They sent for the apostle Peter. He came and prayed for her and she was restored to life again. To her many friends in Joppa, she was indispensable, not alone for what she did, but what she was.

The ministry of Dorcas was one of love and service. She was not lonely for she built bridges instead of walls. "A woman full of good works and almsdeeds" (Acts 9:36) is the way Dorcas's Christian service at Joppa was described. There are many Dorcas Societies today.

The richest personalities are not those who have accumulated and built walls around themselves and their possessions. Rather, the most satisfying life is the one who has built bridges of concern for others. This was the Master's way. By His presence in our lives it can be our way too.

Help me Lord, this day, that I might be ready to help someone along the way who might otherwise fall by the wayside in despair. Through Christ we pray. AMEN.

Wanted – A Man

WANTED—A Man. "I will marry any man who will give my destitute parents $3,500.00. Write for details." Those words appeared in a news paper many years ago. There were no particular qualifications, only a price.

There is a great sign hanging over the door of the universe: Wanted—A Man. Do you know the kind of man the world wants? It is true the world needs more scientists, engineers, doctors, nurses, teachers, ministers, men and women for agriculture, and many other vocations of life. But the need, above all, is for men of character.

Recently, nineteen leading corporations gave the following qualities which they look for in those whom they hope to employ. The qualities are: character, ability to work hard, mental alertness, good judgment, ability to get along with people, and a good appearance.

What kind of men does the world need today? Several years ago, General Omar Bradley spoke words that are still true today. He said, ""We have many men of science, but too few men of God. We have grasped the mystery of the atom, but rejected the Sermon on the Mount. We know more about war than we do about peace; more about killing than we do about living."

When the General reasoned that we have "too few men of God," he was saying that we do not have enough who live by the Golden Rule. We need more men who will let the presence of God be their guide and stay in life.

Where do we find men of God? Someone, long ago, said that we do not find them, we must make them. Those who have helped to make this world as good as it is have been "made." They were dedicated and trained by concerned parents and sincere teachers and called by God.

Sometimes we think that our world is in a sad state of affairs. But, have you ever thought what it might be like if it were not for the Godly characters of those who have been a leavening force in the world?

There is a verse in the book of Ezekiel with a sad yet longing note. It reads, "And I sought for a man among them, that should make up the hedge, and stand in the gap before me for the land, that I should not destory it: but I found none" (Ezekiel 22:30).

Wanted—men and women. Those who love their homes, their country and its future. Men and women who will take their places and stand in the gap and help make up the hedges that reach from earth to heaven. Many through the centuries have done it. Many more are needed. The future of our world's good depends on it.

O God, help us to take our place in a troubled world to live as Christians that we might help to make our age a better one. In the name of Christ our Lord. AMEN.

Why Suffering?

"WHAT HAVE I done that this trouble has come upon me?" Those were the words of a woman who had reared a large family. As I had observed her through the years, she had been a good mother and a faithful wife. Many, many others have, likewise, asked this question.

Why does sorrow and suffering come to us? Is God punishing us for some wrong doing of the past? Have we failed? Is evil in control?

Suffering and heartache comes to almost everyone eventually. Many are not prepared for it and it takes its toll. Others are like the willow in our garden; it bends with the storm but comes back straight and stalwart after each blast of wind. Suffering and trouble changes us. It makes some bitter, but others better.

Paul, the apostle, certainly could witness to the experiences of suffering. He once said, "For we know that in all things God works for good to those who love Him, and are called accordingly to His purpose" (Romans 8:28).

The author of Hebrews also wrote, ". . . for He hath said, I will never leave thee, nor forsake thee. So that wemay confidently say, the Lord is my helper, I will not fear what men shall do to me" (Hebrews 13:5-6).

Seven hundred years before Christ was born, the prophet Isaiah foretold that Christ would be, "a man of sorrows and acquainted with grief" (Isaiah 53:3). Many a person, who has walked through the valley of suffering, has experienced the presence of God's hand upon him. The hymn writer, C. Austin Miles, has expressed the feeling of many of us, when he wrote the comforting words, "And He walks with me and He talks with me; And He tells me I am His own."

Many have suffered due to their unwavering faith in God. These remember that Jesus said, "Blessed are you when men revile you and persecute you and say all manner of evil against you falsely, for my sake. Rejoice and be exceeding glad; for great is your reward in heaven: for so persecuted they the prophets which were before you" (Matthew 5:11-12).

There are those who have been made bitter because of the suffering they or their loved ones have experienced. Others have discovered that God was permitting this suffering, but through it all He was helping them to come out victoriously through discipline and refinement.

We have all known those who, through sickness, disappointment, physical or material loss, have experienced a turning point in their lives. For, rather than blaming God or themselves, they looked to God for His strength to make life really worth the living. Someone has observed that God proves people to improve them. Is not this often the outcome of suffering?

Dear Lord, we pray for those who are suffering and not knowing the answer to it all. Help us to believe that you care and will not forsake us, and we shall give Thee the praise. AMEN.

We Are Able

EVENTS THAT have been taking place in America, recently, have led some to ask, "What is this Country coming to?" Most of us, at times, looking on the dark and negative side of conditions around us, have asked this same question.

It is well that we face up to certain facts and realize that there are conditions that are not as they should be. But history reminds us that our Country has survived many national calamities and regained its former stature. It has done so by its people remembering from whence their nation had come and realizing their dependence on a Power greater than themselves.

It is said that the Chinese had no word for crisis. They used two words to express how they faced crisis. *Wai-Chi* was that combined word. When translated it means Peril-Opportunity.

Our nation was born in the midst of peril. But those founding fathers believed in freedom. Through sweat, tears, and determination they framed the Declaration of Independence, recognizing peril but opportunity also. That spirit has never died. It is one of the anchors that has held our nation together for two hundred years.

America is a great nation, but we must ever be alert to our perils and keep our faith in the opportunities that are ever before us. We are shocked by the violence, the contempt for law and order, and the disregard for religion. We are disturbed by the lowering of ideals, the cynical attacks upon patriotism, the cheap, degrading media called entertainment. There are many other abuses of what good citizens throughout the ages have regarded as the good life.

As we pause to recall from whence we have come and evaluate what we are, we cannot help from thinking of how much we have to be grateful for and recognize the opportunities that are before us.

Back in Old Testament days, when the Israelites were wandering in the wilderness, Moses, their leader, sent twelve men to "search out" the land of Canaan. When they returned, ten of the men were impressed by the fruit of the land, but fearful of the giants they saw there. Caleb and Joshua, the only members of the minority committee agreed with what the others had seen. They, however, had faith in God who had led them thus far.

Caleb stilled the people before Moses and said, "Let us go up at once and possess it; for we are well able to overcome it" (Numbers 13:30).

In times like these a portion of a hymn, written by Earl Marlatt, could very well be our national prayer: "Lord, we are able, Our spirits are thine; Remold them make us like thee divine. Thy guiding radiance above us shall be; A beacon to God, to love and loyalty."

God of our fathers, we humbly recognize our weaknesses but we, likewise, recognize our strength when we trust Thy Holy Spirit and His power working through us. AMEN.

Where Are Our Reserves?

DURING THE Second World War Sir Winston Churchill made one of his visits to France. It was during the dark days just before France collapsed. During this visit, Sir Winston turned to the French generals and asked, "Where are your reserves?" The mournful reply was, "There are none."

This was the main reason for the collapse of France. This is also the primary cause of the failure of any nation or individual.

We know that we cannot write a check on our bank account unless we have made adequate deposits to cover that check. We cannot meet the physical challenges of life unless we practice physical fitness. Nor can we remain a strong nation unless we build up a strong reserve for the dark days. We shall be able to meet all of the demands of life only when we have built up our material, moral and spiritual reserves.

Oliver Wendell Holmes, American jurist, said, "You cannot draw out spiritual funds without replenishing the reserve."

The founding fathers of our Country were concerned that this might be a free nation. They knew that it would continue to be free only as its freedom was preserved. They knew that those reserves could best be guarded by a strong faith in God.

Man has found, many times, that prayer helps to build up a reserve with security. Prayer is not bending God to our will, but rather in getting on God's side. This is not something we stumble on to in the dark. But rather something for which we search. Prayer builds up a reserve for the dark days when the invasion of evil would overcome us. It also gives wisdom to make wise decisions in everyday life.

Abraham Lincoln said, "I have been driven many times to my knees by the overwhelming conviction that I had nowhere else to go. My own wisdom, and that of all about me, seemed insufficient for the day."

Even the Master found it necessary to get alone with His Heavenly Father. There He received the added strength to win the battles that were ever before Him.

Do you remember Jesus speaking of laying up treasures in heaven? I have always felt that those treasures could be drawn upon when we needed them most. Those treasures of patience, forgiveness, kindness, love, and many others. There are times when an extra supply of these are most urgent. These are tangible reserves to have laid away against the day of necessity.

In the days of the famine in Egypt, in the time of Joseph, they had plenty. The were able to say, "In all the land of Egypt there was bread." This, because Joseph heeded the warning of God and prepared for it. We would do well, as Americans, to do likewise.

Lord, we in America seem to have everything, but there are times when there are spiritual famines of the soul. Keep us alert that it may not be so with us. AMEN.

You Are What You Do

LITTLE SARA was proud of her new playhouse. She was pleased with its furnishings, but her greatest pride and joy was a brightly colored alarm clock. There it set on a little table merrily ticking away the time. The only thing wrong with the clock was that the glass on the front was broken and both of its hands were gone. That little clock without hands was a parable of life. It is significant that we be alive, but more so that we are doing something about it. You are what you do.

Ralph Waldo Emmerson, American philosopher and poet, once wrote, "Action is the breathing of the soul, it is the interpreting of our thoughts." It would be interesting to see what lies out there in the future, but it is far more important to do what is clearly at hand. Our value is in our actions, and not alone in our vision.

Jesus was talking about religiion in action, and not alone in words, when He said, "Ye shall know them by their fruits . . ." (Matthew 7:16) He used the tree to express His lesson on fruitfulness. They knew, as we know today, that one does not gather "grapes from thorns, or figs of thistles." Every good tree produces fruit as it is supposed to do.

Elton Trueblood, eminent Quaker professor, once said in my hearing, "Some people make pretty lamps but poor lights." A lamp that is suppose to give forth light is only an ornament until it sheds its light about it. We are what we do.

Faith is an adventure. It only grows by starting. I know something about electricity but not enough, but I do not sit in the dark when I know that all I need to do is to press the light switch to bring light to the room.

The desperate woman who had been ill for twelve years and had found no relief heard that Jesus was to pass her way. She had tried almost everything that she had heard of, now she believed that Jesus could heal her. In her desperation yet with courageous faith, she said to herself, "If I may but touch His garment I shall be whole" (Matthew 9:21).

The miracle was not in the garment but in her faith and action and the Master's compassion on her. Jesus said to her, " . . . thy faith hath made thee whole . . . " (Matthew 9:22) This woman, who acted upon the impulse of her heart was healed, body and soul.

One of life's most proven axioms is that our true character is known by the fruits we produce. We are what we think. We are what we believe. But our whole future's failure or success, depends upon what we do about our thoughts and beliefs.

Lord, help us today to put our creeds into actions, that we may be a doer of our beliefs as well as voicing them. AMEN.

You Are What You Think

A WISE DIETICIAN, who was also one of my teachers, once said, "You are what you eat." She went on to explain that our health, good or poor, depends to a great extent on what we eat.

This is just as true of five words that have held my interest for years; "You are what you think." As the years have come and gone those words have proven themselves to be true many times.

Think illness and one can make himself ill. Think failure and one is defeated already. Think how the great Healer is working through the many avenues of medical science, one's own faith and determination and one can hasten healing and the return to health again.

There are twenty-four hours in a day and night. No more and no less. We can spend those hours thinking about what may happen to us tomorrow. We can think of the trouble that awaits us. We may think how we shall never be able to face the tasks, the debts, or the people with whom we have disagreed. This entire day can be ruined because of our unhealthy thoughts about tomorrow.

Think, there are only so many hours in this day. Live for what you, by God's help, can put into it and tomorrow will take care of itself.

Jesus must have found the thoughts and worries that people had about tommorrow quite prevalent. This was one reason that He said that we were not to take thought for tomorrow, for tomorrow would take thought for itself.

If the great Master has the power to make provision for eternity for "whosoever believeth in Him," then certainly He can provide for our needs a day at a time. Long ago I thought of this and it has meant the difference between peace of mind and doubts and fears.

A famous physician once said that just as there are vitamins good for the body, there are also vitamins good for the mind. "The latter," he said, "are thought vitamins, and they are as essential to health as those taken by mouth."

It was Paul, the apostle, who once said, "Whatsoever things are true, whatsoever things are honest, whatsoever things are just, whatsoever things are pure, whatsoever things are lovely, whatsoever things are of good report; if there be any virtue, if there be any praise, think on these things" (Philippians 4:8).

Thinking will not make us perfect. However, thinking upon the things that are uplifting will make one reach up to Him who can help us to climb that ladder that reaches unto perfection.

The Book of Proverbs has a word that is still true today; "As a man thinketh in his heart so is he."

Dear Lord, and Master of true wisdom, help us to have right thoughts that we shall have Christlike attitudes and actions. AMEN.

"You'll Never Walk Alone"

RODGERS and Hammerstein, as a team, wrote many musicals in their years together. In one of those moving and thrilling productions appears the song, "You'll Never Walk Alone."

It gives one courage to hear the words, "Walk on through the wind, walk on through the rain; Though your dreams be tossed and blown, Walk on, walk on with hope in your heart, and you'll never walk alone."

Alone has always been a sad word to me. I am not thinking of the peace of solitude, but the feeling of being deserted. A good friend of mine once said that she could not bear to be alone. She had to be with others, and better still, in a crowd.

Some of us, however, have found that we are often more lonely in a crowd, in which we are acquainted with no one, than when we are by ourselves.

I think that I shall never forget my first day at school. As I started off for that first day of a new experience as a child, I remember that little hug and that pat on the back; I felt that I was not alone. Mother was with me. From that day to the day I started out for my first church as a young preacher, I was not alone. The prayers of my mother, as long as she lived, were with me.

Ezra Taft Benson, once Secretary of Agriculture, was a member of a family of eleven. He said tht he remembered with consolation that his father and mother lived without frustration and with a deep faith in God.

As the Taft children, one by one, left home to go out into the world, each one was given the following words of wisdom, "Remember that whatever you do, wherever you go, you are not alone. Our Heavenly Father is always near you. You can reach out and receive His aid through prayer."

When it seemed that the world, and even His friends, had forsaken Jesus, He was able to say that His Father who had sent Him was with Him, "He hath not left me alone." Even in the Garden of Gethsemane, when it seemed that all had forsaken Him, Jesus prayed in the confidence that He was not alone. His Father was with Him.

On the third day after the crucifixion, two of Jesus' disciples were going from Jerusalem to Emmaus. The sad memories of Friday were still fresh in their hearts.

What could they do now, these men who had left all to follow their Master? As they reasoned together, Jesus drew near and walked with them. After He revealed Himself to them they were never the same after that hour. Their Master's assurance made them feel that they need never walk alone again. They hurried back to the other disciples to give encouragement to them in their loneliness and disappointment.

Many of us have found that we need not walk alone. We may also reach out through prayer and feel His presence near.

O Master of the lonely road, may we ever be mindful of Thy Presence, walking by our side each day. AMEN.